FROMMER'S

COMPREHENSIVE TRAVEL GUIDE

MINNEAPOLIS & ST. PAUL '91-'92

by Lucille Johnsen Stelling

GW00712392

PRENTICE
HALL
PRESS

NEW YORK • LONDON • TORONTO • SYDNEY • TOKYO • SINGAPORE

FROMMER BOOKS

Published by Prentice Hall Press
A division of Simon & Schuster Inc.
15 Columbus Circle
New York, NY 10023

ISBN 0-13-332990-9
ISSN 1051-6980

Manufactured in the United States of America

J. Asher Dec '92.

CONTENTS

MAPS

For Jean and William Lokos
who still play an important part
in everything I do

ACKNOWLEDGMENTS

Many Minnesotans offered valuable suggestions and information for this book, and I thank them all, particularly Del Stelling, who's been my greatest resource in every sense.

Safety Advisory

Whenever you're traveling in an unfamiliar city or country, stay alert. Be aware of your immediate surroundings. Wear a moneybelt and keep a close eye on your possessions. Be particularly careful with cameras, purses, and wallets, all favorite targets of thieves and pickpockets.

INTRODUCING MINNEAPOLIS AND ST. PAUL

Surely by now you've heard of Lake Wobegon, Minnesota, where "all the women are strong, all the men are good looking, and all the children are above average." Garrison Keillor, the creator of this mythical town, is only one of a number of luminaries who hail from the Twin Cities of Minneapolis and St. Paul. Prince, Loni Anderson, and Nick Nolte were all brought up hereabouts, as were Jessica Lange and Linda Kelsey.

We have notable transplants from other parts of the country as well—Pulitzer-Prize-winning playwright August Wilson, for example. Like so many of us loyal Twin Citians, Wilson arrived originally for what was to have been a short stay—and remained for many years. It's not that we couldn't go home again; it's just that home was never like this.

1. A Natural and Cultural Bounty

Consider the attractions of the area's natural setting. Although every Minnesota license plate declares this the land of 10,000 lakes, there are really more than 12,000 in all—and that's only counting the ones that measure 10 acres or more. It shouldn't be surprising, then, that 31 large lakes lie within the metropolitan area of Minneapolis and St. Paul, making outdoor recreation an important part of Twin Cities life throughout the year. Boating, fishing, and swimming in the summertime, ice skating, ice fishing, skiing, snowmobiling, and ice sailing during the winter—all are just a few minutes away by foot or by car.

With 1 acre of city parkland for every 43 Twin Citians, joggers, walkers, skaters, and bikers can do their thing in picturesque settings throughout the city. Public parks here maintain separate but equal paths for those on foot and those on wheels.

The suburbs offer outdoor attractions of their own: for example, in Apple Valley, cross-country skiers glide past elk, bison, and moose on authentically landscaped terrain at the Minnesota Zoo.

If your favorite sport is hand-to-mouth, you'll find picnic spots aplenty in the beautiful outdoors and, as a matter of fact, in the beautiful indoors as well. Consider the luxuriant glass-enclosed city park atop the shops and offices of St. Paul's Town Square. Here, among trees and shrubs and cascading waterfalls, noontime diners enjoy the finger foods they've brought from home or from one of the fast-food stands in the courtyard four levels below. An added pleasure of passing time in Town Square Park is the periodic lunchtime organ recitals.

Musical performances play a prominent role in Twin Cities cultural life, most notably at two world-class symphony halls: the elegant old-world Ordway Music Theatre in St. Paul and the modern Orchestra Hall in Minneapolis. And there's music for the eye as well as the ear in downtown Minneapolis, where 32 windows of the Schmitt Music Center were bricked up on the parking-lot side of the building to accommodate a mammoth mural of a segment from the score of Maurice Ravel's *Gaspard de la Nuit*. Van Cliburn, in town for an appearance at Orchestra Hall, was so intrigued by the mural that he agreed to perform portions of the piece on a 9-foot Steinway that was pushed out into the parking lot for the occasion.

Perhaps, though, it's theater that has provided the Twin Cities' most significant contribution to culture. *Time* evidently thought so when it highlighted the Tyrone Guthrie Theater in a cover story called "The Good Life in Minnesota," which told the whole world about the remarkably rich quality of life in an area of superb natural beauty, where first-rate sports and recreation coexist amiably with some of the finest art, music, and theater to be found anywhere.

Since its opening performance in 1962, the Guthrie Theater has staged dozens of exciting productions, none more unique, though, than the history cycle which ushered in the 1990-91 season. In fact, by offering *Richard II, Henry IV,* parts 1 and 2, and *Henry V* in rotating repertory, the Guthrie made history of its own. This was the first time that a professional American theater company had ever performed these four great Shakespearean history plays in a single season. But the Guthrie is only one of dozens of playhouses in and around Minneapolis and St. Paul. No city in the country outside of New York has more theaters per capita than you'll find here, and no city except New York spends more on the performing arts than Minneapolis and St. Paul do.

Theater in the Round, near the University of Minnesota main campus, is one of the oldest continuously operating community theaters in the country; the Old Log, on the banks of Lake Minnetonka, houses the longest-lived theatrical stock company; and the Minneapolis Children's, adjoining the Institute of Art, is the largest of all American theaters for children; Great North American History Theater offers original historical plays based on Minnesota events and people.

Art fanciers will find more than 130 galleries throughout Minneapolis and St. Paul and several major museums as well. The Minneapolis Institute of Art and the Walker Art Center are both widely known, not only for their local holdings, but for the successful touring exhibitions that they have originated. More than a quarter of a million people visited the Walker in early 1980 to see 160 Picasso paintings, sculptures, collages, and drawings that the artist had kept for his own collection; later these works were sent to New York City for incorporation into the Picasso retrospective at the Museum of Modern Art.

The hands-on Children's Museum in St. Paul's Bandana Square has an appreciative public of its own, as tomorrow's doctors and dentists, engineers and crane operators, service-station attendants, computer scientists, and TV personnel get to practice their future professions here. The specially outfitted "habitot" offers fun and games to the even-younger set.

The Science Museum of Minnesota attracts audiences of all ages to attend films at its unusual Omnitheater, where panoramic adventures are displayed on a huge domed screen by the special 70-mm OmniMax movie projector. First, though, you have to get by that giant iguana at the museum's front door. A 16-year-old artist created this remarkable and celebrated reptile that sometimes serves as an extended bench for young museum-goers. Popular as he is, though, no one has tried taking Iggy home, maybe because at 40 feet in length and 3,900 pounds in weight, this one-of-a-kind iguana is far from portable. Lighter but no less popular are the dinosaurs you'll find inside the Science Museum, where, in the fascinating "dinosaur lab," visitors can watch the step-by-step reconstruction of one of these extinct reptiles.

For those who prefer competition to culture, four professional major-league teams call Minnesota home. At the Hubert H. Humphrey Metrodome, 55,000 fans can watch the world-champion Minnesota Twins in action. When the Minnesota Vikings are in town, the Dome becomes a gridiron, with seats for 62,000 football enthusiasts. Metropolitan Sports Center in suburban Bloomington draws large crowds for North Stars hockey. The Timberwolves, an NBA expansion team, started their 1990–91 season in a brand-new downtown arena. Out in Shakopee, you can bet your bottom dollar at Canterbury Downs, where thoroughbreds race five days each week from April through October.

If you prefer spending your money on a sure thing, you need look no farther than the suburbs: shopping history was made there in 1956 when Southdale, the nation's first enclosed two-story regional shopping mall, was born. By now suburban malls have become so integral a part of people's lives that many go there on doctor's orders. Long before shops open each day, fitness fans are walking and jogging in the malls' climate-controlled comfort, giving only sidelong glances at the tempting window displays on all sides. And now, one step ahead as usual, the Twin Cities are in the process of bringing shopping malls right into the heart of town, in handsome shopping complexes that have brought us Saks Fifth Avenue, F.A.O. Schwarz, and other nationally known stores.

Maybe the greatest strides in the Twin Cities during the past decade have been architectural. Prize-winning skyscrapers like the World Trade Center in St. Paul and the IDS Building in Minneapolis tower above older, more familiar structures. The Investors Diversified Services Tower, centrally located on Minneapolis' Nicollet pedestrian mall, was designed by famed architect Philip Johnson, who said of its glass expanses, "God changes my wallpaper four times each year." And, in fact, for the benefit of passersby the outer appearance of this handsome reflective structure changes several times each day. Along with the creation of new Twin Cities landmarks, there's a healthy respect here for distinguished old buildings, many of which are listed on the National Register of Historic Places.

In Minneapolis, the shops, restaurants, and galleries of Riverplace reside in restored brick and limestone warehouses and mills on the banks of the Mississippi, not far from the waterfalls that powered Minneapolis' early industries.

The historic World Theatre in St. Paul is where Garrison Keillor used to host the phenomenally popular "Prairie Home Companion." Touring shows now keep this grand old building a very vital part of downtown St. Paul.

In both cities, at any time of year you can walk from one end of downtown to the other with no concern for rain or snow or anything else the weather forecaster might dream up: the skyways are absolutely weatherproof. In Minneapolis, the network of glassed-in second-story thoroughfares extends for 21 blocks, making it the world's longest privately owned skyway system. Measuring 3 miles, St. Paul's skyway system is the world's largest publicly owned one.

Certainly mobility is one of the prime perks offered by these enclosed second-story glassed-in walkways. Another is the view they provide. In Minneapolis you'll be able to look down on the busy Nicollet Mall, surrounded by striking new skyscrapers like the Conservatory, the IDS Tower, and City Center. St. Paul has some skyscrapers of its own for skyway viewing: the new World Trade Center and Town Square, among others. But nothing here can beat the St. Paul Skyway view of the magnificent Minnesota State Capitol.

In both downtowns, architectural beauty is complemented by the natural beauty of the Mississippi, just a short walk away. In fact, it was this mighty river that first brought white men to these shores, as they searched for a water route to fabulous wealth in the mysterious Orient.

---

2. History

French explorers, traveling south from Canada, thought the Mississippi River might be their Northwest Passage toward the opulent East of which Marco Polo had written such tantalizing accounts. During the 17th century at least one of these adventurous souls, the self-confident Jean Nicolet, brought along on his expedition a change of clothes that he must have considered appropriate for the pomp and circumstance of his arrival in China. Imagine his chagrin and the open-mouthed astonishment of passing Dakota tribespeople when Nicolet stepped ashore in an intricately decorated robe "all strewn with flowers and birds of many colors."

Disappointed in their search for a new continent, these explorers may have found some consolation in the abundance of furs that awaited them much closer to home. Also waiting were Native Americans who were more than willing to exchange their beaver and muskrat pelts for blankets, knives, tobacco, tools, and other unfamiliar and intriguing items.

In time the Ojibwa tribes from the east joined the Dakota, moving into this area in advance of white men who had given them rifles, liquor, and other trappings of civilization. The name "Ojibwa" sounded like "Chippewa" to white men's ears, and that's the name by which the tribe is still known today. These advancing tribes disparaged the Dakota, calling them "Nadouessioux" or "little vipers," a name the white men shortened to "Sioux." Different from each other in language and customs, the Sioux and the Chippewa waged fierce and bloody warfare that threatened not only the white men's fur trade but also their settlements.

French dominion over this area came to an end in 1763, at the conclusion of the French and Indian War, when France surrendered to Great Britain all the land east of the Mississippi River. British rule was short-lived, however. Just 20 years later Britain relinquished this land to the newly formed United States of America, and in 1803, by terms of the Louisiana Purchase, Napoleon sold to the United States the territory that would one day include the state of Minnesota.

Now it was time to establish a permanent official presence here, and President Thomas Jefferson sent army troops out to prepare for the construction of a "center of civilization" at the juncture of the Mississippi and Minnesota Rivers. Fort Snelling became a refuge for traders, explorers, missionaries, and settlers, among them several Swiss families that had earlier been lured by promises of a bright future in Canada. Essentially squatters on land that had been ceded to the military by the Sioux, these families made their homes and livelihood in the protective shadow of the fort until a treaty with the tribes in 1837 officially opened new lands for settlement. The families then crossed the Mississippi to live and work on land that was to become St. Paul.

Awaiting the settlers when they arrived was an unsavory Canadian voyageur, Pierre "Pig's Eye" Parrant, who did a brisk business bootlegging rum to soldiers. The new settlement was known as "Pig's Eye" until 1841, when Father Lucien Galtier named his recently constructed log chapel in honor of St. Paul. Townspeople made that the name of their community as well.

Until as late as 1848, many of the inhabitants of this area spoke only French, but when Minnesota became an American territory in 1849, settlers from the eastern United States began to arrive in large numbers. And then came immigrants from elsewhere in Europe. During the decades between 1860 and the turn of the century, thousands of newcomers arrived from northern European countries, including Sweden, Norway, Denmark, and Germany, along with some from the British Isles, particularly Ireland. Pamphlets printed in a variety of languages and distributed abroad bore offers that were impossible to refuse—reduced ship and railway rates and reduced costs for food, clothing, and shelter while the newcomers searched for land.

St. Paul, now the port of entry to the frontier beyond, was also the acknowledged center of business and culture in the new territory. Incorporated as a city in 1854, St. Paul became the state capital in 1858.

Minneapolis, off to a somewhat slower start, didn't become a city until 1867, but in 1872 it absorbed the village of St. Anthony, whose waterfall powered the sawmills and flour mills that would make the "Mill City" a prosperous industrial center. By the end of the decade, Minneapolis was declaring itself superior to St. Paul in numbers as well as importance. Competition grew more and more intense, and finally, in 1890, sibling rivalry erupted into internecine warfare when census results showed the population of Minneapolis to be 40,386 greater than that of St. Paul. Amid cries of foul play, a recount showed that both cities had substantially inflated their numbers. The results: While Minneapolis was in fact the more populous of the two, its original total had been padded by 18,386 votes, with St. Paul's initial claim 9,425 over the recounted figure. Mutually embarrassed, the cities were mutually forgiving. Angry headlines gradually faded away, and so, too, did the free-swinging antagonism that had marked the recount of 1890.

3. The Twin Cities Today

Through the years, Minneapolis and St. Paul have developed individual styles that complement rather than conflict with each other. More traditional than her younger sister, St. Paul is often called "the last city of the East." And if St. Paul reminds you a bit of New England, Minneapolis, "the first city of the West," may make you think of fast-paced Los Angeles.

Which of the two will you prefer? That's a question that needn't be answered—or even asked. One of the best things about the Twin Cities is that you don't have to choose between them. With their downtown areas only ten minutes apart, they combine to offer a remarkable diversity of activities and attractions, and that's what makes them such an extraordinary vacation value. It's two great destinations for the price of one when you visit Minneapolis and St. Paul.

II

ARRIVING AND GETTING ACQUAINTED

1. GETTING TO THE TWIN CITIES
2. GETTING AROUND
3. BEFORE YOU GO . . .
4. GETTING ACQUAINTED
5. TWIN CITIES FAST FACTS

Situated midway between the Atlantic and the Pacific, Minneapolis and St. Paul are readily accessible from anywhere in the world.

Northwest Airlines brings international visitors here daily from Europe, Asia, Mexico, and the Caribbean, with nonstop flights from London, Tokyo, and Hawaii. And Continental Airlines arrives daily with travelers from Australia and New Zealand.

Domestic visitors often arrive by rail and by road. Amtrak maintains a large Twin Cities terminal in the Midway District between Minneapolis and St. Paul. Greyhound Bus Lines has a terminal in both St. Paul and Minneapolis as part of its coast-to-coast service. And for travelers who prefer to do their own driving, major Interstate highways converge in the Twin Cities, making this area easy to reach and easy to get around in after you've arrived.

1. Getting to the Twin Cities

BY AIR

Because nearly two dozen international, national, and regional airlines serve the Minneapolis–St. Paul airport, it should be possible to make specific recommendations concerning rates and schedules. But of course airline fare schedules are relatively complex, with fares on any one flight varying wildly depending on the day of the week that you'll be traveling, the length of your stay, and the advance notice you can provide. Your trusty travel agent should be able to help find you the best possible flight at the best possible rate.

When your plane arrives in the Twin Cities, you'll be landing at **Minneapolis–St. Paul International Airport,** located just 10 miles from downtown Minneapolis, 8½ miles from downtown St. Paul. You'll leave your plane on the upper level of the Charles Lindbergh Terminal Building, dedicated to the Minnesotan who in 1927 became the first man ever to fly solo across the Atlantic Ocean. If you're arriving from another country, you can use the Mutual of Omaha currency exchange (tel. 726-5848), located near the Travelers Aid and Information desks; it's open from 6 a.m. to 6 p.m. seven days a week. Baggage-claim carousels and ground-transportation desks are on the lower level.

Getting from the Airport

After you collect your luggage and leave the terminal building on the ground-floor level, you'll see across the street the freestanding office of a taxi dispatcher at the head of a line of waiting cabs. **Taxi** fares to downtown Minneapolis average about $17 and to St. Paul about $13. At this writing, a 10% discount is available from Airport Taxi (tel. 721-6566) if you phone for an assigned cab number after picking up your luggage. You'll be picked up by your designated taxi near the phone booth just beyond the taxi dispatcher's office.

Across from baggage carousel no. 10 on the lower level of the terminal, you can arrange for **limousine service** to Minneapolis at the Minneapolis & Suburban Airport Limousine Service desk (tel. 827-7777). Service to downtown Minneapolis is $7.50. For limousine service to St. Paul, go to the St. Paul & Suburban Airport Limousine Service desk (tel. 726-5479) across from carousel no. 6. The fare to downtown St. Paul is $5.50.

The Metropolitan Transit Commission (tel. 827-7733) runs **buses** from the airport to Washington Avenue in downtown Minneapolis and to Robert Street in downtown St. Paul for $1.00 or 75¢, depending on whether or not you're traveling during the rush hour. Bus no. 7 will take you to downtown Minneapolis at varying intervals from 4:11 a.m. to 12:13 a.m. daily. Service to St. Paul is more limited. For nearly an hour, from 3:43 to 4:33 p.m., you can get a no. 62 bus directly to downtown St. Paul. At other times, take the no. 7 bus for about one mile until you reach the Federal Building, where you transfer to a no. 9 bus that will take you to downtown St. Paul. These no. 9 buses leave the Federal Building from 4:35 a.m. through 11:39 p.m. each day. (You'll know large MTC buses by their color. Newer ones are white; older ones are red. All are marked with a large "T" on the side.)

BY TRAIN

Amtrak passengers to the Twin Cities arrive in St. Paul at the St. Paul/Minneapolis Minnesota Midway Station, 730 Transfer Rd., St. Paul (tel. toll free 800/872-7245), located about 10 minutes from downtown St. Paul, 20 minutes from downtown Minneapolis. Present round-trip Amtrak fares to Minneapolis and St. Paul from New York are $327; from Chicago, $132; from Los Angeles, $339, and from Miami, $269. Call Amtrak for the latest discount information. Cab service from the Amtrak terminal is $1.10 per mile.

BY BUS

Greyhound/Trailways serves the Twin Cities. In Minneapolis, the **terminal** is at 29 N. 9th St. (tel. 371-3320); the St. Paul address is 9th Street at St. Peter Street (tel. 222-0509). The current round-trip rate from New York is $198, from Chicago it's $99, from Los Angeles, $228, and from Miami, $198, with a bargain fare to customers who order their tickets 30 days in advance—$118 round-trip to anywhere Greyhound/Trailways goes.

BY CAR

As for highway accessibility, Interstate 35, which extends from the Canadian border to Mexico, and Interstate 94, which extends from the Atlantic to the Pacific, intersect in downtown Minneapolis about ten miles from downtown St. Paul. Within the Twin Cities, I-35 divides, becoming I-35E in St. Paul and I-35W in Minneapolis: I-35E goes nearly all the way through St. Paul, except for about one mile which remains to be completed, while I-35W goes north to south through Minneapolis. Interstate 94 goes through both cities in an east-west direction. A Belt Line freeway system encircles the Twin Cities area, with I-494 extending through the southern and western suburbs and I-694 traveling through the eastern and northern suburbs. The Belt Line has interchanges with all the major highway routes.

A new interstate, I-394, now runs from the Lowry Hill tunnel off I-94 in Minneapolis west to I-494. (In the stretch where it extends over Hwy. 12, it's called both I-394 and Hwy. 12.) Old County Rd. 18 is now Hwy. 169, which runs between Hwy. 100 and I-494.

---

2. Getting Around

BY CAR

Unless you plan to spend all your time downtown, you'll want to rent a car for at least part of your visit to the Twin Cities. Otherwise you'll miss some of the many attractions and activities hereabouts. Metropolitan Transit Commission buses are the only form of mass transportation, and although they're efficient and reliable, their schedule may not coincide with yours.

Local car-rental companies include **National Car Rental,** Minneapolis–St. Paul International Airport (tel. 726-5600); **Dollar Rent-a-Car,** Minneapolis–St. Paul International Airport (tel. 726-

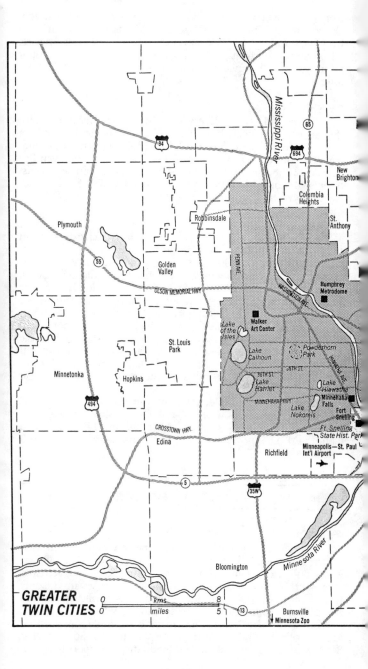

GREATER TWIN CITIES

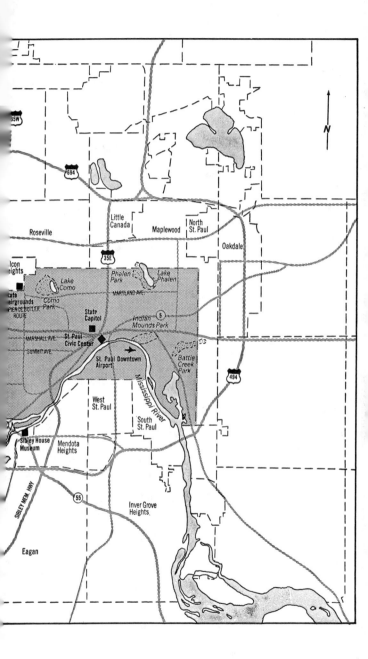

9494); **Hertz Rent-a-Car,** Minneapolis–St. Paul International Airport (tel. 726-1600); and **Avis Rent-a-Car,** Minneapolis–St. Paul International Airport (tel. 726-1526).

BY BUS

If you're going to spend the day or the evening downtown, one thin dime will take you to most offices, restaurants, and businesses, thanks to the Metropolitan Transit Commission's **"Dime Zone."** You don't even need to remember route numbers, just the direction in which you want to travel the cities' major streets.

For longer MTC expeditions, you can get **maps,** pocket schedules, and tokens in St. Paul at Town Square, 7th Street and Cedar Avenue. In Minneapolis, you'll find them at the MTC Transit Store, 719 Marquette Ave.

Fares range from 60¢ to $1.25, depending on the time of day and distance traveled. You'll need the exact change when you board the bus unless you've purchased a token or a Commuter Ticket. They don't reduce the cost of your MTC ride, but they might reduce the scrounging for change you'd otherwise face when you get on the bus.

For Metropolitan Transit Commission **information,** phone 827-7733.

BY CAB

Cab fares are $1.10 per mile. Cab companies include **Airport Taxi** (tel. 721-6566), **Suburban Taxi** (tel. 888-9199), and **St. Paul Yellow Cab** (tel. 222-4433).

---

3. Before You Go . . .

A FEW WORDS ABOUT THE WEATHER

The common perception of Twin Cities' winters is that they're comparable to what you'd find in outer Siberia or, closer to home, at International Falls, the northernmost Minnesota town whose bonechilling temperatures regularly make national news. Actually, weather in Minneapolis and St. Paul tends to be similar to that in other northern American cities, except that for most of the year there's relatively little humidity in these parts, so you probably won't feel as warm or as cold as the thermometer might indicate.

WHAT TO BRING ALONG

Casual clothing is appropriate for most activities throughout the year, but if you're planning an extra special evening out, you'll want something a bit more formal. Some restaurants do require that men wear jacket and tie for dinner. Remember to bring a pair of shorts for your summertime stay and a light sweater or jacket for those cool summer evenings. Whatever the winter weather, many Twin Citians go through the entire season hatless and scarfless. A warm coat's a necessity, though, and so are gloves and boots—

unless the winter of 1986–1987 plays a return engagement. Finally, of course, for this and every other trip, a pair of comfortable walking shoes can make all the difference.

---

4. Getting Acquainted

Although they share many miles of common border, Minneapolis and St. Paul are not Siamese twins: they're separated here and there by the Mississippi River, which saw the cities' earliest settlements on its banks. To this day, parts of downtown Minneapolis and downtown St. Paul overlook the majestic Mississippi. A more modern, man-made form of transportation has also become dominant in the Twin Cities during the past couple of decades—those glass-walled skyway systems, heated in the winter and air-conditioned in the summer, which connect miles of downtown shops, offices, restaurants, and entertainment areas. By now, these second-story walkways are an important part of life in the cities. In fact, it's said that the skyways are to Minneapolis and St. Paul what the canals are to Venice.

The creation of the skyway systems was the first move in a continuing crusade by local community leaders to prevent in the Twin Cities the kind of deterioration that has plagued downtown areas elsewhere. One measure of their success is a recent building boom unprecedented in Twin Cities history, adding dozens of handsome office buildings, high-rise condominiums, and enclosed shopping centers to the downtown areas. Returnees to the Twin Cities are astonished at the way the skylines have changed during the past several years. First-timers are impressed by the dramatic beauty of gleaming glass-and-steel structures, many of them designed by internationally recognized architects.

I'll choose the tallest, most centrally located building in each city as the focal point for your Twin Cities orientations. In each case, the focal point is set squarely in the center of the city's downtown area—not surprising, for in this part of the country each city's downtown begins on the banks of the Mississippi River and then extends from there into clearly definable sections and neighborhoods.

MEET MINNEAPOLIS

One of the first things you'll notice about downtown Minneapolis is the **Nicollet Mall,** with its trees, flowers, decorative street lamps, and—weather permitting—dancing fountains. This is the nation's longest major pedestrian mall, extending about one mile down fashionable Nicollet Avenue, and it features heated bus shelters and a farmer's market on Fridays during the summer. Halfway down the mall, between 7th Street and 8th Street South, stands one of the city's most imposing buildings, the 57-story **Investors Diversified Services (IDS) Tower,** which rises from the midst of the bustling **Crystal Court,** a three-story center of shops and eating places.

Two major department stores, Dayton's and Carson Pirie Scott, stand on either side of 7th Street South, across the mall from the IDS Tower and connected via a skyway. Dayton's is freestanding; Carson Pirie Scott is part of a large enclosed complex known as **City Center,** which contains three stories of smart shops, fine restaurants, and assorted fast-food stands. Among the most famous tenants of City Center are an elegant Marriott Hotel and a charming Laura Ashley boutique, with its fine line of British apparel and accessories. City Center occupies one square city block between 7th and 6th Streets and between Nicollet and Hennepin Avenues.

Two more prestigious shopping centers have recently opened. Directly across Nicollet Mall from Carson's is **Gaviidae Common,** whose anchor is Saks Fifth Avenue. Across 6th Street from Dayton's stands the **Conservatory,** with the Sharper Image and F.A.O. Schwarz among its upscale tenants. (You'll find more about all these shopping centers in Chapter 10.)

The Warehouse District

If you follow 6th Street past City Center and across Hennepin Avenue, you'll find, one block beyond, on 6th Street and First Avenue North, **Butler Square,** the start of the first neighborhood on our tour, the historic Warehouse District. Butler Square is a handsome office and commercial complex that started life in 1906 as a sprawling warehouse. Now it stands at the edge of several blocks of carefully restored turn-of-the-century structures that house restaurants, bars, nightclubs, shops, and galleries.

The Warehouse District is a popular gathering place for nearby office workers and, in fact, for Twin Citians in general. Toward the eastern edge of the district you'll find antiquers, in shops that have established their own niche here.

St. Anthony Falls, the cities' earliest source of water power, is nearby, its size surprisingly modest considering the monumental part it played in the development of this area.

St. Anthony Main and Riverplace

Before there was a city of Minneapolis or a city of St. Paul, there was the village of St. Anthony, with its cobblestone Main Street. When the business district moved across the Mississippi and beyond toward the end of the 19th century, Main Street fell into disrepair. During the 1970s, though, its cobblestone surface was restored, and it has since become the site of a multiuse complex housing offices, restaurants, and retail stores known as **St. Anthony Main.**

More recently, an upscale mall called **Riverplace** opened nearby with its own mix of restaurants, bars, and shops. This area's blend of the historic and the contemporary has made it popular with home folks and visitors alike. (If you visit the Twin Cities during the Christmas season, be advised that the gloriously decorated courtyards at Riverplace rank high among holiday must-sees here.)

A block beyond the historic riverfront district, you'll find University Avenue. Follow it east, and you'll pass by fraternity and sorority houses on your way to the main campus of the University of Minnesota, which has buildings on both the east and west banks of the Mississippi River.

The University of Minnesota Area

A hub of activity in any university town is the campus, where interesting people gather to share their knowledge and their talent. Imagine, then, the variety and vitality to be found here in the Twin Cities, home of one of the largest universities on one campus in the United States.

There's an assortment of architecture to be admired on the campus of the **University of Minnesota,** extending from venerable old buildings like Eddy Hall on the east bank of the Mississippi to sleek new complexes like the west-bank Humphrey Institute of Public Affairs. Particularly interesting to visitors is the Civil and Mineral Engineering Building, which extends six stories underground, tunneled out of natural bedrock.

University-related shopping and entertainment draw students and their elders to two stimulating areas on opposite sides of the Mississippi, **Dinkytown** on the east bank and **Seven Corners** on the west. At Seven Corners, you'll find a particularly lively atmosphere in an area that's recently been designated the West Bank Theater District. Popular after-hours hangouts abound, and you'll find here some of the best theater, music, and stand-up comedy in town.

Between Seven Corners and the downtown Nicollet Mall stands the **Hubert H. Humphrey Metrodome,** a sports facility which is beloved by some, bemoaned by others. It's not the prettiest structure in Minneapolis, but the Dome does draw large crowds to games played by the Minnesota Vikings, the Minnesota Twins, and the University of Minnesota Golden Gophers. Out-of-towners here for a brief stay seem to like the Dome, if only because they can be sure their game won't be rained out. Don't worry about being unable to find the Metrodome; you can't miss it—a huge white mushroom planted on the eastern edge of downtown Minneapolis.

A Cultural Corner of Downtown Minneapolis

Returning now to the IDS Building and proceeding southward on the mall to 12th Street South, you'll pass the sleek, modernistic **Orchestra Hall,** home of the internationally famous Minnesota Orchestra. Just a few blocks farther ahead, lovely **Loring Park,** named for the founder of Minneapolis's extensive park system, provides a beautiful border to the southern edge of downtown. Loring Park is also the site of a pedestrian bridge that provides passage over Hennepin and Lyndale Avenues to the **Minneapolis Sculpture Gardens,** a brand-new area of outdoor statuary facing the **Tyrone Guthrie Theater,** with its famous repertory company, and the **Walker Art Center,** with its renowned collection of modern art. (A more traditional collection can be found at the distinguished Minneapolis Institute of Art, still farther to the south.)

On the hilly terrain behind the Walker-Guthrie complex, over-

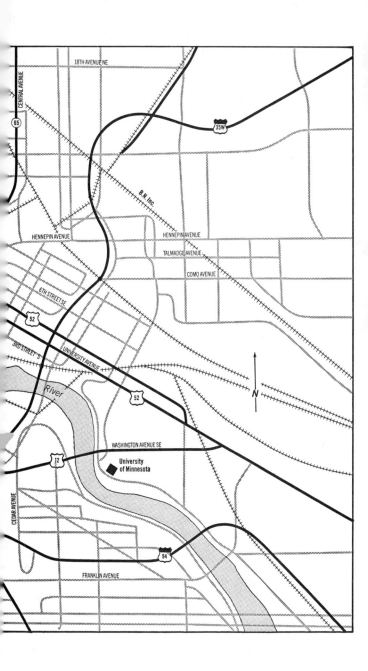

looking downtown, are two of the city's prime residential areas, Lowry Hill and Kenwood Parkway. **Lowry Hill** is famous for its 19th-century mansions, many of which had third-story ballrooms because in those days people entertained at home. The homes in nearby **Kenwood** are lovely, but less elaborate. Still, one of them has gained a bit of fame as the place where Mary Richards (a.k.a. Mary Tyler Moore) used to live. (By the way, it was at the IDS Tower's Crystal Court that Mary threw her hat up in the air week after week!)

Uptown and the Lake District

Following Hennepin Avenue southward through about two tidy miles of stores, restaurants, and multiple dwellings, you'll find yourself in the heart of a smart residential and commercial neighborhood long known as **Uptown** and more recently dubbed "Yuptown." The well-heeled young urban professionals who now live and work here spend a lot of time in local classic movie houses, ethnic restaurants, and trendy bars. **Calhoun Square,** at the corner of Hennepin Avenue and Lake Street, is a fashionable shopping mall that adds further to the magnetic charm of Uptown. Another major draw is the annual outdoor Uptown Art Fair, which attracts craftsmen each summer from throughout the country.

Hennepin Avenue ends a few blocks farther south at **Lakewood Cemetery,** where a large and memorable graveside plaque marks the burial place of Hubert H. Humphrey, formerly mayor of Minneapolis, U.S. senator from Minnesota, and vice president of the United States. And a few blocks farther to the west, in one of the most picturesque parts of the city, you'll find the start of a chain of popular neighborhood lakes: **Lake Calhoun, Lake Harriet,** and **Lake of the Isles.** On the north side of Lake of the Isles, Kenwood Parkway will take you back to the vicinity of the Guthrie Theater, and then, via Hennepin Avenue, you're on your way back to downtown Minneapolis.

A VIEW OF ST. PAUL

And now for your introduction to St. Paul. Like other older "river towns," downtown St. Paul defies directions based strictly on north, east, south, and west designations because its streets and avenues were originally set up to run parallel with and perpendicular to the meandering Mississippi.

An appropriate focal point for your St. Paul orientation is the striking, centrally located Saint Paul Center, housing the **World Trade Center,** a towering complex of offices at 8th Street between Cedar and Wabasha Avenues. Standing on the Wabasha Avenue side of the World Trade Center, whether you're looking north toward the State Capitol or south toward the Mississippi, you'll see the series of second-story skyways that link one side of this busy avenue to the other.

The 40-story World Trade Center, opened in late summer of

1. Minnesota Office of Tourism
2. Ordway Music Hall
3. Civic Center
4. St. Paul Public Library
5. State Capitol
6. St. Paul Cathedral
7. Minnesota Museum of Art
8. Minnesota State Fairgrounds
9. Minnesota World Trade Center
10. Science Museum of Minnesota
11. 3M William L. McKnight Omnitheatre
12. Union Depot Place

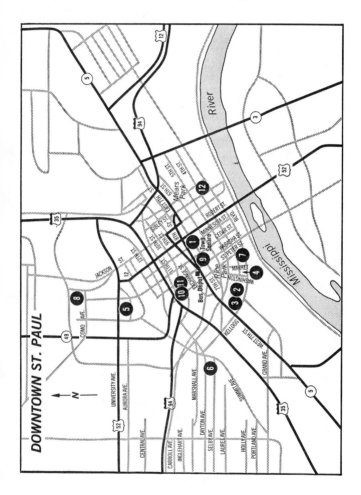

1987, is designed to promote and extend trade between the upper Midwest and foreign markets throughout Europe, Asia, and Central and South America. The Twin Cities, known widely as a computer capital, already do a brisk business with overseas markets. The fact that so many major corporations headquarter here—Honeywell, Control Data, 3M, Northwest Airlines, General Mills, and Pillsbury, among others—makes Minneapolis–St. Paul an especially appropriate headquarters for international trade.

Toward the State Capitol

One block north of the World Trade Center, at the corner of Wabasha Avenue and Exchange Street, stands the **Science Museum of Minnesota,** home of Iggy, the giant iguana, among other impressive creatures and exhibits. Diagonally across the street you'll find the exquisite **World Theatre,** where Garrison Keillor's "Prairie Home Companion" was broadcast live each week to radio fans throughout the nation. From this corner, looking north, you've got a picture-perfect view of the superb **State Capitol** of Minnesota and of its famous dome, the largest unsupported marble dome in the world. At the base of the dome, a group of graceful gilded figures represent *The Progress of the State:* a charioteer holds up a horn of plenty, prancing horses represent the power of nature, and two majestic women embody the spirit of civilization.

Historic Lowertown

To the east of the World Trade Center, the past and the present blend harmoniously in a restored area known as Lowertown. Venerable buildings like the old **Union Depot** and **Galtier Plaza,** both of which played an important role in St. Paul's earlier history, now house fine restaurants, shops, and galleries. And in this area, the practices of an earlier day are revived on Saturday mornings from April to October, when the **Farmer's Market** offers for sale a variety of fresh produce, bakery items, and flowers. Handcrafts from the newest Minnesotans, the Hmong and other Southeast Asians, are also displayed.

Toward the Mississippi

On your way south from the World Trade Center, proceeding along Wabasha Avenue, you'll reach **Kellogg Boulevard,** a broad thoroughfare that parallels and overlooks the Mississippi River; on the way, you'll pass some of the best shopping in downtown St. Paul, including Dayton's and the department stores and specialty shops at **Town Square.** In St. Paul as in Minneapolis, Carson Pirie Scott has chosen to be part of a major center; you'll find this fine department store in the Town Square complex. A tourist-information desk on the street level of Town Square will provide answers to your questions about the city.

Farther south on **Wabasha Avenue,** toward the riverfront where excursion-boat tours are a popular summertime attraction, you'll see the **St. Paul City Hall.** This is the home of one of the state's most beloved statues, a 36-foot-high, 60-ton onyx American Indian called *The God of Peace.*

A few blocks west on Kellogg Boulevard, beyond the modernistic **Minnesota Museum of Art,** you can follow Market Street on your right to **Rice Park,** a verdant square block surrounded by four of St. Paul's most important structures: the graceful new Ordway Music Theatre, the meticulously restored Landmark Center, the distinguished St. Paul Public Library, and the elegant Saint Paul Hotel.

Summit Avenue and Beyond

North of our vantage point at the World Trade Center and directly in front of the splendid State Capitol building, you'll find one of the shortest streets in this or any other city. **John Ireland Boulevard** extends just half a mile from the State Capitol to the magnificent **St. Paul Cathedral,** which overlooks all of the downtown area. Archbishop John Ireland, a dynamic cleric who used his considerable influence and powers of persuasion to create a stately cathedral modeled after St. Peter's in Rome, dedicated it in 1915 to the people of St. Paul. In front of the cathedral, John Ireland Boulevard runs into Summit Avenue, one of two streets in the United States designated a Monumental Residential Boulevard.

Extending for five miles until it ends at the Mississippi River, **Summit Avenue** is the address of some of the nation's stateliest Victorian mansions, among them the home of James J. Hill, founder of the Great Northern Railroad, and the more modest digs of F. Scott Fitzgerald, who wrote parts of *This Side of Paradise* while living here. The official residence of the governor of Minnesota is also on Summit Avenue, and farther on you'll find the campuses of two famous Midwestern colleges, Macalester and the College of St. Thomas.

Running parallel to and south of Summit is **Grand Avenue,** St. Paul's version of Minneapolis's Uptown, a trendy neighborhood that's popular for its distinctive dining, shopping, and entertainment and for its annual summertime festival, Grand Old Day.

Farther to the northwest is **Como Park,** with its popular lake, zoo, and conservatory, and nearby there's the **Bandana Square Complex** with the Children's Museum for kids of all ages. (The complex formerly housed Northern Pacific Railroad trains, which were painted and refurbished there.) Kids of all ages also enjoy the 17 miles (at scale) of tracks, trains, and landscaping set up by members of the Twin City Model Railroad Club in the nearby Bandana Square Shopping Mall.

The **State Fairgrounds** lie in this area too, not far from I-94, which will take you back to downtown St. Paul.

5. Twin Cities Fast Facts

The following is a quick rundown of information that should prove helpful to you while you're in the Twin Cities. The listings are alphabetical, but you might want to turn first to "Tourist Information," where you'll find how very welcome a guest you'll be.

The local tourism offices have put together a really impressive array of guides and services for you, and have made them readily accessible through toll-free "800" phone numbers. In fact, the Minnesota Office of Tourism also maintains a data base which will identify for you, before you leave home, accommodations that offer the special amenities you're interested in, everything from baby-sitting services to honeymoon packages to senior rates. They touch virtually all bases! You can even have a personalized printout mailed to you. Now that's hospitality, Minnesota-style.

Of course, the concierge and front-desk personnel of your hotel will be helpful too, once you've settled in. They know the area and can point you in the right direction, whether you're looking for a local place of worship or a place to have your hair cut, your shoes shined, or your photos processed.

AIRPORT: The Minneapolis–St. Paul International Airport is about a 15-minute drive from both downtown Minneapolis and downtown St. Paul. With more than 500 flights arriving and departing each day, this is the 24th-busiest airport in the world.

AREA CODE: The telephone area code throughout the Twin Cities area is 612.

CALENDAR OF EVENTS: You'll find upcoming events listed every Friday in the daily newspapers, the *St. Paul Pioneer Press* and the *StarTribune*. There are, in addition, a number of widely available weekly and monthly local periodicals, some of them free, that provide useful information on current activities and performances.

In Chapter XI you'll find the approximate dates for annual events like the Minnesota State Fair, the Minneapolis Aquatennial, the St. Paul Winter Carnival, and the Renaissance Festival. The dates vary from year to year, so once again local newspapers and magazines, tourist information offices, and hotel personnel will be able to give you timely specifics.

CAR RENTALS: Most national car-rental companies have offices in the Twin Cities, including **National Car Rental** (tel. 726-5600), **Hertz Rent-A-Car** (tel. 726-1600), **Dollar Rent-A-Car** (tel. 726-9494), and **Avis Rent-A-Car** (tel. 726-1723).

CLIMATE: In the Twin Cities there are four distinct seasons, with average monthly temperatures (in degrees Fahrenheit) as follows:

January	12°	July	72°
February	17°	August	70°
March	28°	September	60°
April	45°	October	50°
May	57°	November	32°
June	67°	December	19°

Of course the actual temperature on any given day can vary quite a bit from these averages. But whatever the weather, you'll be comfortable downtown because of the extensive skyway system.

If you're visiting during the summertime, the shade trees and the lakes serve as natural air conditioners, so unless the weather's humid, you'll find that ordinary summer clothing will keep you quite comfortable. And should the temperature soar, you're only a step away from climate-controlled comfort. All public buildings are air-conditioned, of course.

During the wintertime, the temperature may sound more frigid than it feels. Generally it's a still, dry cold, unlike what you've experienced in windy cities like Chicago or oceanside cities like New York. On days when the temperature really dips, the temptation is to stay indoors, but as often as not, proper clothing will enable you to enjoy the clean, crisp invigorating outdoors.

The number of the **weather bureau** is 725-6090.

CLOTHING: Twin Citians tend to dress for the season, so during the summertime don't be surprised to see shorts worn by men, women, and children in city locations as well as suburban ones. You'll probably want to dress more formally if you're going to a restaurant or to an office, but by and large, dress tends to be casual in these parts. Light clothing will see you through every warm-weather occasion, but remember that evenings tend to be cool and so do some air-conditioned buildings, so bring along a light jacket or sweater.

During the wintertime you'll certainly want to bring a pair of boots to keep your feet dry in case of snow. In fact here, as in metropolitan centers around the world, women's boots have become a fashionable wardrobe accessory, and you'll see certain styles indoors day and evening. What you probably won't see, except maybe on the slopes or the rinks or the cross-country ski trails, is earmuffs. You really should bring a woolen hat, though, and of course warm gloves and a warm coat or jacket. Then you'll be ready for anything that might be on the bill during what's been called our "theater of seasons."

CREDIT CARDS: Most establishments, with the exception of a few restaurants, accept all major credit cards and, with proper identification, personal checks.

DRINKING AGE: The legal drinking age in Minnesota is 21. Identification is required in nightclubs and bars.

EMERGENCIES: Here, as in so many other areas of the country, a phone call to 911 will bring help for **fire, police, or ambulance emergencies.** There's another number you should know, as well. Abbott Northwestern Hospital (tel. 863-4095) offers **24-hour telephone consultations.** Prescription medicine, emergency-room visits, or hospital care can be provided as needed, and specialist referrals can also be arranged at competitive fees. VISA, MasterCard, and personal checks are accepted, and insurance forms will be completed if requested.

FILM DEVELOPING: There are now several one-hour color-print developing and printing companies in the Twin Cities. Many of them operate seven days a week in shopping centers. Proex, one of the first and still one of the best, prides itself on redoing without charge any prints that customers find unsatisfactory.

HOTEL TAX: The hotel tax in downtown St. Paul and on the Bloomington "strip" is 11%; in downtown Minneapolis, 12%.

POST OFFICE: The main U.S. Post Office in Minneapolis is located at South 1st Street and Marquette (tel. 349-4970); in St. Paul it's at Kellogg Boulevard and Jackson Street (tel. 293-3011). There's 24-hour postal service available at the airport.

SAFETY: You'll feel relatively safe in the Twin Cities, but remember that whenever you're traveling in an unfamiliar city or country, you should stay alert. Be aware of your immediate surroundings. Wear a moneybelt and keep a close eye on your possessions. Be particularly careful with cameras, purses, and wallets, all favorite targets of thieves and pickpockets.

SALES TAX: The 6% Minnesota state sales tax does not apply to clothing, prescription drugs, and food that is purchased in stores. At hotels, restaurants, and bars within the city limits of Minneapolis you'll pay an additional ½% tax on the same items that are subject to the state 6% sales tax.

TELEVISION: You'll find all the major TV networks in the Twin Cities, but here's a reminder that may keep you from missing your favorite show: unless you hail from the same time zone (Central Time), the program you want to watch may be aired one or two hours earlier or later than what you're used to. Just check the TV pages in one of the local newspapers. There are six TV channels available here: Channels 2 (PBS), 4 (CBS), 5 (ABC), 9 (Independent), 11 (NBC), and 17 (PBS). Cable is available too.

TIME: Minnesota is in the Central Time zone, one hour behind the East Coast and two hours ahead of the West Coast (if it's 8 p.m. in New York, it's 7 p.m. in the Twin Cities, 6 p.m. in Denver, and 5 p.m. in San Francisco). It observes Central Standard Time in the fall, winter, and spring, and Central Daylight Time (daylight savings) in summer.

TIPPING: The usual tip for service well rendered is 15%.

TOURIST INFORMATION: The Minnesota Office of Tourism (tel. 612/296-5029, or toll-free 800/657-3700) is unique in the services it provides to tourists even before they arrive in the Twin Cities. A toll-free phone call will put you in touch with a travel counselor who can answer your questions and, with regard to accommodations, can key into a data base listing the hotels, motels, resorts, and campgrounds that offer the specific amenities and options you desire. Among the specific information you can get by phone or mail are listings of accommodations with no charge for children, weekend packages, senior citizen rates, pets permitted, baby-sitting and day care available, indoor pool, whirlpool, tennis, waterbeds, limousine and shuttle service, and scheduled entertainment. Also, a seasonal travel newspaper, the *Minnesota Explorer,* and a variety of informational brochures will be sent to you free of charge, at your request.

The **St. Paul Convention and Visitors Bureau** (tel. 612/297-6985, or toll free 800/627-6101) maintains a comprehensively stocked Visitor Information Booth on the street level of Town Square, at 7th Street and Cedar Avenue, with brochures and guides designed to make it easier for tourists to make their choice among the diversity of attractions available. Hours are 8 a.m. to 5 p.m. Monday through Friday.

The Greater **Minneapolis Convention and Visitors Association** (tel. 612/348-4313, or toll free 800/445-7412) has information for you 8 a.m. to 5 p.m. Monday through Friday.

Among the many useful free guides awaiting you at both these offices are brochures (published quarterly) providing day-by-day listings of dance, music, sports, and theater presentations.

MINNESOTA MISCELLANY

And now, a few facts I'd like you to know about this Land of 10,000 Lakes:

The **state bird** is the loon, a sleek black-and-white waterfowl whose haunting, unforgettable call can be heard on the lakes of northern Minnesota.

The **state fish** is the walleye pike. Although it's little known beyond state borders, walleye makes delicious, delicately flavored seafood. Try it—chances are you'll discover a new favorite.

The **state tree** is the Norway Pine, named not for the country of Norway, but for the city in Maine where it grows profusely and where many of our early lumberjacks lived before heading west.

The **state flower** is the pink-and-white ladyslipper, a large, lovely wildflower that flourishes in northern and eastern Minnesota. You mustn't pick one, though—that's against the law.

The **state gemstone** is the Lake Superior agate, a reddish stone with white stripes that's found in central and northern Minnesota. It polishes up into all sorts of distinctive jewelry that you'll find in souvenir shops throughout Minneapolis and St. Paul.

The **state grain** is wild rice, a staple among Ojibwa Indians for centuries and presently a gourmet delight among diners in Minneapolis, St. Paul, and far beyond.

And finally, the **state motto,** "L'Etoile du Nord," is expressed in the language of those hardy French explorers who first discovered these shores back in the 17th century. "Star of the North" is what Minnesota was then and what it remains to this day.

Come and see for yourself.

III

TWIN CITIES ACCOMMODATIONS

1. EXPENSIVE
2. MODERATE
3. BUDGET

Two types of accommodations, in three primary locations, have developed in the Twin Cities over the years: large, expensive, rather formal hotels in downtown Minneapolis and downtown St. Paul, and smaller, more casual, more moderately priced motels elsewhere, particularly along the strip of I-494 (Bloomington) that links the southern and western suburbs to the Minneapolis–St. Paul International Airport. Generally hotels and motels on the "strip" are 15 minutes or less from the airport, 30 minutes or less from downtown Minneapolis and St. Paul.

Recently, larger and pricier hotels have begun making their appearance beyond the city limits, but in general it's safe to say that you'll pay more for accommodations downtown than in the suburbs, and, according to recent studies, you'll pay more in Minneapolis than in St. Paul.

If you're going to be carless for most of your stay, you may be better off in one downtown or the other, where you can get around by foot or by bus to many of the most popular local attractions. Destinations that lie outside downtown areas are readily accessible by cab, and frequently by bus.

On the other hand, if you're going to have the use of a car you might consider heading for the "strip," where hotels and motels offer free parking and easy access from I-494 to the network of beltlines, freeways, and Interstates that connect the cities and suburbs. If you're here on business, you'll find that many of the corporate offices in the Twin Cities are located in suburban rather than downtown areas.

I've selected hotels and motels in three price categories: expensive, moderate, and budget. Admittedly, one person's moderate is another person's expensive and a third person's budget, but let's use these dollar amounts, including tax, as guidelines: **expensive** hotels charge $85 and more per night double occupancy, **budget** lodgings run $50 and less, and **moderate** choices cover anything in between.

Of course there are variables here and there. For example, at Embassy Suites, prices are pushed into the expensive category by the 11% **hotel tax** in Bloomington and St. Paul. (In Minneapolis, the hotel tax is 12%.) The final cost is very moderate indeed when you factor in those complimentary cooked-to-order Embassy breakfasts, nightly cocktail parties, and free parking. Free parking in either downtown area is a rarity.

By the way, don't hesitate to ask about discounts when you're making reservations, especially if you'll be here on vacation. Weekend rates, senior citizens' rates, and children's rates, among others, are widely available and can make a big difference in your total tab.

The **Minnesota Office of Tourism** (tel. 612/296-5029, or toll free 800/328-1461; 800/652-9747 in Minnesota) will prepare a customized printout for you of hotels and motels offering the kinds of amenities you're most interested in.

1. Expensive

Luxury abounds at the downtown **Hyatt Regency Minneapolis,** 1300 Nicollet Mall, Minneapolis, MN 55403 (tel. 612/370-1234, or toll free 800/228-9000). A handsome fountain sculpture is the focal point of a large, decorative lobby where there's plenty of comfortable seating for prime people-watching. This is a hotel that's as popular with the home folks as with guests to the city. Two of the finest restaurants in town adjoin the main lobby of the Hyatt Regency. The Willows, an elegant contemporary dining room with mirrored pillars and ceilings, is famous for its daily smorgasbord, a dazzling array of pâtés, seafood and vegetable marinades, mousses, salads, and more—a best buy at $7.25. And the Terrace is one of the more popular casual dining spots in town.

But for visitors to the Twin Cities, one of the major attractions at the Hyatt Regency may be the guest membership in the excellent Greenway Athletic Club, located on the 6th floor of this 24-story building. Local members enjoy the finest of fitness facilities here, including weightlifting, racquetball, tennis, squash, a running track, sauna, and Jacuzzi; the price for all this is $8.50 per visit. There's also a large swimming pool available to all Hyatt Regency guests.

Nonsmokers have several floors all to themselves, and women travelers often ask for the rooms outfitted with hair dryers, lighted cosmetic mirrors, and clothesline reels. All rooms enjoy delightful views of the city and provide in-house pay movies, complimentary HBO and cable news, AM/FM clock-radios, and for that special homey touch, living greenery. Rates are $145 single occupancy, $165 double. Senior citizens get a real bargain here: $62 for either single or double occupancy, subject to availability. Inquire about discounted weekend rates.

You'll find a beautiful blend of the old and the new at the

downtown **Saint Paul Hotel,** 350 Market St., St. Paul, MN 55102 (tel. 612/292-9292). Back in 1910 this was St. Paul's premiere hotel. Now, after an extensive renovation in 1982, it has taken its place once more as a distinguished grand old hotel that offers superb accommodations and services to those who expect and appreciate the best. Looking across Rice Park toward the Ordway Music Theatre, the Saint Paul Hotel is adjacent on one side to the beautiful St. Paul Public Library and on the other to Landmark Center, the restored Old Federal Courts Building which, after its dedication in 1896, became headquarters for all federal offices in the Upper Midwest.

But if the Saint Paul Hotel maintains close ties with the city's past, it's also an integral part of St. Paul's burgeoning present. Situated at one end of an extensive skyway system, it offers guests climate-controlled access to 38 downtown blocks of shops, banks, restaurants, and varied forms of entertainment.

Accommodations at the Saint Paul Hotel are appropriately elegant. Once past the lobby, with its antique crystal chandeliers, its turn-of-the-century love seats and chairs, and its giant oriental screen, you'll find that the rooms, each decorated uniquely, contain either a king-size bed or two double beds, along with two comfortable chairs and an ample table. Superior rooms cost $99 single occupancy, $114 double. Deluxe rooms, outfitted with a love seat in place of the two chairs, cost $114 single occupancy, $129 double. On weekends, superior rooms are $69 and deluxe $79, for single or double occupancy. Extra guests are always $15.

If you enjoy shopping, you'll be well located at the **Minneapolis Marriott,** 30 S. 7th St., Minneapolis, MN 55402 (tel. 612/349-4000, or toll free 800/228-9290). Rising above the three-level City Center downtown shopping mall, this luxury hotel is connected to Carson Pirie-Scott, one of the city's best department stores, and is just skyway-steps away from perennially popular Dayton's and the brand-new Conservatory fashion center. There's a diversity of fine specialty shops accessible by skyway as well. But that's only part of the fun of staying at this sleek, modernistic 32-story triangular tower.

The decor in the Marriott's public places is stunning throughout, starting—if you can believe it—with the infinitely mirrored, spacious elevators, which serve as conversation pieces as well as transportation.

Colors throughout the hotel have been keyed to the natural and seasonal colors of Minnesota: maroons for the autumn leaves, gray-beiges for the boulders, and greens for grass and shrubs and trees. Put them all together and they spell serenity—a truly relaxing atmosphere that blends with a light-hearted approach to hospitality.

The hotel boasts two superb restaurants, Gustino's and the Fifth Season. The tunes of Gustino's singing servers add a musical touch from time to time, as do the piano melodies from the lobby lounge below.

There's a well-equipped health club with whirlpool and sauna free to guests, and there are four floors reserved for nonsmokers.

Guest rooms here are luxurious; many boast upholstered chairs and matching ottomans, built-in oak desks, and oversize beds. Also notable is the lighting provided by illuminated wall coves, which casts a soft glow over rooms that look out day and night on beautiful cityscapes.

Rates are $144 single occupancy, $164 double; members of the American Association of Retired Persons pay $108. When available, weekend rates offer spectacular savings—$69 nightly for two, with breakfast and complimentary parking. If you arrive on Thursday, you must stay for two nights. For this rate on Friday, Saturday, and Sunday nights, a one-night stay will qualify.

A long-standing Twin Cities tradition was renewed in March 1987 with the opening of the **Radisson Plaza Hotel Minneapolis,** 35 S. 7th St., Minneapolis, MN 55402 (tel. 612/339-4900, or toll free 800/333-3333). Since 1909 there's always been a Radisson Hotel on this site, and many qualms were expressed when the decision was made in 1981 to tear down the old familiar structure and replace it with a bigger and better one—the flagship of a Minneapolis based chain with over 200 hotels and affiliates worldwide.

The Radisson Plaza Minneapolis occupies one of the most centrally located sites in the Twin Cities: across the street from City Center, half a block from the Nicollet Mall, and attached by skyway to downtown's shops, offices, restaurants, and more.

The first thing you'll notice as you approach the Radisson Plaza is its elegant recessed entryway; the second, in the main lobby, is a 1,200-pound marble pedestal, on which a huge, 2,750-pound marble ball floats on half an inch of water. (It's 65 pounds of water pressure that keeps the ball suspended, in case you wondered—I did.)

The effort here has been to contrast the elegance of the public spaces with the residential feeling of the guest rooms. How residential it feels will depend a lot on your own residence, of course. The colors throughout the hotel combine teal and mauve; the French provincial and Chippendale furnishings have the look of the Old World but offer the convenience of the New: for example, the mahogany armoires have color TV sets hidden inside. Each bathroom has a TV speaker and telephone. Large desks are provided for business travelers, and maids switch the phones from the bedside table to the desk when they're making up the room each day.

A state-of-the-art fitness center is available to guests at no extra cost. Facilities include an aerobics room with daily classes, computerized rowing and treadmill equipment, and a cross-country ski machine. Rates are $121, single or double, with other accommodations higher—up to $335 for a very special suite. Seniors receive a 25% discount. Weekend rates for guests of all ages range from $79 to $109.

---

2. Moderate

A winning combination of downtown location and suburban rates is available at the three-story, 193-room **Regency Plaza Best Western,** 41 N. 10th St., Minneapolis, MN 55403 (tel. 612/339-

9311, or toll free 800/523-4200 in the U.S., 800/423-4100 in Minnesota, or 800/633-4300 in Canada), located at the end of Hwy. 12 on the edge of downtown Minneapolis.

Wood paneling and marble give the lobby a classical look; so does the library beyond. The rooms are large and pleasant, many of them enhanced by the beautiful prints of Les Kouba, a popular Minnesota painter of nature. The raspberry and royal-blue color combination carries through all the rooms, as do the light-oak furnishings. There's a large indoor swimming pool, a children's wading pool, and a whirlpool, and in each room you'll find color TV and free in-house movies.

There are two attractive restaurants here—the Regency Café, serving breakfast, lunch, and dinner from 6:30 a.m. to 7 p.m. weekdays, 7:30 a.m. to 5:30 p.m. weekends, and Harrigan's Dining Room, serving burgers, steaks, seafood, and other American fare from 5 to 10 p.m. The Hub Cap Pub is open from 11:30 a.m. to 1 a.m. Monday through Friday, 5 p.m. to 1 a.m. on Saturday, and 5 to 10 p.m. on Sunday. Soup and sandwiches are served there from 11:30 a.m. to 2 p.m. Monday through Friday. Happy hour, with discounted bar prices, runs from 3 to 6 p.m.

There's free shuttle service in a 35-passenger van to any downtown destination within a 3-mile radius—and that includes Riverplace and St. Anthony Main, the Metrodome, the Guthrie Theater, and the IDS Tower. Rates range from $56 for a single to $85 for a mini-suite and $125 for a bridal suite. On weekends, AARP members receive a 10% discount.

Late 1986 marked the arrival of the Twin Cities' first bed-and-breakfast hotel when **Bradbury Suites,** 7770 Johnson Ave., Bloomington, MN 55437 (tel. 612/893-9999), opened its canopied front doors to surprised and delighted travelers. What's different about this kind of accommodation? Well, for the price of a single room, you'll be staying in a two-room suite with a small refrigerator and two TV sets, one that's visible in both the bedroom and the sitting room, and a tiny one for the counter in the bathroom.

The suites, all done in shades of green and mauve, are comfortable and spacious enough for an evening "at home," with dinner delivered by nearby Mother Tucker's, the Lincoln Del, or T.G.I. Friday. And if you'd rather pass the time with cribbage or Trivial Pursuit than with TV, just check out the game of your choice from the "comfort chest" in the lobby. You'll find other useful items there as well—everything from hair dryers to throat lozenges. Consider yourself at home.

Rates are moderate: $67 single, $77 double per night, Monday through Thursday; $39 single, $49 double, Friday through Sunday. For seminars, the cost is $49 anytime. Complimentary admission to the nearby U.S. Swim and Fitness Club is provided, and so is a shuttle to the airport and nearby restaurants.

Like many other moderate and economy-priced motels, the **Dillon Airport Inn,** 814 E. 79th St., Bloomington, MN 55420 (tel. 612/854-5558, or toll free 800/253-7503), has no restaurant of its own. But it's only a few steps away from several informal and popular eating places. Complimentary coffee is offered around the clock at this comfortable inn, which also provides shuttle service to the airport from 5 a.m. to midnight.

You'll feel welcome at once in the attractive lobby, with its sunken sitting room, brick-walled fireplace, and comfortable burgundy-and-beige seating. There's cable TV featuring Showtime in each of the 136 rooms here, and you can choose one with a king-size bed, a water bed, or two double beds. All rooms contain a pair of upholstered chairs and a small desk; some rooms have a balcony.

Rates are $53 single occupancy, $59 double occupancy, Sunday through Thursday; $49 for a room serving one to four adults on Friday and Saturday. Inquire about two-night weekend rates as well. Seniors receive a 10% discount Sunday through Thursday, a 25% discount on Friday or Saturday. There's no charge for a rollaway.

You'll find one of the largest swimming pools on the Bloomington "strip" at the **Holiday Inn Airport 2,** 5401 Green Valley Dr., Bloomington, MN 55437 (tel. 612/831-8000, or toll free 800/HOLIDAY). You'll also find a whirlpool and sauna in the new west wing of this sprawling six-story complex. Located 7½ miles from the Minneapolis–St. Paul International Airport, this Holiday Inn does a lot of fly-and-drive business: if they stay for at least one night, guests can leave their cars in the parking lot and take advantage of the free 24-hour airport shuttle service, thereby saving the cost of airport parking. Shuttle service is also available to nearby shopping malls and nearby restaurants.

There are two on-site restaurants here. Marti's serves moderately priced lunches daily from 11 a.m. to 1:30 p.m. and dinner from 5:30 to 10 p.m.; the Coffee Shop, serving three meals a day, is open from 7 a.m. to 10 p.m. And Partners, the cocktail lounge, is open from 11 a.m. to 1 a.m., with live entertainment from 8 p.m. until closing.

Standard rooms with two twin beds, a work table, and two chairs cost $61 single occupancy, $69 double. AARP members get a 10% discount. There's an especially good weekend discount here—$42.34 for up to four people in a room.

You'll find a lot more than a comfortable and convenient place to stay at the **Thunderbird Motel,** 2201 E. 78th St., Bloomington, MN 55420 (tel. 612/854-3411). Located just 5 miles from the Minneapolis–St. Paul airport, with complimentary shuttle service to the airport 24 hours a day, the Thunderbird is one of dozens of motels on the Bloomington strip, but it has certain notable features. A towering statue of an Indian chief dominates the front lawn, and a graceful Apache rides his steed atop a granite pedestal near the main entrance. These are an introduction to the kind of art that draws thousands of visitors from throughout the area each year to see the largest collection of authentic Indian artifacts and animal mountings in the upper Midwest.

In addition to authentic likenesses of Native Americans, there are likenesses of many of the animals that shared the wilderness with them. In the Totem Pole dining room, for example, two stalwart braves paddle a birchbark canoe while a nearby wolf bays at the ceiling.

A Special-Value Chain Hotel

If you live in one of the 26 states with **Embassy Suites** hotels, you'll be glad to know that there are three of them here in the Twin Cities: one in downtown St. Paul at 175 E. 10th St., St. Paul, MN 55101 (tel. 612/224-5400); one near the airport at 7901 34th Ave. S., Bloomington, MN 55420 (tel. 612/854-1000); and one in suburban Bloomington at 2800 W. 80th St., Bloomington, MN 55431 (tel. 612/884-4811). The toll-free number for all three is 800/EMBASSY.

These value-packed hotels have effectively countered the old admonition: "If you want the comforts of home, stay home." Actually, the comforts awaiting you here may rival what you've left at home: not one but two handsomely furnished rooms with a TV set and a phone in each, a kitchenette whose facilities include a microwave oven, and decor to suit your individual preference, with whole floors devoted to rooms decorated in tones of mauve, green, or blue. Just choose your floor and you choose your color.

A full cooked-to-order breakfast is yours each morning, and at the end of each day you can have your favorite drinks at the two-hour cocktail party held in the attractive skylit indoor courtyard. Here brick pillars, tile floors, fountains, and even a waterfall will remind you of your last visit to the Mediterranean, or of the visit you've yet to make.

Rates vary according to availability; call the toll-free number for specifics. Basic prices are $119 single, $129 double, Sunday through Thursday; $89 to $122 Friday and Saturday for up to four adults. Members of AARP receive a 10% discount. Complimentary transportation to and from the airport is available to guests 24 hours a day.

Throughout the complex are items from the collection—from a beautiful porcelain collection of figurines to the massive buffalo head mounted in the ballroom. The theme extends to guest rooms as well, where paintings, draperies, and even the carpeting show an Indian motif.

But there are 20th-century trappings at the Thunderbird too. This is the only motel on the strip with both an indoor and outdoor swimming pool. You'll have the use of a heat lamp, a whirlpool, a kiddie pool, and picnic tables in the vicinity of the spacious kidney-shaped indoor pool. And across the hall from these, a sauna and exercise room are available without extra charge to guests of the motel.

The Totem Pole dining room is open from 11 a.m. to 10 p.m. Monday through Friday, with weekend dinners served from 5 to 10:30 p.m. and all-you-can-eat brunches from 10:30 a.m. to 2:30 p.m. Rates are moderate: $61 to $68 for a single, $67 to $74 for a double. Weekend packages are available at $55 for one to four persons. Shuttle service to the airport is available 24 hours a day.

The convenience of a motel and the appearance of a hotel are what you'll find at the **Comfort Inn,** 1321 E. 78th St., Bloomington, MN 55420 (tel. 612/854-3400 or toll free 800/228-5150). Rooms are attractively furnished in a variety of decors, and if you order king-size accommodations, you'll find a leisure recliner waiting along with the standard furnishings. Each of the rooms in this five-story complex offers free HBO.

Located on the Bloomington "strip" just 5 miles from the airport, the Comfort Inn provides free transportation to and from the Minneapolis–St. Paul International Airport 24 hours a day. Rates range from $51 to $58 for single accommodations, $53 to $60 double. Weekend rates are $51 to $58 single, $53 to $60 double. Seniors receive a 10% discount.

You'll find attractive, moderately priced accommodations at the suburban **Hopkins House Hotel,** 1501 Hwy. 7, Hopkins, MN 55343 (tel. 612/935-7711 or toll free 800/328-6024). Located about 10 miles from Lake Minnetonka, the largest lake in Minnesota, and 20 minutes from downtown Minneapolis, this seven-floor, 164-room complex offers an indoor pool, sauna, exercise room, and table tennis. The color scheme features shades of rose and blue, starting with the deep-rose cushioned couches and soft-blue table lamps in the lobby. Oak end tables and a brass ceiling punctuated with modern open globe lights complete the bright, cheery decor. Your own room will doubtless be decorated in combinations of rose and blue as well, and if you like, it can also contain a heart-shaped waterbed; just ask for a "happy-tub room." You'll find basic cable color TV here plus free HBO and ESPN sports. Rates are $49 single, $55 double. The happy-tub room goes for $85. A complimentary Continental breakfast is offered and so is a 4-to-7 p.m. happy hour with free hors d'oeurves. Guests receive free daily passes to the Medalist Tennis Club, located about 1 mile from the hotel.

One of the most central locations in the Twin Cities is offered by the **Holiday Inn Metrodome,** 1500 Washington Ave. S., Minneapolis, MN 55454 (tel. 612/333-4646, or toll free 800/HOLIDAY). Situated on the eastern edge of downtown Minneapolis, with the University of Minnesota campus on one side and the Metrodome on the other, this hotel stands right at the hub of the Seven Corners area, with its top-notch ethnic restaurants and bars. Grandma's Restaurant is right next door, an exciting place famous for its hodgepodge of historical artifacts and its menu featuring a wide variety of basic American food and drink. You're right in the heart of the West Bank theater district here, with the satiric productions of Dudley Rigg's Experimental Theatre Company (E.T.C.) next door and a miscellany of shows by local troupes at the Southern Theater just around the corner. Across the street, you'll find the famous Theater in the Round, and don't overlook the delightful entertainment that's available to you on the four stages of the nearby University Theatre and at their summertime stage on the Centennial Showboat, docked on the east bank of the Mississippi River.

In the lobby as well as in the guest rooms, you'll find decor that's been described as "subtle art deco." Amenities include an indoor pool, whirlpool, sauna, and exercise room, all on the 14th floor with an exceptional view of the city. Rates are $79 to $82 single, $89 to $92 double. Discounted weekend rates are $69.50.

There's the ambience of romantic Old Spain at the large and

lovely **Seville Hotel,** 8151 Bridge Rd., Bloomington, MN (tel. 612/830-1300). Orange, brown, and yellow dominate the large lobby, while guest rooms are done in softer earth tones of beige and brown. A pool, sauna, and whirlpool are available here, as are a popular lounge and dining room. Located right on I-494, the Seville is about 20 minutes from the airport, 30 minutes from downtown Minneapolis and St. Paul. You're also close to fine suburban shopping at the nearby Southtown Center and just a bit farther away, at the legendary Southdale, with its satellite centers, Galleria, Yorktown, and Southdale Square. Rates at the Seville are $55 single, $63 double. Weekends, rooms with one king-size bed run $40, with two beds $45, for up to four guests.

The amenities are exceptional at the **Holiday Inn International,** 3 Appletree Sq., Bloomington, MN 55420 (tel. 612/854-9000, or toll free 800/HOLIDAY).

The 13-story, 431-room building boasts a truly imposing lobby with two-story atrium and furnishings done in tones of peach and green. These colors give an air of tranquility to the lobby and to the guest rooms too. You won't have to forgo your fitness regimen here, thanks to an Olympic-size swimming pool, a superbly equipped fitness center complete with Nautilus equipment, and aerobics classes. There's no extra charge for these or for the use of the whirlpool and sauna, but if you decide on a suntan, the booth will cost $6 to $10, depending on how long you want to bask. (By the way, an on-site "hair design studio" can put your coiffure back in shape if all the foregoing proves too much for it.) Two restaurants, the moderately priced Applebutter and more elegant Pippins, are popular with hometown folks as well as with visitors. That's true of the Greenhouse lounge as well. There's free 24-hour shuttle service to the airport, leaving every half hour.

Rates for a standard room with two double beds are $63 for one person, $72 for two people. Rooms with king-size beds are $66 for one person, $75 for two people. Weekend rates are $49 per room.

For decades, visitors to the Twin Cities have been made welcome at the **Normandy Inn,** 405 S. 8th St., Minneapolis, MN 55405 (tel. 612/370-1400). The rustic, Swiss-chalet look of the exterior of this four-story building stands in sharp contrast to the high-rise structures that have grown up around it. The interior has a country look, with dark woodwork, marble tile floors, and a graceful central fountain. Guest rooms are done in earth tones of rust and beige.

Among local folks, the Normandy is best known for its moderately priced restaurant, which features high-rise popovers at dinnertime and beer-cheese soup and pecan pie both afternoon and evening. Located four blocks from the Nicollet Mall, the Normandy is within walking distance of the Convention Center and Loring Park. Economy rooms are $44.50 single, $54.50 double; deluxe rooms run $62.60 single, $68.50 double.

Twin Citians out for a special evening or event are apt to come to the **Northstar Hotel,** 618 Second Ave. S., Minneapolis, MN 55402 (tel. 612/338-2288, or toll free 800/THE-OMNI). The reason for this handsome hotel's local popularity is the presence of a five-star restaurant called the Rosewood Room. Live entertainment is offered nightly in the restaurant and in the popular Rosewood Lounge.

The lobby is done in muted shades of beige and peach, and guest rooms feature muted browns and beiges. A drive-up area makes for convenient arrivals; another gracious feature is the presence of uniformed doormen on duty 24 hours a day. Although there are no athletic facilities on the premises, a $2 guest-entrance fee provides you with temporary membership at the International Fitness Center or the YMCA, both of which are located on the downtown skyway system. Rates at the Northstar are $105 single, $120 double. AARP members receive a 50% discount.

When you see a big bubble in the sky, you'll know you've arrived at the **Ambassador Resort Motel,** 5225 Wayzata Blvd., Minneapolis, MN 55416 (tel. 612/545-0441, or toll free 800/535-1808). The huge glass dome covers the largest tropical indoor-pool court in the state of Minnesota. The palm trees, ranging from 20 to 60 feet in height, will put you in a frolicsome mood; so will the large whirlpool, which accommodates 20 wet and happy people. Other popular features include two saunas, a shuffleboard court, Ping-Pong tables, a putting green, and pool tables. And there's a video-game room as well as two restaurants and a lounge featuring live entertainment.

In the unlikely event that you'd ever wish to leave the premises, a courtesy van will take you to shopping centers within a 5-mile radius, including two of the area's best: Ridgedale and Bonaventure.

The Ambassador lobby is a bright, cheerful place with natural light streaming in through glass walls. Guest rooms are cheery, done in beiges and natural woods. TV includes complimentary Showtime. Room rates are $55 single, $65 double, plus 6% hotel tax.

For nearly 20 years visitors to the Twin Cities have enjoyed staying at the **Sheraton Airport Inn,** 2525 E. 78th St., Bloomington, MN 55420 (tel. 612/854-1771, or toll free 800/325-3535). Now a second beautifully landscaped brown-brick four-story structure has been built adjacent to the original two-story building. Still present and popular in the huge lobby are the cozy nooks and crannies that businesspeople find useful for private conferences.

Another feature of the lobby is the abundance of couches and coffee tables, set amid fresh green plants and palm trees. There's an indoor pool, whirlpool, and exercise room here, as well as free cable TV that includes ESPN, Showtime, and CNN channels. A full-service dining room, the Timbers, is popular; also a favorite is the live musical entertainment and the lounge, with big-screen live TV coverage of major sporting events.

Rates for the individually decorated rooms are $63 single, $69 double. Weekend discounts depend on availability. Phone for specific information. Free transportation is provided 24 hours a day to and from the international airport, located just 3½ miles away. If they don't pick you up from the airport within 12 minutes of your initial call, your first night is free.

3. Budget

If you're interested in economical accommodations with cooking facilities, you'll be glad to learn about the **Friendly Host Inn,** 1225 E. 78th St., Minneapolis, MN 55420 (tel. 612/854-3322, or toll free 800/453-4511). Single-bed rooms with a two-burner stove, small sink, and refrigerator rent for $37 single occupancy, $42 double. Much larger two-bed rooms contain a four-burner stove, small refrigerator, and double cupboards. The cost for these rooms is $47 double occupancy ($4 extra for each additional adult). Without cooking facilities, the one-bed room goes for $32 single occupancy, $37 double; two-bed rooms are $42 double ($4 each additional adult, children free). Families pay $42 for standard two-bed rooms, $47 for rooms with cooking facilities. The seventh night is free in all rooms.

Decor varies here, but the rooms are all attractive and comfortable and the motel is well located, just 5 miles from the airport. Free airport limousine service is provided 24 hours a day. An indoor pool and whirlpool are available on the premises.

The **Exel Inn,** 2701 E. 78th St., Bloomington, MN 55420 (tel. 612/854-7200), is located just 4 miles from the Minneapolis–St. Paul International Airport and provides complimentary airport shuttle service 24 hours a day. This 205-room brick complex of two two-story buildings offers attractive rooms at reasonable rates. Prices range from $36.50 for one person to $48 for king-size accommodations for two. The rooms, decorated in shades of brown and peach, are kept scrupulously clean. Cable color TV is available in each room, including HBO at no additional cost.

Day's Inn/University, 2407 University Ave. S.E., Minneapolis, MN 55414 (tel. 612/623-3999, or toll free 800/325-2525), is located at University and Washington Avenues six blocks east of the University of Minnesota's Minneapolis campus. Guest rooms, done in earth tones of rust, brown, and orange with touches of blue, offer two large chairs, a desk, and a credenza; most have a vanity area separate from the bath. There are no restaurants on the premises but there's a branch of the Embers chain right across the street. A free Continental breakfast is available each morning. Rates are $38 to $50 for a single, $44 to $60 double. Free local phone calls, free shuttle service to the university and to local hospitals, and two nonsmoking floors are also offered here.

Low-cost weekly accommodations are available near the university at the **Gopher Campus Motor Lodge,** 925 S.E. 4th St., Minneapolis, MN 55414 (tel. 612/331-3740), with rates at $31 for one person, $36 for two.

Card-carrying members of American Youth Hostels may be able to secure a place to stay in the Twin Cities for a maximum of three nights at $12 per night or less, depending upon availability. Contact **American Youth Hostels,** Minnesota Council, 2395 University Ave. W., Suite 302, St. Paul, MN 55114 (tel. 612/659-0407).

TWIN CITIES DINING

The good news about dining out in the Twin Cities is that there's something here to suit every taste and every budget. Far from being the land of lefse and lutefisk, Minneapolis and St. Paul are remarkable for the variety, the quality, and the cosmopolitan nature of their restaurant cuisine. Actually, they're a little short on Scandinavian dining places, but there is plenty of good French and German, Greek and Italian, Chinese, Japanese, Vietnamese, and other ethnic fare to be found here. And there are fine eating spots that have a special way with basic American steaks and chops and seafood, as well as with vegetarian foods.

A number of Twin Cities restaurants have won national and international awards, and they'll be called to your attention, along with those that have become favorites among knowledgeable hometown folks. Many of the places listed here, in fact, are the ones to which local hosts generally bring their own out-of-town guests.

I'll let you in on the not-to-be-missed restaurants in various parts of the cities and suburbs. They'll be listed in each area pretty much from the top down, the most expensive to the least expensive. Bear in mind that geographically some areas are relatively confined —the downtown Minneapolis, Warehouse, and Mill districts, for example. Others, like Minneapolis South Suburban, are rather spread out. Do use the maps in this book to get oriented before you set out.

Two reminders about price: First, even the costliest eating spots tend to be moderately priced at lunchtime. Thus you can enjoy the finest in ambience, cuisine, and presentation for a nominal noonday cost, and you can also turn these lunches into scouting expeditions for that extra special evening out, when memories—not money— become the prime consideration. Second, prices in the Twin Cities restaurants tend to be lower than in other metropolitan areas, so the "expensive" choice may seem quite reasonably priced to you. All the better. It's just one more benefit for visitors to these fair cities.

---

1. Minneapolis and Minneapolis South Suburban

DOWNTOWN MINNEAPOLIS

Let's start right at the top. No restaurant in the Twin Cities has proved more popular with the public and the press than **D'Amico Cucina,** 100 N. 6th St., Minneapolis (tel. 338-2401). Situated across the street from the recently constructed Timberwolves sports arena, D'Amico Cucina has been an unqualified winner since it was opened in September 1987 by longtime restaurant consultant and manager Richard D'Amico, his brother, executive chef Larry D'Amico, and their colleague Steve Davidson. The result of their collaboration is a handsome, casually sophisticated restaurant where the cuisine is imaginative, the service impeccable, and the atmosphere everything you could desire, whether personal or professional reasons have brought you to this tree-lined, brick-walled section of the Warehouse District. D'Amico Cucina is, in fact, a graceful blend of the old and the new. A brick wall and wood-beamed ceilings hearken back to the building's warehouse days; a blend of peach and gray in the marble floor and wall coverings is accented by steel and black leather chairs and set off by a variety of Italian artifacts. The colorful, artistically presented fare enhances an ambience as comfortable and congenial as you could wish.

You're free, of course, to order as much or as little as you like, but the menu choices here are many, varied, and eminently tempting. The wine list, also, is extensive. *Antipasti* include the miniature thin-crusted pizza of the day, timbale of prosciutto, and charcoal grilled eggplant ($8.50), while *primi* include a delicious version of the standard Italian "comfort food," potato gnocchi with tomato, basil, thyme, and romano cheese ($8). Another notable item is the savory quadrucci with chicken, walnuts, and sage ($9).

Of the *secondi,* favorites include pork tenderloin with garlic, red beans, and smoked bacon ($15.50) and grilled lamb with crispy lentils and black olives ($20). The menu changes several times a year, so you may not find these particular items available when you arrive, but the common wisdom hereabouts is that chef Greg Westscott and sous-chef Whitney Gaunt can do no wrong, and I subscribe to that view. Daily specials here are always worthy of careful consideration, and so are the pastries, custards, gelati, and sorbetti, all of them prepared on the premises.

Hours are 5:30 to 10 p.m. Monday through Thursday, 5:30 to 11 p.m. Friday and Saturday, and 5 to 9 p.m. Sunday, when one of the best bargains in town is offered: the family-style dinner that includes soup, a tasting of antipasto, pasta, and risotto at $12 per person. (By "family-style," the D'Amicos mean the platter is passed around the table just as you'd do at home. The quantity on the platter, of course, depends on the number of people in your party.) For Sunday family dinners as well as for dinners on every other day of every week, reservations at D'Amico Cucina are highly recommended.

A few blocks away, on the top level of Gaviidae Common, a more recent enterprise of the D'Amico brothers has gained national recognition. Among its other laurels, the **Azur Restaurant,** 651 Nicollet Mall, Minneapolis (tel. 342–2500), was named one of the best new restaurants of 1990 by *Esquire* magazine. The handsome decor was designed by Richard D'Amico in shades of black, purple, and green; the ambience is bustling and upbeat, thanks in part to the French rock-and-roll music that provides a spirited background. Service, under the guidance of manager Mark Luedtke, is correct but unpretentious. In fact, despite the fact that this is one of the most expensive restaurants in town, you'll eat dinner here without benefit of a tablecloth. Linen napkins are on hand, though, and so are platters and serving utensils for the two, three, or more members of your party who decide on the same dish.

Featured here is chef Jay Sparks's version of the cooking you'd find in southern France's Côte d'Azur. Olive oil, roasted garlic, leeks, and fennel play an important part in Sparks's recipes. Popular dinnertime appetizers range from grilled tomato bread ($5.50) to yellowfin tuna with fried leeks and cucumber-melon sauce ($9). Favorite entrées include gratin of prawns, field mushrooms, and fried artichokes ($16) and duck breast with caramelized balsamic vinegar, black olives, and pine nuts ($22.50.) There's an extensive wine list and a delightful variety of aperitifs and digestives. Lunch is served here Monday through Saturday from 11:15 a.m. to 2:30 p.m., dinner Monday through Thursday from 5:30 to 10 p.m., and Friday and Saturday from 5:30 to 11 p.m. Reservations are recommended. Valet parking is available at $3 in Gaviidae Common's underground garage.

For a special occasion, you can't do better than **Goodfellow's,** 800 Nicollet Mall, Minneapolis (tel. 332-4800). Located on the top floor of the Conservatory, one of downtown Minneapolis's most unabashedly upscale shopping centers, Goodfellow's window walls provide a dramatic view of the Nicollet Mall. The restaurant is accessible by skyway to major hotels and department stores, including Dayton's, and herein lies a tale. Goodfellow's was named after Good Fellow's Dry Goods Store, owned by the great-great-grandfather of John Dayton, co-owner of the restaurant. Dayton's department stores have become synonymous, locally and nationally, with retailing of the highest quality.

Praise for Goodfellow's restaurant has been lavish, from both local and national observers, including Esquire Magazine, which named this one of the best new American restaurants of 1988. No longer brand-new, Goodfellow's has maintained its reputation for impeccable service, cuisine, and ambience. Prices here are relatively high, but the value is second to none. The menu changes seasonally with the availability of ingredients, but game, including venison, is available year round. Particularly popular are appetizers like grilled lamb tenderloin with spinach-and-warm-goat-cheese salad and fried eggplant ($7.50) and fettuccine with grilled shrimp, oven-dried tomatoes, and basil sauce ($9.50). Main-course favorites include braised pork tenderloin with wild rice cake and tomatillo-shallot sauce ($18) and grilled veal chop with herb cheese lasagne and roasted pepper sauce ($28). Desserts are all tempting, but my personal favorite is the delectable lace cookie cup filled with raspberries, cream, and caramel ($6).

The wine list here is widely and justifiably admired and includes over 400 selections, all of them American except for the champagne. (Most of the wines hail from California, a few from the Finger Lakes of New York.) There's a wide variety of nonalcoholic wines and beers as well.

And then there's Goodfellow's vegetarian menu, devised with characteristic attention to detail. Vegetarians will be pleased with dinners featuring items such as roast corn soup with cumin-seared tomatoes and cilantro, mixed green salad with red beet vinaigrette and parmesan cheese, fennel-and-pine-nut-stuffed phyllo leaves with white beans and grilled vegetables, and a choice of desserts or fresh fruit, all at a cost of $30.

Lunch is served from 11 a.m. to 2:30 p.m., dinner from 5:30 to 10 p.m., Monday through Saturday. Reservations are recommended.

Where do celebrities head for lunch and dinner while they're in the Twin Cities? Likely as not, you'll find them at an elegant restaurant known simply as **510,** located at 510 Groveland Ave., Minneapolis (tel. 874-6440). Robert Redford has dined here, and so have Carol Channing, Charlton Heston, Pia Zadora, and Richard Dreyfuss. And while they were appearing in *Foxfire* at the nearby Guthrie Theater, Jessica Tandy and Hume Cronyn were here regularly.

This is probably the premiere special-occasion restaurant in town, the place where lawyers, architects, and businesspeople confer with their peers and where they recruit new members for their firms. It's also a place where tourists come, because they've read or heard about 510 and want to try its admirable cuisine for themselves.

While dinner is big-tab time at 510, lunch tabs can be surprisingly modest. At either meal, the shimmering crystal chandeliers and the sweeping blue-gray draperies provide a gracious and serene setting in which to enjoy the creativity and commitment to quality that have made Kathleen Craig's fine restaurant as popular as it is.

Unpredictability is one characteristic of 510, and your waiter will recite for you the specials of the day, including soups, appetizers, entrées, and desserts, as well as the fixed-price tasting menu, a seven- or eight-course dinner for a price that varies between $40 and $45. Reportedly, the same tasting menu has never been presented twice; certainly there are no reports of diners dissatisfied with any of the tasting menus presented.

It's easy to spend $50 per person for dinner at 510, what with most first courses going for $7 to $9; entrées from $15 to $25; and desserts, $3.50 to $4.50. Add champagne, coffee, a gratuity, and there you are. But again, the cuisine here really excels.

At the very least, you really should consider coming here for lunch, when the top price is $12 for a fresh seafood selection. Lunch is served from 11:30 a.m. to 2 p.m. Monday through Friday, and dinner from 6 to 10 p.m. Monday through Saturday. A three-course theatre menu is available for $22.50 from 5:30 to 6:30 p.m. Monday through Saturday.

The **New French Cafe,** 128 N. 4th St., Minneapolis (tel. 338-3790), with its whitewashed brick walls and exposed wooden beams, is considered one of the smartest dining and drinking spots in the Twin Cities. This is the location of choice for that important breakfast meeting, the perfect spot for a casual lunch or a special dinner, and the place where many local artists get together late at night. It was the New French Cafe that began the transformation of Minneapolis's run-down warehouse district into a Soho on the Mississippi, where nearby art galleries coordinate their openings every few weeks, attracting art crowds that go from gallery to gallery to comfortable eateries like this. The cuisine, authentically French, features both classic and contemporary selections at lunchtime prices that range from $6.95 for a salad of lentils, celery root, mushrooms, beets, and green beans to $11.50 for ragoût of goose with red wine, crème fraîche, mushrooms, turnips, carrots, and leeks served with savoyarde potatoes. Desserts, baked on the premises, are a specialty here, including favorites like eclairs ($2.50) and fresh fruit tarts ($3.25).

On Friday and Saturday, there's a late-night menu offering light fare at prices that range from $3.50 to $7.95. And on Sundays from 5:30 to 9 p.m., you'll find what may be the best buy of all—entrées like pork ragoût and roast chicken for under $10.00. Otherwise, hours of service are as follows: breakfast on Monday through Friday is from 7 to 11 a.m., Saturday and Sunday from 8 a.m. to 2 p.m.; lunch is served Monday through Friday from 11:30 a.m. to 1:30 p.m.; regular dinner hours are Monday through Thursday and Sunday from 5:30 to 9:30 p.m., Friday and Saturday from 5:30 to 10 p.m.

If you enjoy music in the foreground as well as the background when you dine, don't miss **Gustino's,** the popular Italian restaurant on the sixth floor of the downtown Marriott Hotel, 30 S. 7th St., Minneapolis (tel. 349-4075). A dozen talented singing servers are on hand here seven nights a week to bring you a beautiful blend of musical and culinary fare. Gustino's caters to the diverse performing schedules of these singers, who regularly appear in local operatic and musical-comedy productions.

There's a feast for the eye, as well, in this handsome art deco room with its panoramic view of downtown Minneapolis and, from March through October, spectacular Twin Cities sunsets. As you're led to your table through a glass alcove, you'll pass a white grand piano and a floor-to-ceiling triangular glass wine "cellar" displaying more than 200 bottles of Italian wine.

It's northern Italian cuisine that's featured here, so veal is a specialty of the house. You can choose a chop with mushrooms in a light cream sauce, veal scaloppine, veal in marsala sauce, breaded veal scallops with ham, mozzarella, and fresh tomatoes, or a delectable roast veal with the stuffing and sauce of the day. Gustino's offers fine Italian seafood and chicken, too, each entrée served with polenta or risotto and vegetables. You really can't go wrong with any of the soups, salads, pizzas, and pasta on the menu here, but do save room for a slice of pepperoni bread and one of the "painted desserts" concocted daily by the chef. Entrées here average about $20, antipasti about $7, except for the three-level *torre di pisa* (get it?), an extravaganza of assorted antipasti selections for $15. Wine-lovers will enjoy the "wines of the month," two selections that can be ordered by the glass that are ordinarily available only by the bottle. Hours at Gustino's are Sunday through Thursday 6 to 10 p.m., Friday and Saturday 6 to 11 p.m.

For more than four decades Twin Citians have headed to **Murray's,** 26 S. 6th St., Minneapolis (tel. 339-0909). Butter-knife steak is the specialty of this handsome, family-managed restaurant, but you needn't live by beef alone at Murray's. The menu features broiled filet of walleye pike and T-bone veal steak, among other favorites.

Located in the heart of downtown Minneapolis, Murray's has somehow managed to retain its intimacy after being enlarged a few years ago. Mirrored walls, dusty-rose draperies and valances, and wrought-iron chandeliers and balustrades provide the same warm and gracious setting that Art and Marie Murray cultivated back in the forties. Their grandson, Tim, who now runs the restaurant, also kept piano and violin accompaniment to the evening's dining experience.

Dinners here are in the expensive-but-worth-it category. Top items, silver butter-knife sirloin steak for two or chateaubriand for two, served with half a bottle of California wine, will cost about $60. Less costly items are notable too. The Downtowner menu, served from 4:30 to 6 p.m. every day, features, for example, broiled sirloin tips for $13.95 or herb-broiled chicken for $11.75. Dinner includes potato or vegetable and salad, along with another specialty, the famous bread basket of baked-on-the-premises garlic toast, soft pretzels, and assorted rolls and crackers.

Murray's is open seven days a week. Lunch is served from 11 a.m. to 3 p.m., tea from 2 to 4:30 p.m., and dinner from 4 to 11 p.m. Between Memorial Day and Labor Day, Murray's doesn't open on Saturdays until 4 p.m.

You can have your choice of food and drink and ambience at the **Loring Cafe,** 1624 Harmon Place, Minneapolis (tel. 332-1617). Owner/manager Jason McLean has provided a variety of spaces, indoors and out, to suit a wide variety of tastes. The best measure of his success is the year-round popularity of this restaurant, bar, and sometime arts center located in a converted automobile showroom that dates back more than 50 years. Dine on the main floor, in the loft, or, in the summertime, out back in one of the best outdoor settings in town. Notice the large garage doors, now decorated with flowers and candelabra, and recall that long ago this building was a prominent part of "Automobile Row." You'll dine in the back-alley courtyard, next-door to another old building on whose roof a saxophonist appears from time to time, playing some of the sweetest dinner music you're likely to encounter in this or any other town. During less balmy times, other kinds of music are offered at the Loring Cafe—jazz, blues, folk, and classical music in the coffeehouse/bar, whose decor is eclectic to say the least. The multiple uses to which this space has been put are a measure of proprietor McLean's flexibility. During off hours, the bar becomes a large studio available to painters, sculptors, dancers, writers, and other artists. The idea originated with a young waitress and writer named Kelly Shea, who expressed to McLean the need for writers to be able to get together to share ideas and support. As she tells it, he promptly offered the bar as a meeting place, saying "I'd be honored to have the café shelter you and foster your work." One result of McLean's generosity is the wooden box which now stands in the bar with a sign saying "Please Take One." What you'll take is a sheet published every two weeks or so with original writing on one side and a schedule of upcoming cafe events on the other. As you might have guessed, McLean himself has art credentials; he was an actor and director at the Guthrie, the Children's Theatre, and other local playhouses for about 13 years.

But it's the culinary achievements of the admirable kitchen staff that have made everything else possible. Appetizers like focaccia served with roasted garlic bulb and French goat's cheese ($5) are perennially popular. Entrées range from fresh vegetable sauté ($8.50) to veal loin chops with caramelized apples and calvados ($16). And don't overlook the excellent pasta and pizza selections, the imaginative salads, and the long and excellent wine list. Wintertime lunch hours here extend from 11:30 a.m. to 2:30 p.m. Monday through Friday; dinner is from 5:30 to 11 p.m. Monday through Thursday and until midnight Friday and Saturday. During the summer, the Loring Cafe is open until midnight every night.

One of the best bargain buffets in the Twin Cities is the one you'll find at **Ping's,** 1401 Nicollet Ave. S., Minneapolis (tel. 874-9404). Monday through Friday from 11:30 a.m. to 2 p.m., $6 entitles you to unlimited visits to buffet tables piled high with appetizers, fried rice, and assorted entrées. Even more lavish Sunday buffets, served from noon to 3 p.m. and 5 p.m. to 9 p.m., cost $7.95. Pink Chinese kites contrast with gray walls and pillars in this attractive informal dining room, and a pink tile bar serves as a focal point of the lower of two dining levels. Chef Mingh Tran's selections consistently attract downtown businesspeople, local high-rise residents, and more far-flung Twin Citians who savor the spicy Szechuan entrées that are featured here. No need to worry about parking your car when you dine at Ping's; there's complimentary valet parking at their nearby lot.

One of the most renowned specialties is the crispy flavorful Peking duck, an appropriate specialty in a restaurant named for one of the more famous ducks of our time, the protagonist of Marjorie Flack and Kurt Wiese's children's tale "The Story about Ping." In Minneapolis, Ping's Peking duck can be brought to you as an entrée for two for $25 or as appetizers for four or more for $20. Other entrées range from $6.25 for the vegetable stir-fry to $12.95 for sesame beef or chicken. Ping's is open Monday through Thursday from 11 a.m. to 10 p.m., Friday 11 a.m. to midnight, Saturday 4:30 p.m. to midnight, Sunday, noon to 9 p.m.

The French accent at **Jardin** extends beyond the name and the atmosphere of Keith Hudalla's delightful little bistro, located at 1614 Harmon Place, Minneapolis (tel. 338-2363), in full view of picturesque Loring Park. It's the cuisine that counts most, though, and here it's the work of chef David Schauer, who studied at the Cordon Bleu school in France and made a name for himself locally at the New French Cafe, La Tortue, and other notable restaurants.

Schauer cooks everything from scratch, adding no artificial flavor enhancers to the fresh foods that are the mainstay of Jardin's menu. Ingredients here are healthful and natural, even to the sweeteners—apple juice, maple syrup, and the like. A variety of salads, soups, pizzas, pasta dishes, vegetarian dishes, and organic poultry items make this menu among the most varied and healthful in town. There are 37 wines available by the glass, all of them produced without pesticides or preservatives.

Opened in October 1989, Jardin quickly found a loyal following among health-conscious Twin Citians, and you'll enjoy it too. Lunch prices are moderate to high, with wild mushroom linguine going for $7.50 and sea scallops on a bed of spinach served with risotto for $10. But you can get by, too, on some of the lighter fare: a bowl of the soup of the day for $3.25 and provincal pizza for $6. Prices for these items are same at dinnertime; other dinner entrées include shrimp spaghetti ($11) and coho salmon ($13). And then there are those wonderful pastries and other delectable desserts (all $4). Lunch is served from 11:30 a.m. to 2:30 p.m. Monday through Saturday; dinner 5:30 to 9 p.m. Monday through Thursday, 5:30 to 10 p.m. Saturday and Sunday.

You'd have a good time even if you didn't have a single thing to eat at one of the three **Rudolph's Bar-b-que** Twin Cities locations: at Franklin and Lyndale avenues, Minneapolis (tel. 871-8969); 815 E. Hennepin Ave., Minneapolis (tel. 623-3671); and 366 Jackson St., Galtier Plaza, St. Paul (tel. 222-2226). The decor and the food listings are among the wittiest anywhere, based as they are on the good old steamily romantic days when screen idol Rudolph Valentino reigned supreme. In fact, on the oversize purple menu, a photo of the turbaned Valentino and a blonde beauty bears the legend "Your eyes, your lips, your ribs!"

Wit, whimsy, and wonderful ribs are what you'll get at Rudolph's, along with a barbecue sauce that has won innumerable national awards. Owner Jimmy Theros has also won national devotees among rib-fanciers at his Akron, Ohio, restaurant. How to describe Rudolph's ribs? I've got a book to write; you go and taste them for yourself. If you're not a devotee of barbecued ribs, there are plenty of other moderately priced entrées, ranging from Greek-style chicken at $7.95 to New York steak for $12.95. Save room for the "happy ending" desserts. Peach Melba, at $3, is a real treat.

A lavish brunch is available on Sundays. The cost is $11 for adults, $5 for children under 12. On your way out, take a look at some of the wonderful vintage Hollywood photos that line the walls. They're irresistible too. Hours vary by location, so call ahead for specifics.

THE MILL DISTRICT

With the opening in March 1987 of the **Whitney Grille,** 150 Portland Ave., Minneapolis (tel. 339-9300), the Mill District, between the Metrodome and the Mississippi River, got its first luxury restaurant. (Actually, this is both the newest and oldest part of town —newest because it's in the process of redevelopment, oldest because the buildings here date back to the 19th century and reflect the city's role as the birthplace of the grain milling industry in the United States.)

There's an old-world atmosphere at the Whitney Grille, with its fabric-covered walls, African-mahogany woodwork, and marble appointments. The handsome traditional European chairs have been upholstered in tapestry and outfitted with gooseneck arms. An especially nice touch at dinnertime is the piano music that's offered from 6 p.m. Monday through Friday and Sunday, and from 6:30 p.m. on Saturday.

The distinguished cuisine here seems a natural extension of the setting. Executive chef Richard Groshens and executive sous-chef Richard Adams have won enthusiastic reviews for their regional American items, including West Coast halibut bisque, East Coast shellfish terrine, Colorado rack of lamb, and Wisconsin veal T-bone. Desserts are fabulous. A particularly popular summertime item is the exquisite raspberry roulade, a concoction of fresh raspberries and chantilly cream wrapped in sponge cake that's been soaked in Triple Sec.

Cuisine and decor are special here, but so is the atmosphere of warmth and hospitality cultivated by Michael Kutscheid, a maitre d' with a difference. Trained as a lawyer, Kutscheid worked as a waiter during law school. Upon graduation, he discovered he didn't want to leave restaurant work. His dedication to the Whitney Grille is evident when you arrive. "We want people who come here to feel that they're special," he declares.

Breakfast is served from 7 to 10:30 a.m. Monday through Sunday, with prices ranging from $4.50 for pancakes with sliced fruit, maple syrup, and bacon, sausage, or ham, to $8.50 for two eggs served with sirloin steak, scrapple, and toast. Sunday brunches are deservedly popular too.

Luncheon entrées, served from 11 a.m. to 4:30 p.m. Monday through Sunday, range from $8.50 for sautéed boneless breast of chicken to $13.50 for broiled prime sirloin. A selection of appetizers, soups, salads, sandwiches, and desserts is available.

Dinner entrées, served from 5:30 to 10:30 p.m. Monday through Sunday, include Minnesota walleye for $14, veal T-bone for $21, and chateaubriand for two, carved tableside, for $41.

A dimly lit dining room tastefully decorated in warm shades of mauve and gray. Sound romantic? It is, and it's part of what brings diners back again and again to **Yvette,** in Riverplace, 1 Main St. S.E., Minneapolis (tel. 379-1111). There's much to recommend this lovely French-American restaurant that overlooks the Mississippi and historic St. Anthony Falls.

The dry-aged beef steak here is among the best you'll find in the Twin Cities, and the daily seafood specials feature a mouthwatering selection flown in from Boston each day. Desserts are another specialty, with the top draw being the chocolate velvet cake, baked on the premises.

Wines are very much a concern here. The selection ranges in

price from a Canteval house wine for $15 to Chateau Mouton Rothschild Pauillac 1897 for $3,000.

Dinner entrées, served with potato and vegetable, are priced from $9 to $19. This restaurant is open from 11 a.m. to 11 p.m. every day (until midnight on Friday and Saturday), with lunch served from 11 a.m. to 5 p.m. and dinner from 5 p.m. on. There's live music here every night and, when weather permits, there's outdoor dining on a flower-bordered terrace.

If you like seafood, you'll like what's waiting for you at the **Braxton Seafood Grill,** Riverplace, 1 Main St. S.E., Minneapolis (tel. 378-1338), where you'll find one of the most comprehensive seafood menus in the Twin Cities.

This perennially popular restaurant has both British and nautical touches in its decor. Along with the dark-green walls and glowing mahogany woodwork in the Dome Room, there's a huge Tiffany-style glass dome and fluted Tiffany-style lamps. And there's an exquisite display of sterling-silver English antiques.

Each of the dining rooms has attractions of its own. Some tables offer a truly spectacular view of the Mississippi River, cobblestoned Main Street, and the Minneapolis skyline beyond. Other rooms contain private alcoves for parties of six or so. Another, frequently prebooked, seating option is a terrace that offers a breathtaking skyline view, but is only large enough for six tables of fortunate diners.

Mesquite-grilled swordfish is one of the most frequently ordered entrées here, with shrimp scampi not far behind. Blackened catfish is another favorite. All entrées can be blackened upon request, and all are served with the vegetable of the day, a choice of potato or rice, and as many biscuits as you can eat.

Dinner entrées range from $8.95 for seafood and $12.95 for grilled baillard of chicken to $28.95 for steak and lobster served with shoestring french fries, four-grain rice medley, or baby redskin potatoes.

A best-buy for families is the all-you-can-eat Sunday buffet brunch, served from 10 a.m. to 2:30 p.m.; the prices are $11 for adults, no charge for children under 12.

Lunch is served Monday through Saturday from 11:30 a.m. to 2:30 p.m.; dinner, Sunday through Thursday from 5:30 to 10 p.m., Friday and Saturday to 11 p.m.

Japanese cuisine, both traditional and contemporary, is featured at **Kikugawa,** Riverplace, 45 Main St. S.E., Minneapolis (tel. 378-3006). Owner-operator John Omori recalls the reaction of Twin Citians to sushi when it first appeared on the menu during the early eighties, while his restaurant was still located across the river in downtown Minneapolis. "They'd look at the sushi and say, 'Wow!' or 'Yuck!' " he declares with a smile, then adds that the raw-fish delicacy has gone from less than one-tenth of his food orders to about one-third.

This handsome restaurant, with its pale-wood pillars and beams, offers *nabemono* table cookery throughout the different dining rooms. Particularly popular are the tatami rooms, where diners leave their shoes at the door and experience an older era of Japanese dining. In the tatami rooms, the main dining room, or the river-front room, a favored menu choice is beef shabu, paper-thin slices of filet mignon cooked for two or three seconds in hot shabu broth. Currently a favorite in Japan, the dish is particularly popular with the growing number of local residents who have visited the country. Omori has also introduced a yakitori bar, a broiling station for skewered chicken, beef, seafood, and vegetables. And then there's the selection of delicious desserts here, including two inspired in-tercontinental inventions—tempura ice cream and green-tea ice cream. They'll surprise and delight you.

Other items you might try are sukiyaki, priced at $14.75 ($7.50 at lunch) and the *nabemono* table-prepared dishes, including shabu shabu (Japanese fondue) for $16. For haute cuisine Japanese-style, try the combination tempura—seafood, chicken, beef, and seasonal vegetables ($16). It's justifiably famous in these parts. There are other specialties, too, at a range of prices. If you like Japanese food, you'll like Kikugawa.

The restaurant is open for lunch from noon to 2 p.m. Monday through Saturday; dinner hours are Monday through Thursday from 5 to 10 p.m., Friday and Saturday to 11 p.m., and on Sunday from 4 to 9 p.m.

THE WAREHOUSE DISTRICT

Good food and good wine in a comfortable, congenial setting continue to attract diners to **Faegre's Bar and Restaurant,** 430 First Ave. N., Minneapolis (tel. 332-3515). Located on one of the busiest corners of downtown Minneapolis, Faegre's has received awards for its creative Continental and American cuisine and its ex-tensive list of fine California and European wines.

You'll see diners wearing everything from black tie to blue jeans here in a 120-seat dining room that's minimally decorated—white walls displaying works for sale by local artists, indirect lighting cre-ated by a series of reflective ceiling beams, postmodern window-boxes, and large windows looking out on the diversity of Ware-house District passersby.

Specials change here every day, but there's always a vegetarian entrée and the delectable Chinese chicken salad on a bed of Napa cabbage with a savory ginger-garlic-tahini dressing. The Caesar salad has won an enthusiastic following, and so have the French onion soup and the crusty French bread. And speaking of French, how about one of the most surprising items at Faegre's—french fries served with béarnaise sauce! It's reportedly a favorite of French chefs (in the privacy of their kitchens), and it's a favorite here as well.

Everything's made from scratch by a kitchen staff that's as com-mitted to nourishing, flavorful food as owner Sis Longellow is. Prices are moderate. Lunches average $7; dinners, $15. Lunch is served from 11:30 a.m. to 2:30 p.m., and a light menu is available from 2:30 to 5:30 p.m. Dinner is served from 5:30 to 10:30 p.m. Monday through Saturday, until 11 p.m. on Sunday, with a late-night menu served from 10:30 p.m. to 12:30 a.m.

If your silverware's standing in a glass tumbler, and your nap-kin turns out to be a white terrycloth towel, you're at **Monte Carlo**

Bar & Grill, 219 Third Ave. N., Minneapolis (tel. 333-5900). There's some question as to whether this popular art deco hangout is a restaurant with a bar or a bar with a restaurant. When the tin ceilings first went in some 70 years ago, the Monte Carlo was exclusively a drinking spot, and that's what it remained until the Warehouse District turned chic back in the seventies. Now it has broadened its clientele, serving chicken soup, burgers, steaks, chops, and more at lunch and dinner to office workers, antique dealers, sales clerks, and shoppers. The prices are moderate, from $5.95 for a full Caesar salad to $13.95 for filet mignon. The best buy of all is what you'll find here during the extended brunch, 10 a.m. to 4 p.m. on Sunday: all the scrambled eggs, Canadian bacon, sausage, toast, and hash browns you can eat for $4.95.

The copper bar is still the focal point of Monte Carlo, with shelves of more than 500 bottles reaching up to the ceiling. Drinks are served club style—the mixer in a large tumbler, liquor in shot glasses, garnishes at the side.

There's free parking in an adjoining lot. Hours are 11 a.m. to 1 a.m. Monday through Saturday, 10 a.m. to midnight on Sunday.

By the way, there's a relatively quiet front room off to the right as you enter Monte Carlo. It's the preference of those who find the rest of this lively restaurant a bit rambunctious.

There's a lot of coming and going at the **Loon Cafe,** 500 First Ave. N., Minneapolis (tel. 332-8342). Downtown office workers and shoppers find this a good place for a quick lunch. The oblong burger served on a sourdough bun is popular, and so are the "championship chilis" listed on the menu with asterisks to indicate spiciness. There's also a selection of soups, salads, and cold sandwiches. Prices range from $3 to $8.

Primarily, though, this is a bar that sells food, not a restaurant that sells drinks, and the Loon really comes into its own in the evening, when it becomes one of the busiest, noisiest spots in this chic neighborhood. Many young professionals find their way here before heading home. Ticket-holders on their way to or from a performance or a game find this a good place to stop awhile as well. And celebrities, local and national, wander in from time to time: Bob Dylan, Morgan Fairchild, and others have been sighted at the Loon.

Named for the official bird of Minnesota, this cafe displays and sells a variety of wildlife prints as well as sweatshirts and T-shirts bearing the loon's likeness.

Taped music, overpowering when you walk in, soon subsides into the general din and somehow doesn't seem to inhibit conversation. Hours here are 11 a.m. to 1 a.m. Monday through Saturday, 5 p.m. to midnight on Sunday.

MINNEAPOLIS SOUTH SUBURBAN

You can enjoy yourself amidst the art deco decor of **Wellington's,** 12201 Ridgedale Drive, Minnetonka (tel. 593-0000), knowing the food here is not only good but good for you. Chef Dave Antonovitch wouldn't have it any other way. So when regulars come to this restaurant at the Radisson Hotel Minnetonka, those in search of a beef fix can be assured that the certified Black

Angus is waiting for them. But at this self-proclaimed beefeaters' restaurant, house specialties include lamb Wellington and salmon Wellington too, dishes wrapped in puff pastry and roasted until golden brown. Each of these featured items, at $19.95, is served with baked potato, Caesar salad, and baked bagel sticks. Other favorites include a 12-oz. New York strip steak for $14, with a 16-oz. cut available for $17. And then there's a relatively new item on the menu, roasted range chicken in smoked tomato sauce, at $14.25. Range chickens, Chef Antonovitch explains, are free to roam and are, therefore, free of excess fat. Antonovitch, who has banned monosodium glutamate from his kitchen, enjoys the challenge of flavoring foods with fresh herbs rather than chemicals. He's also eliminated oil-based dressings and all deep-fried foods from Wellington's menu; when a recipe requires oil, it's canola oil that's used. And what will you do with all the calories you've saved during dinner? Save them for a serving of raspberry white chocolate torte or Bailey's chocolate cream torte, or, on the lighter side, a fresh fruit torte featuring kiwi, peaches, or strawberries atop fresh whipped cream in pastry shells. Go on. Hours at Wellington's are Monday through Saturday, 6 to 10:30 p.m.

The next best thing to a flight to Italy is a drive to **Cocolezzone,** 5410 Wayzata Blvd., Golden Valley (tel. 544-4014). Inspired by and named for a popular trattoria in Florence, this large, lively, and very beautiful spot was an instantaneous success when it opened its doors in June 1985. With marble floors, beeswax-finished walls, and a plenitude of imported artifacts, Cocolezzone is a casual, sometimes clamorous, but altogether delightful place where pizzas fly through the air on their way to oak-fired ovens in the large display kitchen.

Because northern Italian fare is featured here, be prepared to see, along with the usual tomato-laden toppings, such relatively unfamiliar sights as seafood pizza and pizza with spinach, cheese, and a cooked egg in the center. Tomatoes, of course, make many appearances here, most notably perhaps in tortellini rosa, a delectable meat-filled pasta in a tomato and cream sauce.

Dining here can be a very expensive or a remarkably inexpensive experience, depending on how you approach the lengthy à la carte menu. Sharing is encouraged by the waiters, who delight in guiding you through the traditional succession of courses. The lunchtime menu lists a variety of antipasti, or you may prefer to select your own assortment from the tempting display case. Next comes the pizza, followed by soups, primi (a selection of pastas), meat, fish, and, finally, salad—for reasons of digestion, you'll be told.

For dinner, when the prices and portions are somewhat greater, the courses include antipasti, pizzas, primi, secondi, contorni, and dolci. The average dinnertime tab comes to about $20, exclusive of wine. For lunch, $12 is the average amount.

Lunch is served at Cocolezzone from 11 a.m. to 5 p.m. Monday through Friday, from noon to 4 p.m. on Saturday. Dinner is served from 5 to 11 p.m. Sunday through Thursday, until midnight on Friday and Saturday.

1990 marked the fifteenth anniversary of the first **Hotel Sofitel** to be built on American soil—right here in Minnesota at the juncture of I-494 and State Highway 100. (The exact address is 5601 W. 78th St., Minneapolis; tel. (612) 835-1900 or toll free 800/876-6303). Three Sofitel restaurants in three different price ranges quickly took their place as Twin Cities favorites, and their popularity continues to this day. In fact, three-fourths of diners at this elegant hotel are local folks who return again and again for informal sidewalk café dining at **La Terasse,** for the ambience of a true French brasserie at **Chez Colette,** or for the ultimate in elegance at **Le Café Royal.**

Flavorful and healthful dining are the preoccupations of Chef Gerard Thabius as he creates dishes for all three Sofitel restaurants. His skilled use of fresh herbs, for example, would render superfluous the use of MSG, which he's banned from his kitchen because of its reported effect on blood pressure. All the baked goods served here are made on the premises daily. Croissants, a particular favorite, are prepared the old fashioned way, layer by layer. Sausages are made in these kitchens too, and salmon is smoked right on the premises in the bona fide French manner. The French accent extends to the wines too: the red, white, and rosé house wines are bottled and labeled for the Sofitel in France; the champagne bearing the Sofitel label is imported directly as well. (While French wines are prominent on the extensive list, California wines have a place too, as befits a hotel chain which now has properties in Los Angeles and San Francisco as well as Houston, Miami, and Chicago.)

At La Terasse, when weather permits, outdoor tables are much in demand (though reservations are not accepted), but the atmosphere of a French sidewalk café remains throughout the seasons. At Chez Colette, where reservations are recommended, a traditional French brasserie, friendly and casual, has been duplicated, even to the brass hat, coat, and newspaper racks you'd find in the Parisian original. For elegant and formal occasions, Le Café Royal, with its tableside flambé service, is sure to suit your taste. (Do phone ahead for a reservation.)

Lunch prices at Le Café Royal range from $7 to $13, dinner prices run from $21 to $44; at Chez Colette, you'll pay $5 to $10 for lunch, $13 to $20 for dinner. Prices at La Terasse range from $5 to $12. The hours of the three restaurants are as follows: La Terasse is open continually from 11 a.m. to 1 a.m.; Chez Colette is open for breakfast from 6:30 to 11 a.m., for lunch from 11:30 a.m. to 2:30 p.m., and for dinner from 5:30 to 11 p.m.; Le Café Royal is open for lunch from 11:30 a.m. to 2:30 p.m., for dinner from 6 to 11 p.m.

Phone early for a reservation at **Kinkaid's,** 8400 Normandale Lake Blvd., Bloomington (tel. 921-2255). This beautifully appointed steak-and-seafood house—an elegant assemblage of marble, brass chandeliers, and cherrywood furnishings in a parklike indoor setting—describes itself as "behind the times and proud of it." For all its vaunted traditionalism, though, Kinkaid's is at least partially the product of some very contemporary marketing research, employed before its opening in October 1986 by Restaurants International. The data showed Twin Citians to be "value oriented," willing to spend, but only when they feel they're getting their money's worth. What they get at Kinkaid's is a choice of top-notch steaks, chops, and fish, mesquite-grilled at high temperatures to sear the flavorful juices in. And there's a variety of fine pastas, sauces, soups, and desserts as well.

Luncheon entrées, served with vegetable and herb pan-bread, range from $7.50 for fish-and-chips to $12 for boneless New York steak. Dinners, served with a choice of chowder or salad, range from $12 to $20. The chatty dinner menu, which includes a lengthy wine list along with recipes for some of Kinkaid's most notable entrées, also carries a money-back guarantee that your steaks, chops, and roasts will be moist, flavorful, and tender. An elegant back bar has a dining area of its own, and a separate bar features fresh oysters flown in daily from all over—the East Coast, West Coast, Canada, and New Zealand, for instance. Desserts are delicious too. Lunch is served from 11 a.m. to 2 p.m. Monday through Saturday; dinner 5 to 9:30 p.m. Monday through Thursday, 5 to 10:30 p.m. Friday and Saturday, and 5 to 9:30 p.m. on Sunday. The "blueberry" brunch is served Sundays from 10 a.m. to 2 p.m.

You'll think you've come to a small rustic restaurant as you approach **Gregory's,** 7956 Lyndale Ave. S., Bloomington (881-8611), but wait till, you get inside! There are three floors of dining rooms and bars here, making Gregory's one of the largest and most popular restaurants in this burgeoning suburb.

The Old West lives again in the main dining room, with its split-log walls and wagon-wheel chandeliers. The other rooms offer diverse decor and ambience: the elegance of the Ritz, with its mahogany furnishings; the turn-of-the-century Parlor, warm and inviting with its frosted gaslight globes and hand-carved fireplace; the trendy black leather upholstery and stained glass windows of the Rafters.

But it's the food, not the furnishings, that account for the enduring popularity of Gregory's. You'll find a touch of Cajun here, a bit of nouvelle cuisine there—Gregory's doesn't aim to be left behind—but primarily this is the kind of place for prime rib, walleye pike, chicken, shrimp, and duck. There are soups made from scratch and three luncheon specials every day. The next day's specials are noted in each luncheon menu, so regulars can plan accordingly.

Lunch prices range from $5.95 for burgers and fries to $8.95 for broiled walleye. Dinnertime entrées, served with salad and potato or rice, range from $8.50 for baby beef liver to $15.95 for cajun shrimp. Feel free to come as you are to Gregory's. You'll see everything here, from formal attire to sweaters and slacks. Lunches are served 11 a.m. to 3 p.m. Monday through Friday; dinners from 4 to 10:30 p.m. Monday through Saturday. The bar remains open until 1 a.m. Gregory's is closed on Sundays.

Pearson's Family Restaurant, 3803 W. 50th St., Edina (tel. 927-4464), features the kind of down-home cooking that many Minnesotans grew up with. Paul Pearson, second generation owner-manager of the establishment, got started in the business as a toddler, back in the fifties, when a picture of him, dressed in diaper and

Indian headdress, was used on Twin-Cities billboards promoting an earlier family venture, the first electronic drive-in in the Upper Midwest. Now Paul and his brother Marston share responsibility for Pearson's, which their parents opened in 1973 as a coffee shop near one of the most valued streetcorners in the state of Minnesota—50th and France in the affluent suburb of Edina. That small diner has since been joined by the Oak Room and the Oak Room West, two elegant, handsomely paneled dining rooms, with large stone fireplaces and brass chandeliers.

Local families enjoy Pearson's because the menu is varied enough so that everyone in the clan can find something to his or her liking, including the basic hamburger, omelets, or salad. Breakfasts are well under $5, most lunches and dinners under $10. Swedish meatballs, baked chicken, and roast prime rib rank high among the favorites here; and the pastries and soups, even the salad dressings and dinner rolls, all of which are made on the premises, come in for high marks. The diners here are 90% steady customers, Paul Pearson reports. But there is competition now and then from a source that's difficult to combat: "When Mount Olivet Church gives a lutefisk dinner, our business goes down," Pearson declares. Hours are 7:30 a.m. to 9 p.m. Monday to Saturday, 9 a.m. to 7 p.m. Sunday. Pearson's is closed on major holidays.

SOUTH MINNEAPOLIS

The handsome German castle you'll see pictured on an outdoor wall of the **Black Forest Inn,** 1 E. 26th St., Minneapolis (tel. 872-0812), says a lot about this popular restaurant and its clientele. It was a local artist and set designer, Jack Barkla, who painted the distinctive mural, and it's artists and theater folk like Barkla that you're likely to encounter at the Black Forest when evening performances are over. Audience members find their way there too, for the informal atmosphere and the extensive selection of domestic and imported beers and wines, served amid the dark woods and stained glass of an authentic German "gasthaus." Families and couples find this a comfortable setting for a lunch or dinner of German specialties or more familiar fare.

Luncheon entrées include wienerschnitzel and sauerbraten, as well as chicken wings and corned beef on rye. The more comprehensive dinner menu includes German favorites like schweinbraten (roast pork with apple dressing and red cabbage) and gefuellte krautrolle (stuffed cabbage with rice); entrées are served with a vegetable and often a potato pancake or spaetzel. The Black Forest features a long list of German, French, and California wines, as well as a variety of liqueurs, brandies, and cognac. Luncheon prices range from $2.85 to $10; dinner entrées run from $4.50 to $13.30. During warm weather, an enclosed courtyard becomes a convivial beer garden. Lunches are served from 11 a.m. to 5 p.m. Monday through Saturday, dinners from 5 to 11 p.m., with a late night menu from 11 p.m. until midnight. Sunday dinner is served from noon to 10 p.m., with a late night menu available from 10 until 11 p.m. Reservations are available for parties of five or more.

You'll find a lot more than the name implies at the **Malt Shop,** 809 W. 50th St., Minneapolis (824-1352). Famous for its hamburgers and ice cream desserts, the Malt Shop also offers an array of international specialties—everything from bird's nest salad to feta salad. All soups, dressings, and sauces are made by the Malt Shop. Salads come in two sizes and so do the "gourmet hamburgers," which come in many variations. Daily specials ($6), served with soup or salad and a grilled onion roll, vary from Monday's lasagne to Sunday's chicken Monterey. Popular box lunches include sandwich, potato chips, fruit or feta salad, chocolate-pecan cookie, and condiments and utensils for $4.75. Hours vary, so call for specifics.

NORTHEAST MINNEAPOLIS

When lawyer/legislator Joseph Kozlak and his wife Gertrude decided to open a Minneapolis restaurant back in 1943, they were able to seat 56 diners at **Jax Cafe,** 1928 University Avenue N.E., (tel. 789-7297). Today, the much-enlarged Jax, owned and operated by the founders' son Bill and his wife Kathy, can seat 300 people on each of its two floors, with room for 50 or so more on the beautifully landscaped patio. (Jax was reportedly the very first restaurant in the Twin Cities to offer outdoor dining.) Although about 75% of Jax customers come here regularly, this handsome restaurant is known widely as a special-occasion place, where proms, weddings, anniversary celebrations, and other festive goings-on are enhanced by an ambience of dark woods, soft lighting, and impeccable service. The music is soft here and, if you're in town on the right evenings, live. (On ten or twelve occasions during the year, you can dine to the romantic strains of the Golden Strings, a gifted ensemble whose appearances here are always sellouts.) Although Jax was known for decades primarily for its sizzling steaks, choices have become more numerous as dining and drinking habits have changed. There's a growing emphasis here on keeping things interesting for those who these days might be more tempted by special appetizers or desserts than by alcoholic beverages. The temptations are many, but do consider the Bailey's Irish cream banana torte, which recently won first prize in a cities-wide competition and a place on the menu of the annual gala Symphony Ball. Before dessert, though, there are other choices to be made: "classic cut" tenderloin, chicken marinara, broiled filet of walleye pike—the list is long and varied. Entrées are served with soup or salad and rice, pasta, potato, or vegetable. At lunch entrées run from $6.50 to $10.50, at dinner from $11 to $20. Lunch is served seven days a week from 11 a.m. to 3 p.m.; dinner hours are from 3:30 to 11 p.m. Monday through Saturday, from 3:30 to 9 p.m. on Sunday. On Sunday a buffet brunch ($12.50) is served from 10 a.m. to 3 p.m.

MINNEAPOLIS UPTOWN

Figlio's, 3001 Hennepin Ave., Minneapolis (tel. 822-1688), is a bustling beauty of an Italian restaurant, albeit one with a marked California accent. One of Figlio's dining rooms overlooks busy Lake Street, which has some of the best people-watching hereabouts. The other, larger room has a view of its own—of the busy demonstration kitchen with an oversize built-in wood-burning oven flanked by brick walls on which pizza paddles hang suspended.

The northern Italian cuisine is overseen by executive chef Rex Retneyer, famed locally for his version of carpaccio, paper-thin slices of raw beef tenderloin marinated in olive oil, shallots, capers, and herbs, topped with thinly sliced parmesan cheese, and assembled into open-faced sandwiches on Italian bread, with three kinds of mustard at the ready.

Another specialty is something called morto nel cioccolato, "death by chocolate," of which happy locals contentedly declare, "What a way to go!" Do consider a portion of this extravagantly rich and utterly delicious concoction composed of alternating layers of sublime chocolate cake and heavenly chocolate-amaretto gelato, served with a thick chocolate sauce.

The rest of the menu is a wide assortment of Italian and American favorites, from fettuccine Alfredo and stuffed tortellini to grilled swordfish and ten-ounce burgers.

There are a lot of nice touches to the service here, including the heated plates that keep your selection piping hot. Outdoor dining on Lake Street, take-out service, and Sunday brunch (from 11:30 a.m. to 2:00 p.m.) are some of the features that keep Figlio's popular.

Prices are moderate, with pizzas running $6 to $7 and dinner entrées running $5.95 to $14.95. Hours are 11:30 a.m. to 1 a.m. Monday through Thursday, 11:30 a.m. to 2 a.m. Friday and Saturday, and 11:30 a.m. to 6 p.m. on Sunday.

2. St. Paul and Outer St. Paul

DOWNTOWN ST. PAUL

One of the loveliest Victorian houses in the Twin Cities, **Forepaugh's,** 276 S. Exchange St., St. Paul (tel. 224-5606), is also one of its finest French restaurants. Built in 1870 by businessman Joseph Lybrandt Forepaugh, this three-story mansion faced the home of Alexander Ramsey, first territorial governor of Minnesota. Both houses, now listed on the National Register of Historic Places, are popular with visitors seeking fine examples of Victorian architecture and decor, but at Forepaugh's it's possible to enhance the experience with a meal in one of nine lovely dining rooms, each with its own special attraction, and each named for a past governor of Minnesota.

From the Pillsbury Room you can enjoy a panoramic view of downtown St. Paul; in the Olson Room you can admire the richness of fine mahogany paneling; and in the Sibley Room you'll view a bit of the past in the historic photographs of Victorian tea parties, which were held across the street in Irvine Park late in the 19th century.

The state fish takes on a delectably French aspect here in a dish called walleye meunière; New York sirloin, prepared to taste with a tangy green peppercorn sauce (entrecôte au poivre vert), is a favorite too.

Entrées, served with salad, potato, and vegetable, average $11.25 to $16.95. Lunch is served Monday through Friday from 11:30 a.m. to 2 p.m.; dinner, Monday through Saturday from 5:30 to 9:30 p.m., on Sunday from 5 to 8:30 p.m.; Sunday brunch is offered from 11:30 a.m. to 2 p.m.

You've got a lot of choices to make at **Spazzo,** a unique Italian-American restaurant located at Town Court, part of the World Trade Center complex at 30 E. 7th St., St. Paul (tel. 221-1983). First, there's a long list of Italian and American menu selections listed under such headings as "Appetizers," "Entrées," and "I Just Want a Sandwich." And then there's the matter of plate size. Diners here are encouraged to sample a variety of different dishes, so rather than order a large entrée and a small side plate, you might choose several small ones. Or if you're not feeling particularly hungry, you might settle for just one small plate—and that's fine too.

Most diners at Spazzo enjoy sampling a number of selections, and that requires another choice. Do you have your plates brought to the table all at once, or do you take them in succession? The mixing and matching opportunities are many, delectable, and sometimes surprising.

An appetizer that has caught on quickly here is buffalo mozzarella with roasted sweet peppers, olive oil, and fresh basil. And spaghettini with artichoke hearts, goat cheese, and sun-dried tomatoes tossed in cream, parmesan, and egg is a newly popular entrée. Old favorites are available as well—everything from hamburgers, small and large, to calves' liver, to grilled New York sirloin.

Prices are moderate to high, depending on your selections. Pasta ranges from $5 for a small plate of fettuccine Alfredo with four kinds of cheese to $7 for fresh linguine with bay scallops, clams, and shrimp tossed in cream, parmesan, and egg. Entrées, which come in one size only, range from $10 for the boneless breast of chicken to $14 for medallions of tenderloin.

Hours are 11 a.m. to 10 p.m. Monday through Thursday, 11 a.m. to 1 a.m. Friday and Saturday.

You don't have to be Irish to love **Gallivan's,** 354 Wabasha, St. Paul (227-6688). This St. Paul landmark underwent major expansion in 1982 and is now owned by Lloyd Urbain, a well-known St. Paul restaurateur. What had been a dining room and bar has now become three separate dining rooms with an adjoining bar and lounge. The spacious main dining room features dark woods and subdued lighting; the intimate library boasts a functioning fireplace along with bookshelves stocked with histories, biographies, law books, and encyclopedias.

The loyal clientele here is composed largely of folks who work in the neighborhood—lawyers, judges, and civil servants from the nearby Court House and City Hall, as well as journalists from the *St. Paul Pioneer Press,* the local Knight-Ridder newspaper with offices a block away.

There are few surprises on the menu here, and that's just the way the regulars like it. Actually, the prices may prove a pleasant surprise to first-timers. Entrées, which include a choice of soup or salad and a choice of pasta, french fries, or au gratin or baked potato, range from $12 for a crisp chicken half to $21 for T-bone steak. If you're a liver-lover like me, you'll cheer for the broiled baby beef liver with bacon and onions; the broiled walleye pike is a favorite too. There's a long wine and liquor list here. Hours are 11 a.m. to 1 a.m. Monday through Saturday.

MIDWAY ST. PAUL

Every large city has a restaurant like the **Blue Horse,** 1355 University Ave., St. Paul (tel. 645-8101), an elegant, expensive Continental dining spot that's frequented by a clientele for whom quality and consistency are more important than cost. John Warling is the second generation owner-manager of this internationally honored restaurant. As you wait for your table in the arched brick entryway, you can read citations from *Cartier's, Esquire,* and *Travel & Leisure.* Established in 1963, the Blue Horse has undergone a "lightening" of its menu since the 1983 arrival of chef Peter Grise. While retaining its long-standing reputation for superlative steaks and seafood, the Blue Horse now offers popular specialties that have been sautéed or stir-fried, and sauces that are more frequently thickened by reduction than by roux. Despite his abiding interest in innovation, Grise has retained perennial Blue Horse favorites like the old-fashioned corned beef hash, for which he "inherited" the recipe. Newer favorites include osso bucco, Florida stone crab, and veal Antonio.

There's a strong legislative and business presence here at both lunch and dinnertime, but one part of the population is conspicuous by its absence, according to Grise. "We don't get yuppies here," he says. "We serve the people yuppies hope they're going to become." Actually, Grise is something of a yuppie himself. After earning a degree in art and a reputation as a gourmet cook, he realized that "cooking is a studio art, involved with texture, color, and form." At the Blue Horse, he creates works of culinary art. Along with food and service second to none in the Twin Cities, the Blue Horse is known for its extensive and selective wine list. (John Warling points out that Minnesota ranks fifth in the nation for per capita consumption of premiere varietal wines.)

Luncheon specials, served with soup or salad, range from $8.50 to $11.95. Dinner entrées, served with the famous Blue Horse Caesar salad and a choice of vegetable, rice pilaf, or potato, range from $14.95 to $30.95.

Lunches are served 11:30 a.m. to 4:30 p.m., dinners 5 to 11 p.m., every day but Sunday.

The accent is all-American at the **Dakota Bar and Grill,** 1021 E. Bandana Blvd., St. Paul (tel. 642-1442), a gathering place that's won many local awards in two categories: "best restaurant" and "best nightspot." The menus (the chef dates and signs a new one each day) feature a full complement of seafood, beef, chicken, lamb, and pork, along with tasty vegetarian dishes that have converted many a hard-core carnivore. Most dishes are made with ingredients from Minnesota and Wisconsin.

Executive chef Ken Goff's imaginative use of spices and garnishes excels in popular items like brie-and-apple soup. Another popular creation is fresh walleye in a toasted wild rice crust with cucumber-tarragon tartar sauce.

The wondrous desserts include a tart cherry rice pudding with almond crust and caramel and—if calories are absolutely no object —chocolate mousse with strawberry cream.

For lunch, consider two other unusual entrées, fresh salmon hash with wild rice, sweet peppers, and mint, or grilled smoked ham with raspberry-rhubarb sauce. A Sunday brunch buffet features assorted muffins, granola, coffee cakes, yogurt, and several hot entrées. Outdoor dining is popular here during spring, summer, and early fall, when flowering shrubs enhance the setting.

Prices for lunchtime sandwiches are under $6.50; grilled meats and fish cost less than $9 at lunch and less than $20 at dinnertime. Lunch is served 11:30 a.m. to 2:30 p.m. Monday through Friday; dinner from 5:30 to 10:30 p.m. Monday through Thursday, 5:30 to 11:30 p.m. Friday and Saturday, and 5:30 to 9:30 p.m. Sunday. Brunch is served Sunday from 10:30 a.m. to 2:30 p.m.

The jaunty carousel horses that hang suspended from the ceiling of **Filbert's,** 1021 Bandana Blvd. E., St. Paul (tel. 644-1442), are probably the first thing you'll notice about this popular restaurant and nightspot, but it's people who have earned Filbert's the "place to be seen" award in local newspaper polls. Who you'll see here, though, varies widely according to the time of day or night.

By day this is an attractive suburban dining place with a beautifully landscaped outdoor dining plaza that's much in demand during warm weather. A variety of popular salads, sandwiches, and burgers is available for $6.50 or less. Luncheon entrées range from $5 to $10. Dinners are in the $5-to-$11 range.

But it's what happens after dinner that has given Filbert's its reputation, for late-night dancing, drinking, and high-energy fun that brings the 25- to 45-year-old crowd back again and again. Dining hours are 11:30 a.m. to 9 p.m. Monday through Thursday, 11:15 a.m. to 10 p.m. Friday and Saturday.

ST. PAUL HIGHLAND

There's good news and bad news concerning **Ristorante Luci,** 470 S. Cleveland Ave., St. Paul (tel. 699-8258). The good news is that Lucille and Al Smith, after living in Italy for eleven years, decided after his retirement from 3M to open a small restaurant featuring the kind of food that Italians really eat. The bad news is that since opening their tiny trattoria they've turned away several times the number of diners they've served. Reservations are required here, but if you're only in town for a short time, take a chance and call, especially if you're trying for a weekday evening. Cancellations do occur from time to time, and you might get lucky. The decor is simple here—white walls, black wrought-iron light fixtures, white tablecloths on tables that can accommodate groups of eight.

The menu, which changes two or three times a year, is simple too, divided into sections for antipasti, soup, salad, pasta, meat or fish, and dessert. There's also a four-course "taster's dinner," which includes the day's antipasti, pasta, and fish special with a choice of soup or salad, all in reduced portions. Featured on the menu are antipasti like bruschetta con pecorino fresco (grilled home-baked bread with fresh goat cheese and dill) for $4.50, gazpacho neapolitan style for $2.65, rigatoni alla bolognese (with ground veal, lamb, and beef simmered with tomatoes, red wine and fresh herbs) for $7.95, and linguine alla puttanesca (fresh tomatoes, olive oil, garlic, Calamata olives, and capers) for $6.50. Secondi (meat and fish courses) include pollo piacere (sautéed chicken breast) prepared in a variety of ways—with a leek piccata sauce, with a tomato sauce with fresh herbs and balsamic vinegar, or with a marsala wine sauce, for instance. And then there are the sweets—Luci cheesecake, flourless chocolate torte, made daily with Belgian chocolate, and a variety of fruit tarts.

The carefully selected wine list has been growing steadily; at this writing it includes a pleasing selection of about a dozen house wines—red, white, and nonalcoholic—ranging from $5 to $7 per half carafe, $10 to $12 per carafe. They're all $2.50 per glass. (My own favorite among the white house wines is the Chardonnay Folonari 1987, and, among the reds, Zinfandel/Pinot Noir, Seghesio.) Bottles of Italian wine range from about $14 to $50 or so.

Luci oversees the menu, Al the wine list, and their six children anything and everything that suits their fancy and their rapidly increasing skills. One bakes the bread each day, one makes the pasta (by hand—no pasta machines on these premises!), others take turns at the register and at the tables. Since their parents seem resolute in their determination to keep Ristorante Luci small, it may fall to the upcoming generation to open another restaurant in some other part of town. (Mine, I hope.) Hours here are Tuesday through Thursday 5 to 9 p.m., Friday and Saturday 5 to 10 p.m.

GRAND AVENUE

The Lexington, 1096 Grand Ave., St. Paul (tel. 222-5878), is an institution in the Twin Cities, an elegant and gracious, sprawling yet intimate restaurant with a long-standing reputation for fine food, beautiful surroundings, and reasonable prices.

It started out decades ago as a one-room tavern serving steak sandwiches and hamburgers, and has since evolved into a 360-seat restaurant with an extensive menu. You'll find traditional American fare at the Lexington: New York sirloin and spring lamb chops, Dover sole and lobster tails, chicken Kiev and barbecued ribs. And then there are the specialties of the house—medallions of beef bourguignon glazed with a sauce of red wine, veal scaloppine sautéed in butter and simmered with sherry and mushrooms, Minnesota ringneck pheasant braised in a sauce of cream and brandy and served over wild rice. Entrées, served with a choice of potato and a choice of salad, range in price from $9 for braised short ribs or lamb shank to $23 for "bone-in steer tender," a first-choice beef filet.

The setting here is as carefully designed as the menu: dark polished woods, gleaming crystal chandeliers, fine oil paintings, and a variety of rare artifacts—from the bronze relief in the main dining room depicting an elderly couple sharing a bit of snuff to the jovial gargoyle now putting in his time as a wine tureen in the Williamsburg Room. There's really no lovelier setting, no friendlier service, no finer food than you'll find at the Lexington, where families, business associates, and newcomers in search of the flavor of Minnesota are attentively and graciously served.

After you've enjoyed your entrée, try one of the splendid desserts, which have garnered a following through the years. The incredibly creamy cheesecake amaretto is always in demand, but you won't go wrong with the carrot cake, pecan pie, or anything else on the menu.

This restaurant accepts no credit cards except the ones they themselves issue, but you can pay by check. Food is served from 11 a.m. until midnight Monday through Saturday.

For more than a decade, one of the most popular ethnic restaurants in the Twin Cities has been the **Acropol Inn,** 748 Grand Ave., St. Paul (tel. 298-0151). Now this fine Greek-American restaurant is one of the handsomest, too. Etched glass is prominent in the new decor: Juno greets you at the front door, while large figures of Zeus and Dionysus dominate the first of two spacious dining rooms. Greek landscapes are illuminated by spotlights and taped Greek music adds to the effect. The final, convincing touch comes when you taste the homemade fare, prepared for you by Aris and Cassandra Apostolou and served, likely as not, by their son George or daughter Vicki.

Early each morning Cassandra Apostolou begins baking the day's supply of bread, baklava, and assorted pastries, while Aris readies the soups, roasts, salads, and other specialties. Lamb, roasted on a spit, is favored here; so are the seafood, beef, and chicken entrées prepared American style. But mostly it's the authentic Greek dishes that keep people coming back again and again—everything from moussaka (ground meat, fried eggplant, and a special topping) to dolmades (ground meat and rice wrapped in grape leaves and topped with lemon sauce) to stefado (beef in wine sauce with potatoes and onions). The Greek salads are delectable too, enhanced with imported feta cheese and olive oil. Dinner prices range from $9 to $13 including soup, salad, and homemade bread. Luncheon entrées range from $5 to $9.

Maybe the best news of all is that for less than $6 you can lunch on a gyro sandwich with soup; many local diners consider it the perfect combination. Hours are 11 a.m. to 9 p.m. Monday through Thursday, 11 a.m. to 10 p.m. Friday and Saturday.

THE CATHEDRAL AREA

One hundred years ago everybody in the elegant Ramsey Hill neighborhood of St. Paul knew that an establishment named for pharmacist W. A. Frost stood on the corner of Selby and Western Avenues. That's true today too, but now it's a restaurant, **W. A. Frost and Company,** 374 Selby Ave., St. Paul (tel. 224-5715), located in the restored Dakotah Building, not far from the state capitol and on the edge of one of the country's best-preserved enclaves of Victorian residences. The ambience of bygone days dominates here, with tin Victorian ceilings, marble tables, oriental rugs, and iluminated oil landscapes that date back to the turn of the century. There are two functioning fireplaces as well, a popular feature during the winter months. As the seasons change, though, diners look forward to some of the Twin Cities' most picturesque outdoor dining, amid flowering bushes and trailing vines, under a living canopy of trees.

The menu is eclectic, offering a variety of European, Asian, and American dishes. Favorite appetizers include the savory smoked salmon and cream cheese torte ($5.50) and crispy Chinese chicken wings ($4.25). A wide range of seafood is served here, everything from walleye to monk fish. And there's a variety of beef, chicken, and pasta dishes as well. This is one fine restaurant where people customarily come just as they are; don't be surprised to see a casually clad neighborhood couple fresh from working in their garden, while at a nearby table the governor or a bevy of businessmen or legislators sit in somewhat more formal attire.

Prices at W. A. Frost are moderate, ranging from $8 to $20 for an entrée that includes potato and fresh vegetable. You'll also find one of the largest selections of imported beers and fine liquors in the area. Lunch is served Monday through Saturday from 11 a.m. to 2:30 p.m., dinner daily from 5:30 p.m. on.

MACALESTER-GROVELAND

Faculty members and students from nearby Macalester College and St. Thomas University make up more than half the regular diners at the **Khyber Pass Cafe,** 1399 St. Clair Ave., St. Paul (tel. 698-5403). But diners come from throughout the Twin Cities to check out for themselves the high praise they've seen and heard since this small, neighborhood restaurant opened in June 1986.

Afghani articles decorate the white walls, and strains of Afghani music provide an exotic background in the spare, comfortable dining room. Owner Habib Amini, who does all the cooking, explains that unlike other Middle Eastern cuisines, Afghani cooking uses relatively few spices and aims to enhance rather than overpower the food's natural perfume. Chicken, lamb, and vegetarian dishes are among the favorites here. One popular selection is the *kebob-e murgh,* chunks of boneless chicken cooked on a skewer and served with tomatoes, onions, and chutney; *korma-e sabzee* is a delicious spinach dish served with chunks of lamb; *korma e dahl,* another popular entrée, features chunks of lamb with yellow lentils cooked in onions and garlic.

Luncheon entrées range from $4.50 to $6.25. Dinner entrées, served à la carte with flat bread, are $5.25 to $5.95. A full dinner, served with basmati rice, salad, chutney, and flat bread, runs from $7.25 to $8.95. Desserts are delicious. If you like puddings, you're bound to enjoy the *firni,* rich and creamy and flavored with a blend of cardamom, rosewater, and pistachios. If you're a yogurt lover—and even if, like me, you're not—try a glass of *Doh,* plain yogurt diluted with water, mixed with cucumber, and garnished with mint.

Delightfully refreshing! Lunches are served from 11 a.m. to 2 p.m., dinners from 5 to 9 p.m. Khyber Pass is closed on Sundays and Mondays.

OUTER ST. PAUL

Dining doesn't get much more pleasant than the experience you'll find at **Kozlak's Royal Oak Restaurant,** 4785 Hodgson Rd., Shoreview, (tel. 484-8484). Whether your table is indoors in one of the handsome two-tiered dining rooms with arched windows overlooking the colorful outdoor gardens, or you're seated on the canvas-topped, screened-in veranda, you'll be pleased by the attentive service and reliable cuisine that has distinguished this family's name for decades. Diane Kozlak, whose parents, Jack and Ruth, founded the Royal Oak in 1977, is now co-owner with her brother-in-law, chef Mark Satt.

Four-course jazz brunches are particularly popular here, where your tab will depend on the entrée you select, from eggs Benedict ($8.95) to veal and fettuccine or "brunch steak" ($14.95). The meal is modeled on the jazz brunches offered at Brennans in New Orleans.

Lunchtime prices fall between $6 and $9, while dinner entrées range from about $14 for sautéed chicken breast to $24.95 for broiled choice T-bone steak. Your entrée is complemented by a trip to the salad bar or, if you choose, a house salad or a cup of the Boston clam chowder.

Flexibility is the operative word here, and you can call ahead for everything from box lunches to full dinners at home, a particular favorite with two-job couples who enjoy entertaining but don't relish the work that entails. The cost for take-out is about $3 less per dinner entrée, making for an even more attractive alternative. Lunch is served Monday through Saturday from 11 a.m. to 2 p.m.; dinner, Monday through Thursday from 4 to 9:30 p.m., Friday and Saturday from 4 to 10:30 p.m.

You'll see a variety of collections when you visit the **Lake Elmo Inn,** 3442 Lake Elmo Ave., Lake Elmo (tel. 777-8495). In the main dining room owner John Schultz displays an impressive assemblage of salt and pepper shakers, and you're welcome to a free dessert or cocktail if you donate a set of your own. There's also a nutcracker collection clustered on the wall. And, if you chance to be in Lake Elmo at Christmastime, you'll receive a complimentary beverage at the bar in exchange for a Christmas ornament that will be hung on the tree until after the holidays and then be suspended from the ceiling ever afterward as part of the perpetual collection of Christmas decorations.

But the most important collection at the charming Lake Elmo Inn consists of the great number of satisfied diners who have made it unnecessary for John and Kathy Schultz to advertise for the past five years. Word-of-mouth has kept people coming in ever increasing numbers, for what the Schultzes sum up as "friendliness and food as good as anyone's ever had, served well at reasonable prices." You'll do well to phone for reservations, especially if you're coming out during the summertime. This lovely area served a century ago as a resort for wealthy St. Paulites, and is still a popular warm-weather destination. If you're coming on Saturday night anytime during the year, better call a week in advance.

As an inn, established in 1881, this building had served as a stagecoach stop and later a railroad stop, where a boardwalk provided convenient passage down to the lake. At present, John and Kathy Schultz and their three small children live on the second floor of the inn.

Dining-room specialties include the flavorful spedini appetizer —for $3.75 you'll get French bread topped with garlic, parmesan, anchovies, pine nuts, and mozzarella. Of the excellent soups, my own favorite is the wild rice and duck soup, at $3.50 a bowl, $2.50 a cup. Among the dinnertime entrées, there's a particularly attractive vegetarian plate featuring stuffed tomato with fresh spinach, wild rice, a medley of vegetables, stuffed mushrooms, asparagus, and linguine, for $9.95. Or try the salmon Wellington, a filet beautifully prepared with spinach and wrapped in puff pastry ($16.50) or the chicken Alfredo, a winning combination of mostaccioli, chicken, and parmesan cream sauce ($10.95). Desserts here are spectacular, particularly at the Sunday "champagne brunch" when 20 or so are presented for your selection.

The Lake Elmo Inn is open seven days a week, serving lunch from 11 a.m. to 2 p.m. Monday through Saturday, dinner from 5 to 10 p.m. Monday through Thursday, from 5 to 11 p.m. Friday and Saturday, and from 4:30 to 8:30 p.m. on Sunday. The very popular Sunday champagne brunch is served from 10 a.m. to 2 p.m. Do make reservations!

For more than 60 years, the Vitale family has done business at the site of the **Venetian Inn,** 2814 Rice Street, Little Canada (tel. 484-7215), about 5 miles north of downtown St. Paul. Now readily accessible to both Twin Cities, less than 2 miles from both I-694 andHwy. 36, this location was largely rural when Congie and Joe Vitale opened a small vegetable stand offering produce they'd grown themselves.

Today, three sons, Pat, Joe, and Jim, and their families, own and operate the Venetian Inn, along with their widowed mother, now in her eighties, who remains active and involved. She's also become the namesake of a successful line of frozen foods marketed statewide as "Mama Vitale" products.

Today, after a succession of remodelings and additions, the Venetian Inn dining room seats 300 people, with room for 600 in the banquet halls. And nearly 200 more attend performances in the Venetian Playhouse, where "Nunsense" has lately been enjoying a successful run.

You'll be offered a bib with your order of ribs or pasta, both of which rank high with Venetian Inn regulars. Seafood is a specialty as well, and so are Italian dinners including veal scaloppine, eggplant parmigiana, and chicken cacciatore. Dinner includes an antipasto tray, tossed salad, and Italian bread; some dishes also include a side of spaghetti or baked potato. Prices range from $7.25 for rigatoni with meatballs to $26.95 for a seafood platter that includes haddock, stuffed shrimp, whitefish, scallops, and lobster tail.

The Venetian Inn is open for lunch from 11 a.m. to 3 p.m. daily; dinner is served from 3 p.m. to 10 p.m. Monday through Thursday, 3 p.m. to 11 p.m. Friday and Saturday.

---

3. The Chain Restaurants

There's something for everybody at **T.G.I. Friday's,** with three locations, 7730 Normandale Blvd., Bloomington (tel. 831-6553); 5875 Wayzata Blvd., St. Louis Park (tel. 544-0675); and 2480 Fairview Ave. N., Roseville (tel. 631-1101).

As the name implies, this is a place for unwinding after work is done. It's also a place for lunch or dinner, weekdays and weekends alike. The extensive menu, in effect throughout the day and evening, features nearly 10 pages of suggestions for dining and drinking, either at the large, square, center bar or in one of the elegantly cluttered dining rooms, which abound with Tiffany-style lamps, stained-glass windows, mounted animal heads, and assorted antiques. The red and white striped tablecloths are a signature item at T.G.I. Friday's throughout the country.

Best described as an American bistro, this congenial gathering place is remarkable for its selection of nonalcoholic drinks. Friday's Flings are a delightful alternative to the liquor that used to be considered a social necessity. Flings are particularly popular at lunchtime with office workers and at any time with those who enjoy the atmosphere at the bar but don't care to drink alcohol. Drinks are not discounted for the popular daily happy hour, but a wide assortment of hors d'oeuvres is.

Prices here are easy to take. Burgers with all sorts of extras go for $5.50. Beef, chicken, and seafood entrées range from $8 to $12. A delightful children's coloring menu, reportedly designed by children, features everything kids love best, from hot dogs to grilled cheese to pigs-in-a-blanket. Prices are in the $2 range. Friday's is open seven days a week: Monday through Friday from 11 a.m. to 1 a.m., Saturday from 10 a.m. to 1 a.m., and Sunday from 11 a.m. to 1 a.m.

There hadn't been a Chinese buffet in the Twin Cities until Leeann Chin opened one back in 1980. Now there are three branches of **Leeann Chin Chinese Cuisine:** 1571 Plymouth Rd., Minnetonka (tel. 545-3600); 214 E. 4th St., Union Depot Place, St. Paul (tel. 224-8814); and 900 Second Ave. S., International Center, Minneapolis (tel. 338-8488). There are also nine take-out kitchens, located throughout the Twin Cities and suburbs.

Chin is the author of two best-sellers: "Betty Crocker's Chinese Cookbook: Recipes by Leeann Chin" and "The New Chinese Cookbook." This unassuming woman's achievements are the more remarkable because she spoke no English when she first arrived with her five children in 1955. She could sew, though, and she ultimately established a small dressmaking and alterations business. In the late 1970s she hosted a luncheon for the women she'd sewn for, and their requests for lessons in Chinese cooking led ultimately to an invitation to teach classes at the Bonaventure Center in suburban Minnetonka. The rest, as they say, is culinary history.

Certain signature items have evolved in Leeann Chin's restaurants during the years. Shrimp toast and cream cheese, lemon chicken, and Szechuan beef rank high as favorites. Buffet selections change from day to day, but you'll always find three appetizers, two entrées, and fried rice at the long, fully laden tables. In addition, you'll be served your choice of Chinese soup or salad, and of course, tea. Happily, there's no limit on the number of trips you may take to either the appetizer or the entrée tables.

Prices are $7 for the luncheon buffet, $13 for the dinner buffet. Hours vary by location, so call ahead. By the way, be sure to look closely at the exquisitely carved ivory and jade artifacts in each of the restaurants—they're exceptional!

You'll have a sense of déjà vu when you get your first look at a **Pannekoeken Huis Restaurant,** at 1505 S. Robert St., West St. Paul (tel. 455-1653); 2217 Hudson Rd., St. Paul (tel. 735-8860); 3020 W. 66th St., Richfield (tel. 866-7731); and 9830 Aldrich Ave. S., Minneapolis (tel. 881-5635). Then you'll remember where you saw this trim, pretty blue-and-white building before. It was on the last piece of Delft porcelain you admired.

The most popular item on the menu in these popular and picturesque family restaurants is, of course, the pannekoeken, a soufflé-style pancake that is baked in the oven, flipped, and then rushed to the table before its puffiness disappears. The average deflation time is 20 seconds, and that's why, from time to time, you'll see a waitress dashing from the kitchen with a plate held aloft as others clear out of her way. You can choose from 11 different toppings for your pancake or choose to eat it plain with powdered sugar and lemon wedges. You'll love it either way.

There are other delights here as well—hearty Dutch stews and soups and omelets, for example. But much of the menu is Dutch-American: metworst sausage and eggs, pannekoeken burgers, Netherlander sandwiches. And, finally, there are wholly domestic items, like grilled Reuben sandwiches, barbecued ribs, and batter-fried chicken strips. So maybe you won't find a truly authentic Dutch experience here after all. What you will find is tasty, healthful fare in delightful surroundings at modest prices: a $6 top tab for entrées. Soups, accompanied by a house salad and a thick slice of fresh-baked nine-grain bread, are well under $4.

And save room for some of the imported candies and fresh pastries you'll be invited to take with you on your way out. You'll be glad you did! Hours are 6 a.m. to 11 p.m. Sunday through Thursday, 6 a.m. to 1 a.m. Friday and Saturday.

For the past 30 years **Nora's,** 2107 E. Lake St., Minneapolis (tel. 729-9353), has been serving Twin Citians wholesome fare at exceptional prices in a beautifully appointed setting downtown. Now there's a second Nora's at 3118 W. Lake St. (tel. 927-5781), just a block from Lake Calhoun and about a mile from the heart of Uptown, and thus squarely within one of the most popular and interesting parts of Minneapolis. Where else can you enjoy three pieces of fried chicken, french fries, soup or salad, toast, vegetable, and a small ice-cream sundae for $4? Or shrimp in garlic butter baked in wine sauce, with potato, soup or salad, vegetable, toast, and a sundae for $6? Or an eight-ounce tenderloin filet with the same sort of accompaniments for under $8?

The breads, soups, and sauces are made on the premises, and so are the popular onion rings, which come fully into their own only when they're dipped into the drippings of a broiled-to-order steak (just a personal observation I'd like to pass along). Another popular item is "Uncle Nels" broiled sandwich, a combination of turkey breast, mushrooms, cheddar cheese, and a light wine sauce on toast. According to owner Nora Truelson, it came into being as a bribe to one of her five sons: "We'll name the sandwich for you if you'll work tonight." He did and they did. Nora's is open from 11 a.m. to 10 p.m. everyday.

Six years after the first **Old Country Buffet** opened at 9 E. 66th St., Richfield (tel. 869-1911), there are eight more doing SRO business at suburban locations throughout the metropolitan area: 2480 Fairview Ave., Roseville (tel. 639-0088); 6540 University Ave., Fridley (tel. 572-8627); 4801 Hwy. 101, Minnetonka (tel. 474-1684); 14150 Nicollet Ave. S., Burnsville (tel. 435-6711); 5526 W. Broadway, Crystal (tel. 536-8497); 3000 White Bear Ave., Maplewood (tel. 779-1957); 3071 Coon Rapids Blvd., Coon Rapids (tel. 421-2150); and 2005 S. Robert St., West St. Paul (tel. 457-9832).

You'll understand their overwhelming success when you visit one of these clean, pretty family restaurants featuring country-style decor in shades of blue, rust, and white, and an abundance of booths and tables to accommodate parties of any size—and parties of absolutely any size do dine regularly at Old Country Buffet.

Certain items regularly appear, afternoon or evening, on the succession of buffet tables. You'll always find fluffy mashed potatoes and golden fried chicken, along with gravy, vegetables, salads, breads, beverages, desserts, sundaes, and hot cinnamon rolls. But those are only the starters. There's a long list of daily specials—meatloaf on Monday, fried cod on Tuesday, Asian fare on Wednesday, lasagne on Thursday, Swedish meatballs on Friday—and that's only at lunch. For dinner, seven nights a week, you can have roast beef or ham carved to order, along with the daily dinner specials.

If you try Old Country Buffet once during your visit to the Twin Cities, you'll probably come back. It couldn't be more pleasant or more budget-pleasing. Complete lunches are $4; dinners, $5.40. Sunday breakfast, served from 8 to 10:30 a.m., is $4. Lunch is served Monday through Saturday from 11 a.m. to 3:30 p.m.; dinner hours are Monday through Thursday from 4 to 8 p.m., Friday and Saturday 4 to 9 p.m. Sunday and holiday hours are from 11 a.m. to 8:30 p.m.

Budget dining doesn't get any better than at **Lotus,** with locations at 3037 Hennepin Ave., Minneapolis (tel. 825-2263); 313 Oak St., Minneapolis (tel. 331-1781); 3907 W. 50th St., Edina (tel. 922-4254); and Sioux Trail, Burnsville (tel. 890-5573). Don't be put off by the decor—or the lack of it—at these casual, congenial Vietnamese restaurants. The large white oriental lamp shades are about as far as Le and Hieu Tran went in 1983 when they decorated the first of what would become four busy neighborhood eating places.

Because sharing is encouraged, you can try a number of savory, nutritious entreés, from beginners' fare, like chicken or beef with vegetables, to less familiar selections, such as curried mock duck sautéed with onion, garlic, and lemon grass and served in a spicy coconut gravy. The chow mein here is delectable—a hearty mixture of chicken, beef, and shrimp with crunchy slabs of cabbage, carrots, celery, onion, and broccoli that in no way resembles the gelatinous mound you'll find in many Chinese eating places. The menu indicates which items are hotter than others, but the dishes can be adjusted to taste.

Although Le and Hieu Tran and their four children have made many friends in the Twin Cities, few people are aware of the symbolism in the name and the logo of the Lotus restaurants. This flower, like so many refugees from Vietnam, survives and grows in harsh conditions. And the blue curve of neon beneath the illuminated flower in the window of each Lotus restaurant symbolizes the ocean from which the Trans and other desperate boat people were rescued before being flown to the United States. You may have to wait for a table at the Lotus restaurants, but the food and the value reward a little patience. Entrées range from $4 to $7.45. Hours vary from restaurant to restaurant.

---

4. Restaurants by Cuisine

Afghani

American

Chinese

Continental

Jardin (page 43)   M

Dutch-American
Pannekoeken Huis Restaurant (page 64)   B

Eclectic
Azur Restaurant (page 39)   E
Goodfellows (page 39)   VE
Gregory's (page 51)   M
Loring Cafe (page 42)   M
Malt Shop (page 53)   B
T.G.I. Friday's (page 63)   M
W.A. Frost and Company (page 59)   M

French
Le Café Royal (page 50)   VE
Chez Colette (page 50)   M
510 (page 40)   VE
Forepaugh's (page 54)   M
New French Cafe (page 41)   E
La Terasse (page 50)   M
Yvette (page 45)   M

German
Black Forest Inn (page 52)   M

Greek
Acropol Inn (page 59)   M

Italian
Cocolezzone (page 49)   M
Figlio's (page 53)   M
D'Amico Cucina (page 38)   E
Gustino's (page 41)   E
Ristorante Luci (page 57)   M
Spazzo (page 55)   M
Venetian Inn (page 62)   M

Japanese
Kikugawa (page 46)   M

Steak and Seafood
Braxton Seafood Grill (page 46)   M
Kinkaid's (page 50)   M
Wellington's (page 48)   M

Vegetarian/Health Food
Faegre's Bar and Restaurant (page 48)   M
Goodfellows (page 44)   VE
Jardin (page 43)   M

Vietnamese
Lotus (page 65)   B

VE = very expensive, $30 and up
E = expensive, $20–$30
M = moderately priced, $10–$20
B = budget dining, under $10

(approximations for one dinner without alcohol)

THE SIGHTS OF MINNEAPOLIS AND ST. PAUL

A beautiful blend of the old and the new is what you'll find here in the Twin Cities. Many of their proudest buildings, like the splendid mansions on St. Paul's Summit Avenue, have been listed on the National Register of Historic Places; many other buildings, newer than tomorrow, will dazzle you with their soaring expanses of reflective glass. Don't miss Gaviidae Common, City Center, and Phillip Johnson's award-winning IDS Tower in downtown Minneapolis. Be sure to visit Town Court, part of the handsome Town Square Center not far from the State Capitol in downtown St. Paul. Note, too, that the internationally famed arts of the Twin Cities are often housed in buildings that are themselves works of art.

Not all the Twin Cities' sights are man-made, however. The lakes of Minneapolis and St. Paul are legendary, not only for their beauty but for the many popular activities that take place there throughout the year.

Let's start our mini-tour in St. Paul, because that's where the Twin Cities started.

1. Historic St. Paul

THE STATE CAPITOL

The grandest of all Twin Cities sights is the Minnesota State Capitol, built in 1905 on a hill overlooking downtown St. Paul. Approached by a succession of broad, gray-granite terraces and crowned by the world's largest unsupported marble dome, the magnificent structure at 700 Wabasha St., was the design of Cass Gilbert, a young St. Paul architect whose later work included the Woolworth Building in New York City. At the base of the dome, modeled after the one Michelangelo created for St. Peter's in Rome, is a dramatic grouping of gilded figures titled *The Progress of the State*. Four prancing horses, symbolizing the power of Nature, are held in check by two women, representing Civilization. A charioteer, Prosperity, holds aloft a horn of plenty in one hand, and in the other he grasps a banner bearing the inscription "Minnesota."

The interior of the capitol building is equally impressive, with its marble stairways, chambers, and halls, and its diversity of fine oil paintings depicting important events in Minnesota history. Free guided tours through the senate, house of representatives, and supreme court chambers are offered Monday through Friday from 9 a.m. to 4 p.m., on Saturday from 10 a.m. to 3 p.m., and on Sunday from 1 to 3 p.m. Phone 296-2881 for details.

THE CATHEDRAL OF ST. PAUL

On a nearby site, at the corner of Summit and Selby avenues, stands another of St. Paul's proud architectural achievements, the 3,000-seat Renaissance-style Cathedral of St. Paul, constructed of Minnesota granite. John Ireland Boulevard, the street that extends just half a mile from the capitol to the cathedral, is named for the dynamic archbishop of St. Paul who served as a fighting chaplain during the Civil War and later lent his energies and determination toward raising the funds for the creation of this magnificent structure, which he dedicated to the people of St. Paul.

SUMMIT AVENUE

Beyond the cathedral, Summit Avenue, long the most prestigious of St. Paul's addresses, extends 4½ miles to the Mississippi River. On this distinguished street stands the country's longest span of intact **Victorian mansions,** and here, at 240 Summit Ave., you'll find one of the city's perennially popular tourist attractions, the mansion of "empire builder" James J. Hill, founder of the Great Northern Railroad, a network that made possible the development of the American Northwest. (For information about tours, phone 297-2555.) Among the more modest homes on this avenue is the one at 599 Summit, where F. Scott Fitzgerald lived in 1918 while finishing his first literary success, *This Side of Paradise*. And farther down toward the Mississippi, at 1006 Summit, you'll find the governor's stately residence.

Elsewhere on Summit Avenue you'll find several famous colleges and universities—**Macalester College,** at Summit and Snelling avenues; the **College of St. Thomas,** at 2215 Summit Ave.; and, at 875 Summit Ave., arguably the most influential small college anywhere in the country, the **William Mitchell College of Law,** whose graduates include two former colleagues on the United States Supreme Court, Chief Justice Warren Burger and Justice Harry Blackmun.

Distinguished houses of worship stand on the avenue as well, including **Mount Zion Temple,** 1300 Summit Ave., home of the oldest Jewish congregation in the state of Minnesota. Members of the congregation, which dates back to 1856, selected the architect Frederick Mendelsohn to design their new temple for them in the early 1950s. Mendelsohn had gained international fame earlier for his work in pre-Nazi Germany. Tours of this beautiful building are popular with Gentiles and Jews alike. Call 698-3881 for more information.

DOWNTOWN RESTORATIONS

In the downtown area, two twin-towered churches are particularly interesting and photogenic. **Assumption Church,** 51 9th St. W., was constructed in 1873 for the city's German-speaking Catholics, and it looks like a bit of Bavaria transplanted to a midwestern American city. That may be due to the fact that this picturesque church was designed by Joseph Reidl, architect to the king of Bavaria. Relatively austere on the outside, it contains within a wealth of beautiful statuary, magnificent murals, and an exquisite gilded back altar. The **Saint Louis Catholic Church,** 506 Cedar St., is a quietly elegant structure of red brick and limestone. It was built in 1909 for French-speaking parishioners.

The **St. Paul Union Depot,** at the corner of East 4th and Sibley streets, is a massive sandstone building with an imposing columned entrance that once welcomed train travelers to the Twin Cities. The Union Depot was opened to the public in 1920, then reopened in 1983 after it had been restored and refurbished. Now it houses one of Leeann Chin's phenomenally popular Chinese restaurants. (See Chapter IV for more specific information on this delectable subject.)

Elsewhere in Lowertown, at Mears Park, Sibley and 6th streets, stands **Park Square Court,** the 19th-century warehouse credited with having inspired the redevelopment of St. Paul's historic Lowertown. Now primarily an office complex, Park Square is accessible by skyway.

Nearby **Galtier Plaza,** on Sibley Street between 5th and 6th streets, is now an entertainment, retail, restaurant, and residential complex.

But perhaps the most dramatic of all St. Paul's restored structures is the **Landmark Center,** facing Rice Park at 106 W. 6th St. This massive early French Renaissance structure with Gothic towers and pillars, turrets and gables, 20-foot ceilings and hand-carved mahogany and marble decoration, served for decades as the Federal

Courts Building and Post Office. Eventually it fell into disrepair, and it was slated for demolition when a determined coalition of private citizens and public officials intervened and prevailed. In 1972 the building was taken over by the city, and today, returned to its former grandeur, it houses a diversity of arts and civic offices and is open to the public for free guided tours.

The Landmark Center is just one of several significant structures that encircle **Rice Park,** the oldest of St. Paul's urban parks and a treasure in itself, with its lovely central fountain and meticulously manicured lawns.

On another side of the park you'll find the **St. Paul Public Library** and the **James Jerome Hill Reference Library,** both housed in the same exquisite building. Hill funded the library bearing his name, which contains his own reference collection. (Hill's donations also played a major role elsewhere in the city, most notably in the establishment of the College of Saint Thomas and the Cathedral of St. Paul.)

Forming the fourth "wall" around Rice Park is the restored and refurbished **Saint Paul Hotel,** which has made a graceful transition from its turn-of-the-century origins to its present-day role as host to visitors to this city (see Chapter III for details).

THE WORLD THEATER

It was St. Paul's favorite son, Garrison Keillor, who spearheaded a national crusade to save the World Theater, one of the city's most beautiful and beloved restorations. The World, built in 1910 by Sam S. Schubert, and originally named for him, was for decades an upper Midwest showplace for stage productions and cinema. Ultimately it became the home of Keillor's "Prairie Home Companion," the radio show that provided weekly reports on Lake Wobegon, the mythical town "where all the women are strong, all the men are good-looking, and all the children are above average." By 1977, when plaster started falling from the ceiling, safety officials demanded that the theater be closed, so a massive fund drive got under way that ultimately led to the World's rehabilitation and then to its gala reopening in April 1986. Today, restored to its original splendor, the World is one of the country's few remaining two-balcony "dramatic house" proscenium theaters, with none of its 925 seats more than 87 feet from the stage.

2. The New St. Paul

THE ORDWAY MUSIC THEATRE

The Ordway received national attention when it opened on January 1, 1985. Its grace and grandeur led to comparisons with the grand old concert halls of Europe, but the expanses of its glass walls provide a distinctly contemporary touch to the exterior of the structure. These glass walls also provide a superb view of the city for those within. (See Chapter VII, "Music, Dance, Museums, and Galleries," for details.)

TOWN SQUARE

At the heart of St. Paul's extensive skyway system is the remarkable four-story Town Square, with its shopping, office, dining, and entertainment facilities. Easily the most beautiful part of Town Square, though, is still unexplored territory to many Twin Citians. Tucked away on the fourth level above the retail area is the world's largest indoor public park, with lush greenery, dancing waterfalls, cozy seating alcoves, and even a historic merry-go-round where children can have fun while their elders enjoy the beauty and uniqueness of it all.

THE WORLD TRADE CENTER

Also new on the St. Paul landscape is the nearby World Trade Center, a sleek, imposing 40-story office complex opened in the fall of 1987 for the purpose of encouraging and expediting international trade. Town Court, the adjoining retail complex, includes an indoor fountain, shops, and restaurants.

LANDMARK CENTER

This beautiful castlelike structure was formerly the Old Federal Court Building, where famous gangster trials were held back in the 1930s. The courtroom has been elegantly restored, and so has the magnificent sixth-story courtyard. Landmark now serves as the art center for St. Paul, with one of the main galleries of the Minnesota Museum of Art located here.

THE SCIENCE MUSEUM OF MINNESOTA

Exhibits at the Science Museum, 30 E. 10th St., ranging from the anthropological to the technological, have enthralled visitors of all ages and all backgrounds since 1980. Its distinctive concave entranceway encloses a portion of the circular second-story Omnitheater, where exciting and educational 70-mm OmniMax movies are projected onto a massive tilted screen, providing an image that gives a sometimes scary sense of involvement.

THE MINNESOTA MUSEUM OF ART

Overlooking Kellogg Boulevard and the Mississippi River, the handsome art deco Minnesota Museum of Art, 305 St. Peter, is the repository of a distinguished collection of contemporary paintings, sculpture, photography, and drawings from throughout the world. A large portion of the street level has recently been turned over to the Park Square Theatre, a highly regarded company whose popular productions add yet another dimension to the interesting offerings here.

TWO SPECIAL ST. PAUL STATUES

There are two statues in St. Paul that rank high on any list of sight-seeing attractions.

In the St. Paul City Hall/Ramsey County Courthouse, at

The Skyway System

St. Paul's skyway system has become so integral a part of city life that we tend to forget how remarkable it is. Extending for nearly 3 miles from one end of St. Paul to the other, this is the largest publicly owned skyway system in the world. Built and maintained by the city, St. Paul's skyways, like any other public thoroughfares, are uniform in design and patrolled regularly by the police department. Although hours in different parts of the system vary, depending on the kinds of buildings they're connecting, those that tourists are likely to use are generally open from 6 a.m. to 2 a.m.

The city has made good use of its skyways for festive as well as functional purposes. During one St. Paul Winter Carnival, lines of marchers, musicians, clowns, and tap-dancers started out at the north, south, east, and west corners of the skyway, ultimately convening at the center, Town Square. In the process they made their way into the *Guinness Book of World Records* for having participated in the world's longest indoor parade.

The skyways have made this a second-story city, where a vast majority of retail business is conducted above street level. Visitors needn't worry about the weather as they walk from hotels to shops, restaurants, and theaters. This is, after all, wonderful, weatherproof downtown St. Paul.

Fourth and Wabasha avenues, Carl Milles's majestic 36-foot tall onyx figure, *The Indian God of Peace,* stands in regal splendor. This 60-ton statue, which rotates very very slowly, has been seen and admired by most Twin Cities children and by the grownups who bring them here during viewing hours: Tuesday through Friday from 8 a.m. to 5 p.m., Sunday from 1 to 5 p.m. Many Twin Cities parents saw this statue for the first time when they themselves were children.

And on the slope between the capitol and the cathedral there's an often-overlooked symbolic tribute to a history-making Minnesotan. Charles Lindbergh, who grew up in Little Falls, Minnesota, became in 1927 the first pilot ever to make a nonstop solo flight across the Atlantic Ocean. Sculptor Paul Granlund has honored him by creating two bronze figures, Lindbergh as the young man who observes you as you drive or walk by, and Lindbergh as the small boy who looks the other way, toward downtown St. Paul and the Mississippi River just beyond.

3. St. Paul's Natural Attractions

More than a million visitors a year make St. Paul's **Como Park** one of the most popular of all Twin Cities attractions. The glorious **Como Park Conservatory,** site of innumerable weddings and other festive events, would in itself be a prime attraction, but there's a great deal more to be enjoyed in the vicinity. Adjacent to the conservatory are two smaller but equally beautiful showplaces: the **McKnight Formal Gardens,** with their famous Paul Manship sculpture of an Indian boy and his dog, and the **Ordway Memorial Japanese Gardens,** designed by Masami Matsuda of Nagasaki, St. Paul's Japanese sister city. There is also the long popular **Como Zoo,** not far from a small, privately operated amusement park which has pony rides among its many attractions.

Golfers will be glad to know about the elegant new octagonal clubhouse that overlooks one of the city's best 18-hole **golf courses,** here at Como Park. A vast pavilion, restored to its early-20th-century grandeur, enables Twin Citians to again enjoy seeing and being seen as they promenade and listen to lakeside concerts.

Lake Como provides delightful sunning, and paddleboats are a popular diversion here as well, making their way among the ducks, gulls, and other birds that are at home on the lake.

If you've a question, comment, or concern during your visit, look for one of the park rangers, in their beige-and-brown uniforms; they patrol regularly and are unfailingly courteous and helpful. Como Park is located about 2½ miles north of the juncture of I-94 and Lexington Avenue in St. Paul. See Chapter IX, "Sports and Recreation," for details on park activities, and phone 292-7400 for information on the many beautiful lakes and parks in St. Paul.

4. Fort Snelling

One of the most popular sight-seeing attractions in the Twin Cities isn't properly in either Minneapolis or St. Paul, but in between them at the confluence of the Mississippi and Minnesota rivers (Hwy. 5 at Hwy. 55, one mile east of the Minneapolis–St. Paul International Airport). This is the place where in 1819 Col. Josiah Snelling and his troops began construction of a fort to establish an official presence in the wilderness that had recently been won from Great Britain. President Thomas Jefferson had hoped this outpost would become a "center of civilization," and that's what occurred, as families arrived and built homes on the perimeter of land that had been ceded to the army by the Sioux. In 1837, after a treaty opened additional land for settlement, these families moved across the river to establish a community of their own, one that would later be known as St. Paul.

Fort Snelling continued as a military installation that played an important role in the lives of those who lived and worked there. In 1837 Dred Scott, the slave of an army surgeon, was married in a Fort Snelling lookout built of limestone from nearby bluffs. After the doctor's death in 1846, Scott sued for his freedom on the basis of having lived for a time in the free state of Minnesota, and lost the case. The now-famous Dred Scott Decision is often cited as a contributing factor to the American Civil War.

And in 1864 a young German military attaché named Count Zeppelin ascended 300 feet above the Old Round Tower in a large gas-filled canvas bag. Later, such vehicles, bearing the count's name, served as a common means of aerial transportation.

Since 1937 the Minnesota State Historical Society has maintained a **living museum** at Fort Snelling, where costumed guides re-create the activities and ceremonies of everyday army life during the 1820s. Phone 726-9430 for information about hours and admission; you can get specifics on tours and special events by calling 726-1171. While you're at Fort Snelling, don't overlook the interesting gift shop with its selection of authentic Native American handcrafted jewelry.

---

5. Historic Minneapolis

THE ARD GODFREY HOUSE

In the mid-1800s, on the east bank of the Mississippi River, the village of St. Anthony took its name from the nearby waterfalls, which had earlier provided the power to build Fort Snelling. St. Anthony lost its name and its separate identity in 1872 when it merged with Minneapolis, but its cobblestoned main street remains, and so does the small yellow wooden house that was built by Ard Godfrey, a mid-19th-century millwright from Maine. Prior to this time, most houses in the area were made of log; a few were adobe huts.

The Ard Godfrey House, now located at the corner of University and Central Avenues S.E., reflects the New England heritage of its builder in the cornices, the moldings, and the divided window sashes. Designed in 1848, the 1½-story dwelling was made of lumber from the village's first sawmill—powered, of course, by St. Anthony Falls. Godfrey's house, which originally stood on the corner of Main and 2nd streets, was turned into a museum and moved to its present site in 1909. Somehow in the process its kitchen wing was lost, but much of interest still remains, including original furnishings as well as flags, snowshoes, and the city's first directory, dated 1859. Tour information is available by calling 330-0181 or 870-8001.

OUR LADY OF LOURDES

Just a short walk away, at One Lourdes Place S.E., you'll find the church that's been in continuous use longer than any other in Minneapolis. Our Lady of Lourdes Church, serving parishioners since 1877, is a small, Gothic-style limestone structure that retains its original statuary, tapestries, and stained glass. French carols are presented at Christmas (about 25% of the church's congregation is of French descent). Tours are available by appointment (tel. 333-9016), with a $1 donation requested. Visitors wishing to attend services here are welcome at 5:30 p.m. on Saturday and at 9 and 11 a.m. on Sunday.

The neighborhood in which this dignified historic building now stands would no doubt astound the original French Catholic parishioners. Today Our Lady of Lourdes is surrounded by two bustling shopping and entertainment centers, St. Anthony Main and Riverplace.

THE WAREHOUSE DISTRICT

Although 19th-century Minneapolitans firmly believed that Main Street would remain the city's major thoroughfare, when railroads superseded ships as the primary means of transporting goods, the business and industrial interests moved across the Mississippi River. In what's now known as the Minneapolis Warehouse District, chic restaurants, bars, artists' galleries, and antique shops have moved into the restored sprawling structures that once housed local products awaiting shipment downriver to other parts of the nation.

THE FOSHAY TOWER

The venerable Foshay Tower, at 821 Marquette Ave., is a proud survivor of the past. Built in 1929, the 447-foot-high obelisk was known for decades as the tallest structure in the Upper Midwest. Today it has been dwarfed by its sleek new neighbors, but for one brief shining interlude in 1981 the tower received national attention in newspapers and on TV, when an immense, much-photographed yellow ribbon was wrapped around its upper portion as a welcome-home greeting to America's liberated hostages of Iran.

A DIVERSITY OF DOWNTOWN CHURCHES

Among the distinguished old buildings in downtown Minneapolis, many on the perimeter are, not surprisingly, churches of various denominations and descriptions—the Romanesque Revival **Wesley United Methodist Church** at 101 East Grant St., the imposing **Westminster Presbyterian Church** at 1201 Nicollet Ave., the modified Gothic **St. Mark's Cathedral** (Episcopal) at 15th Street and Hennepin Avenue, the magnificently spired **Hennepin Avenue Methodist Church** at Groveland and Hennepin avenues, and the neobaroque **Basilica of Saint Mary** at 17th Street and Hennepin Avenue.

THE LUMBER EXCHANGE BUILDING

There's an interesting bit of architectural history to be seen at 425 Hennepin Ave., site of the Lumber Exchange Building, built in 1885 and refurbished in 1980. It was in this elegant 12-story structure, fashioned of granite and Lake Superior brownstone, that much of the city's extensive lumber trade was conducted. It currently houses offices, shops, and a nightclub.

THE POWERS DEPARTMENT STORE BUILDING

At 5th Street on the Nicollet Mall stands an old structure that has recently been pressed into new and distinctly unusual service. Powers Department Store, which closed its doors to shoppers in 1985, had long played a significant role in local retailing. It was in this friendly, family-owned department store, for example, that the Twin Cities' first "moving stairway" was introduced to a properly impressed public in 1929. What you'll find at Powers now is an institution dedicated not to shoppers but to scholars. St. Paul's

College of St. Thomas has come across the river to establish in this building off-campus classes for the benefit and convenience of downtown Minneapolis workers and residents. A storefront private college of this kind is a first for the area and represents a superb addition to the mall that has played so central a role in the continuing revitalization of downtown Minneapolis.

6. The New Minneapolis

THE NICOLLET MALL

Here's an important word of warning to tourists taking their first look at the picturesque Nicollet pedestrian mall. Those cabs, buses, and emergency vehicles you see on the mall are the only exceptions to the firmly enforced ban on vehicular traffic. The beautifully landscaped mile-long thoroughfare is primarily for use by pedestrians, and you'll be glad that's so as you enjoy your walk amid the mall's trees, flowers, and graceful statuary.

NEW FACES DOWNTOWN

If downtown Minneapolis looks like a brand-new city, that's because so much of it is. Let's take a walk down the Nicollet Mall, starting at the northern end, not far from the Mississippi River. We'll see along the way some of the award-winning buildings that have changed the face of the city.

The Skyways

As in St. Paul, the first thing you'll notice in downtown Minneapolis is the extensive skyway system. Dating from the 1960s, it was the first such system in the country. It is also the longest privately owned skyway system in the world.

Because the design, maintenance, and security of Minneapolis's skyways are primarily the responsibility of the owners of these linked buildings (there are some public buildings here too), the designs and hours of the individual skyways tend to differ from one another. In general, skyways remain open during the business hours of the buildings they connect. While you're walking through downtown Minneapolis, you'll notice different skyway designs of the different architects engaged by various building owners. One particularly interesting skyway, which links Crossings Condominiums and the Norwest Operations Center, at South Second Avenue near Washington Avenue, looks like the car of a sleek, streamlined train. In fact the skyways have given a sleek, streamlined look to all of well-connected downtown Minneapolis.

Shortly after completion in 1963, the **Northwestern National Life Insurance Company,** at 20 Washington Ave. S., was pictured on the cover of *Time* magazine. Modeled after the Parthenon, this magnificent marble structure with its graceful Doric columns is one of the loveliest and earliest landmarks of the new Minneapolis.

The remarkable 11-story **Federal Reserve Bank Building,** at 250 Marquette Ave., is reportedly the first American building designed on the cantilevered suspension system usually reserved for bridges. It's said that the building could easily support another structure of identical size. **Norwest Center,** at 6th Street and Marquette Avenue, has been called one of the finest works of architect Cesar Pelli. Fifty-seven stories high, its combination of buff Kasota stone and white marble add a decidedly elegant tone to downtown Minneapolis.

City Center, a 6-acre expanse occupying the square block between 6th and 7th streets and Nicollet and Hennepin avenues, houses the Marriott Marquis Hotel, the International Foods Building, and a three-level, atrium-illuminated shopping area that contains dozens of fine shops in addition to one of the city's best department stores, Carson Pirie Scott.

A stunning new downtown addition faces Carson's across the Nicollet Mall. **Gaviidae Common** is an elegant five-level shopping and entertainment complex anchored by Saks Fifth Avenue. Specialty shops and fine restaurants add to the winning combination.

The 51-story **Investors Diversified Services Center,** across the street at 777 Nicollet Mall, contains the **Crystal Court,** which serves as the focal point of the skyway system. Today shops, restaurants, and offices keep this a busy area, but a great number of visitors are here just to see for themselves the Court and the beautiful IDS Building, considered by many the finest work of famed architect Philip Johnson.

The **Conservatory,** a splendid glass-and-marble fashion center at 8th Street on the Nicollet Mall, opened late in 1987 and immediately added to the fun and excitement of shopping in downtown Minneapolis. It contains an upscale collection of shops and boutiques.

Peavey Plaza is a picturesque addition to the Nicollet Mall at 11th Street, where it adjoins Orchestra Hall and serves each year as site for the joyous Sommerfest (see Chapter VII). With its ice skaters in the wintertime and fountains in the summer, the plaza has been called a small version of New York's Rockefeller Center.

Now, walking a few blocks east, we'll find at 222 S. 9th St. the 42-story **Piper Jaffray Tower,** featuring innumerable panes of aqua-blue window glass and providing a particularly dramatic addition to the Minneapolis skyline.

One of the most beautiful lobbies in the Twin Cities can be found at **Lincoln Centre,** at 333 S. 7th St. You'll recognize this building by its elegant exterior—gray granite combined with black, white, and green marble.

Marble and copper-colored glass distinguish the beautiful 17-story curved-glass **Lutheran Brotherhood Building** at Fourth Avenue between 6th and 7th streets.

The **Hennepin County Government Center** links two square blocks of downtown Minneapolis at 5th Street between Third and Fourth avenues. You'll find here beautiful landscaping and lots of benches from which to admire it.

The **Pillsbury Center,** a twin-towered marble structure at Second Avenue South between 5th and 6th streets, is a contemporary example of a famous family's historic commitment to the Twin Cities.

The massive **Northstar Center,** at 110 7th St., where a 10-story hotel sits atop 6 stories of offices and parking ramps, was a harbinger of the exciting things to come when it opened in 1963. This was the first new complex of office, retail, and dining areas in downtown Minneapolis, and its early promise has been more than fulfilled.

The end of this minitour finds you near 5th Street and Chicago Avenue, where the **Hubert H. Humphrey Metrodome** sprawls on the eastern edge of downtown. Tourists and teams seem to like it a lot more than home folks do. But everybody seems to like the new **Timberwolves Arena,** extending between 6th and 7th streets and First and Second avenues north. It's brought a lot of excitement to downtown Minneapolis.

THE ARTS IN MINNEAPOLIS

The Twin Cities is widely known for its wealth of cultural presentations—contemporary, homegrown work and borrowings from other times and places. I'll be telling you more in chapters VI and VII about some of the specific features and facilities that you'll enjoy in the Twin Cities, but here's a quick look at the buildings housing some of the internationally known theaters, museums, and orchestras that await you here.

Located on Vineland Place on the southwestern rim of downtown Minneapolis, the glass-walled **Guthrie Theater** looks bright and welcoming, with its cheerful view of the lobbies and levels within and its colorful banners proclaiming the titles of plays presently in production.

Although the **Walker Art Center** and the Guthrie Theater share the same Vineland Place site and the same outer lobby, they don't share architectural styles. With its brick and concrete exterior, the Walker, despite the color and excitement within, looks relatively austere, even severe, to passersby. Facing the Walker is the well-known Minneapolis Sculpture Garden, which opened in September 1988.

At **Orchestra Hall,** 1111 Nicollet Mall, what you see on the outside is a far cry from what's within, where painstaking and imaginative attention to design has been responsible for superlative acoustics. The exterior, though, brightened only by huge blue ducts, serves simply as an unadorned shell for the massive lobby and 2,200-seat concert hall within.

The classic **Minneapolis Institute of Art,** at 2400 Third Ave. S., is one of the greatest and grandest museums in the country. It shares an outer lobby with the famous Minneapolis Children's Theatre company.

THE UNIVERSITY OF MINNESOTA

Established in 1851 and now one of the largest universities on one campus in the United States, the University of Minnesota has recently gained fame for the organ transplants and other surgical miracles accomplished at its on-campus University Hospital. You probably won't get to watch an operation during your stay, but there are many on-campus activities that visitors can enjoy.

Whether or not you're able to attend a performance, do drive down to the riverfront for a look at the **Centennial Showboat,** docked on the east bank of the Mississippi. This authentic 19th-century sternwheel river packet was secured by the University's theater department for the state's 100th anniversary celebration in 1958. It's been here ever since, staging summertime melodramas and musical olios for booing, hissing, and cheering audiences. There are concerts, recitals, lectures, and exhibits on campus as well, many of them free of charge.

If you'd like to tag along on the campus tours provided for incoming and prospective students, they're conducted daily at 11:15 a.m. and 2:15 p.m. on the Minneapolis campus and at noon on the St. Paul campus. Phone 624-6868 for further information.

---

7. The Lakes of Minneapolis

Three of the most popular lakes in Minneapolis form a chain that's believed to be part of the course followed by the Mississippi River some 25,000 years ago. For information about all the Minneapolis lakes and parks, phone 348-2243.

LAKE OF THE ISLES

Although property close to Lake of the Isles is very expensive these days, you couldn't have given it away 100 years ago. What stood here then was a mess of swamps and marshes that were feared as breeding places for malaria. But after years as a dumping ground, the property was dredged during the late 1880s and by the turn of the century had become valuable real estate. Now a man-made lake, popular with fisherfolk because it's stocked with tasty sunfish and crappies, its small wooded islands are a picturesque part of the city. Lake of the Isles is popular with canoeists too, for its irregular shoreline and varied landscape. (At 20 to 25 feet deep, this is the shallowest lake on the chain.) During the wintertime a regulation hockey rink is set up, along with areas for general skating, and of course a warming house is set up too.

If you decide to walk around Lake of the Isles, remember that the path closest to the shore is for you; the other path is for bicyclists.

LAKE CALHOUN

A channel connects Lake of the Isles to Lake Calhoun, so boaters can paddle from one to the other. (No powerboats are permitted on city lakes, partly because of the noise and partly because the rapid churning of the water erodes the shoreline.) Lake Calhoun is the largest of the chain of lakes, and at 90 to 100 feet, it's the deepest as well. Whatever the season, you're likely to see boats here, lots of one-man skimmers and sailboats in the summertime, iceboats (sailboats on blades) in the winter. This is perhaps the lake most popular with young adults, who do a lot of sunning on its shores, swimming in its depths, cross-country skiing on its ice, and socializing in its neighborhood, the Hennepin and Lake Uptown area.

LAKE HARRIET

The third link in the chain of lakes may have the greatest appeal to families because of its delightful gardens, bird sanctuary, and summertime band concerts at the pavilion, which was remodeled in 1985. The All-American Rose Selection test bed in the **Lake Harriet Rose Gardens** provides an annual display of glorious colors and scents for visitors. The **Lake Harriet Rock Garden** has been popular since 1929; it was refurbished in 1984. And the adjacent **bird sanctuary** features a woodchip path for visitors who enjoy the solitude and serenity of an unspoiled woodland setting, the more remarkable for being located in the heart of a busy metropolitan city.

If you're visiting the Twin Cities during the summer months, from late May until early September, join the many men, women, and children who arrive by boat, by bike, or by automobile, with or without picnic supper, to enjoy the nightly Lake Harriet **bandstand concerts.** And if there are children in your party, remember the restored-streetcar ride that may be the only opportunity today's youngsters may ever have to enjoy that form of transportation (see Chapter XIII, "Family Fun," for further details).

Sailing is another popular recreation at Lake Harriet, one of the city's three sailing lakes. Along with Lake Calhoun and Lake Nokomis, Lake Harriet features weekend sailboat races that draw throngs of participants and observers throughout the summer months.

---

8. Guided Tours

Of course there's more to be seen in the Twin Cities, and one of the best ways of getting your bearings is to make your first order of business the kind of narrated tour that I always seek out in an unfamiliar city. Here are four good ways to go in Minneapolis and St. Paul, depending on your preference and your pocketbook.

GRAY LINES TOURS

As in so many cities across the country, city tours are offered by Gray Lines, which in the Twin Cities is run by Medicine Lake Lines. Tours last about 3 hours and take passengers through both Minneapolis and St. Paul, with time out at Minnehaha Falls and St. Paul Cathedral (if no service is underway). Prices are $15 for adults, $14 for seniors and $7 for children 7 to 14 years of age (children under 7 can ride free as long as they don't take a seat that could go to a fare-paying passenger). Tours run Monday through Saturday during

June, July, and August. In May and September, tour buses run only on Saturdays. Call 591-9099, or ask your concierge or front-desk personnel for further information.

SUBURBAN LIMOUSINE TOURS

If you prefer seeing the cities as part of a smaller group in a smaller vehicle, consider **Twin Cities Sightseeing Tours,** operated by Minneapolis and Suburban Airport Limousine Service. This tour lasts 2½ hours, costs $15 for adults, $12 for seniors and children under 12 years of age, and will take you to many landmarks in both cities, with a stop en route at Minnehaha Falls. Individuals can board at the main office, 3920 Nicollet Ave. S., and leave their cars in the parking lot free of charge, or you can be picked up at a hotel or other location. Call 827-7777 for more specifics. The sights you'll see on a Minneapolis and Suburban Limousine tour are pretty well determined in advance, but you'll find that different drivers bring their individual perspectives to the matters at hand. If your interest is primarily historical or literary, or directed toward some other specific area, you might mention that when you call.

STERNWHEELER BOAT TOURS

For a change of pace, consider a tape-narrated, round-trip boat trip on an old-fashioned riverboat from Harriet Island in St. Paul to Fort Snelling. You'll experience a bit of local history as you travel the Mississippi on the *Jonathon Paddelford* or the *Josiah Snelling,* authentic sternwheelers belonging to the Paddelford Packet Boat Company (tel. 227-1100). The company also operates over in Minneapolis at the Boom Island landing, where you can board the *Anson Northrop* and the *Betsey Northrop* for a ride downriver past Nicollet Island and through the locks at Upper Saint Anthony Falls. Prices are $7.50 for adults; $6.50 for seniors 62 and over; and $5.00 for children under 12. (Children under 2 years old are admitted free.) Snacks are available on all trips (hot dogs are $1.25; individual pizzas, $2.50).

VI

THEATER IN THE TWIN CITIES

1. MAJOR TWIN CITIES COMPANIES
2. OTHER AREA COMPANIES

Though the Twin Cities have long been recognized as a vital center for the dramatic arts, the quality and variety of the theater here may yet surprise you. Over the course of a month you can attend dozens of productions in the metropolitan area. The quality is high, and the cost of tickets is surprisingly low here in the birthplace of American regional theater.

Although Twin Cities theater didn't gain international prominence until the establishment in 1963 of the Tyrone Guthrie Theater, first-rate productions had been attracting theatergoers for a long time before that. The Old Log, one of the country's oldest stock companies, began staging professional productions in 1941. Theater in the Round, one of the country's longest-lived community theaters, staged its first performance in 1952. The Brave New Workshop, the country's oldest satirical revue, was founded in 1958, five years before Chicago's Second City got under way. And the University of Minnesota Theatre consistently drew audiences from throughout the Twin Cities for a wide variety of productions that were popular not only at home but also on the road.

The famous Irish-English director Sir Tyrone Guthrie selected the Twin Cities as the home for his repertory company in part because a committed theatergoing public already existed here. But there was another consideration as well—one that had to do with dollars and cents. "We will put our various skills and experiences at your service," he had declared. "We will create for you a professional theater, which you will own. . . . You, however, must undertake the formidable task of raising the dough."

In Minneapolis, that was no problem: corporate support for the arts is greater here than anywhere else in the country. The "dough" was raised handily and the Guthrie Theater is now an integral part of cultural life in these parts.

What's best about Twin Cities theater is that it's a year-round activity for audiences of widely varied tastes. There's mainstream theater and avant-garde theater, dinner theater and coffeehouse theater, theater in the park and theater in the round, children's theater, historical theater, showboat theater, and a lot more.

In the Twin Cities theater is not primarily a business but an art. As such, it's supported in large part by contributions from individual and corporate benefactors. You'll see the names of some of these patrons listed in the programs of many local not-for-profit resident theaters, including the Guthrie, where actors work for wages far lower than those associated with Broadway's "star system." These factors, plus lower production costs, combine to keep ticket prices relatively low in Minneapolis and St. Paul. A good seat will seldom cost more than $15 to $20 and student, senior citizen, and standby rates are lower still.

Transportation poses few problems here: even outlying theaters are easy to reach by highway and freeway, and parking is either free or inexpensive.

And because the investment of time and money is not as great here as elsewhere, theatergoers can afford to be a bit more adventurous and tolerant than they might otherwise be. That makes experimentation, and therefore variety, more feasible.

All these factors have helped to keep theater alive and well and growing in the Twin Cities. Theater has begotten more theater. The opportunities here have drawn talented artists in great numbers, and this abundance of talent has in turn attracted film and TV production companies to these parts. Casting directors and agents pass through regularly to check performances at the Guthrie and other local theaters—with consequences that have by now become legend.

Loni Anderson, Linda Kelsey, Nick Nolte, Prince, and others who've gone on from the Twin Cities to make national names for themselves, were able to develop their talents at local theaters employing "amateurs," a term that identifies artists not only as unpaid performers, but also as lovers of their craft. Members of the original Moscow Art Theater were amateurs; so were members of the Provincetown Players. And so are members of many troupes in Minneapolis and St. Paul.

While certain Twin Cities actors, writers, directors, and technicians have gone on to spend their professional lives on one coast or the other, many others remain to enjoy fulfilling careers in Twin Cities productions.

It's been said that you can make a fortune in the theater, but not a living. Not so in the Twin Cities, where a great many talented theater people are making a comfortable living. This, in turn, enhances the quality of life for the rest of us.

1. Major Twin Cities Companies

Here's an alphabetical listing of some of the theatrical companies that await you in Minneapolis and St. Paul.

BRASS TACKS THEATER

Patty Lynch, who founded this enterprising company in 1979, remains artistic director to this day. She's also the author of the recently produced *Pretty Girls Aren't That Smart,* a contemporary suspense thriller with a feminist twist. Other hit première productions include actor/director/playwright Jim Stowell's highly praised series of monologues, *Travelling Light,* and a companion piece, *Rio Grande.*

It's the preeminence of language and the commitment to developing dynamic new works that keeps this avant-garde company on the cutting edge of the Twin Cities theater scene. Brass Tacks productions (tel. 341-8207) are staged in a number of spaces around town, but primarily at the Hennepin Center for the Arts in the restored downtown Masonic Building in Minneapolis, or at the Southern Theater, which started life as a vaudeville house near the west bank of the University of Minnesota's Minneapolis campus. The Brass Tacks' address changes regularly, but their phone number remains the same, so call for word on their presentations during your Twin Cities stay. You can count on an interesting and dynamic evening in the theater.

BRAVE NEW WORKSHOP

For nearly 30 years, Dudley Riggs's Brave New Workshop, 2605 Hennepin Ave., Minneapolis (tel. 332-6620), has been fulfilling its self-proclaimed role as loyal opposition to all parties. It is by now the oldest satirical company in the United States. Company members write their own material, and after each evening's series of sketches, the company does improvisations based on audience suggestions. Many of these impromptu skits are in turn developed into titled sketches. Past productions, which have also toured successfully in New York, Boston, Miami, and San Francisco, include *I'm OK, You're a Jerk; National Velveeta, or What a Friend We Have in Cheeses;* and *The Vice Man Cometh.*

You can't miss the storefront theater in which this company performs: the bright lights and red, white, and blue stripes serve loud notice that you've arrived. Performances are at 8 p.m. Tuesday through Thursday, at 8 and 10:30 p.m. on Friday and Saturday. Ticket prices are $10 Tuesday through Thursday, on Friday and Saturday $12. For $6.50 on Sunday, *On the Wall, Off the Wall* offers a combined program of improvisations and award-winning short films.

CHANHASSEN DINNER THEATRE

In 1968 general amazement, if not amusement, greeted the announcement that Herb Bloomberg, a prominent local builder, was venturing into entirely unfamiliar territory. After completing construction of the beautiful Old Log Theater in Minnetonka, Bloomberg decided to open and run a dinner theater of his own at 521 W. 78th St, Chanhassen (tel. 934-1525, or toll free 800/362-3515), some 20 miles from downtown Minneapolis.

Another unlikely announcement followed the first: productions staged here would not be limited to the usual forced feedings of Broadway musicals; the Chanhassen would be offering polished productions of highly regarded theater works in a handsome and congenial dinner-theater setting. One of their earliest hits turned out to be the 19th-century French farce *A Flea in Her Ear*. One member of that cast, incidentally, was TV-star-to-be Linda Kelsey.

Today the Chanhassen has grown into a large theater complex with four playhouses under one roof, offering performances throughout the year. The Chanhassen has consistently earned high marks for the quality and diversity of its productions: *Equus, Loot, On Golden' Pond, The Dining Room,* and *The Foreigner,* among others. There have been superb productions of musicals as well— hits like *A Little Night Music, Camelot, Company, Gypsy, West Side Story,* and *Fiddler on the Roof.* In the last, a dark-haired Loni Anderson acted and sang the role of Tevye's daughter, Tsietel. Recent hits have included main-stage shows like *42nd Street* and *Guys and Dolls,* as well as dramas like *Steel Magnolias* and *A Walk in the Woods.*

The first thing visitors notice as they enter the enormous, but somehow intimate, theater complex is the oversize fireplace in the long lobby that leads to the various theaters, bars, alcoves, lounges, and other gathering places. There's a selection of entertainment here seven days and nights each week, with dinner-and-theater package prices ranging from $24 to $29 for matinees; $28 to $36 Sunday and Tuesday evenings; $30 to $36 Wednesday and Thursday evenings; $37 to $43 Friday and Saturday evenings. The Chanhassen Dinner Theatres are now owned and operated by International Broadcasting Corporation, whose earlier connection with live theatre involved the backing of Broadway shows. They also own IceCapades and the Harlem Globetrotters.

Chanhassen is easily reached at the juncture of Hwy. 5 and Hwy. 11, about 30 minutes from either downtown St. Paul or downtown Minneapolis.

CHILDREN'S THEATRE

Located at 2400 Third Ave. S., Minneapolis (tel. 874-0400), in the huge white-brick building that houses the Minneapolis Institute of Art, the Children's Theatre presents productions geared toward multigenerational audiences—kids of absolutely all ages. The rows in the 746-seat auditorium have been raked with youngsters in mind, so small people can look over the heads of tall ones with no difficulty at all. Plays, based primarily on tales familiar to children and teenagers, are lavishly produced and skillfully acted by a company of child and adult players. Since 1984, when the Children's Theatre School, from which many of the acting company were previously drawn, was discontinued, open auditions have provided young cast members for the productions.

Authors are often invited to participate in the staging of their plays at Children's Theatre; Dr. Seuss (Theodore Geiss) worked with the company on the CTC production of *The 500 Hats of Bartholomew Cubbins,* Astrid Lindgren came to the Twin Cities to advise on the production of *Pippi Longstocking,* and illustrator-author Tomi de Paoli served as consultant for the staging of *Strega Nona.*

Adult prices range from $11.25 to $18.50. Full-time college students, children and senior citizens pay $8.25 to $14.50.

CRICKET THEATRE

At 9 W. 14th St., Minneapolis (tel. 871-2244), the Cricket Theatre concentrates on staging contemporary plays by living playwrights, some of whom have already made a name for themselves, some whose reputations are emerging. Along with contemporary classics like *American Buffalo*, *The Gin Game*, *Streamers*, *Fool for Love*, and *Who's Afraid of Virginia Woolf?* this company has produced lesser-known works by finalists in the New Plays Program, sponsored by the Dramatists Guild and the Columbia Broadcasting System, thus giving fledgling dramatists the chance to watch their plays being brought to life and to work closely with professional theater artists. There have been 13 world premieres and 47 area premieres among Cricket's offerings since the theater was founded by Bill Semans in 1968.

In 1987 the Cricket made two important changes: it moved to a new home in a beautifully renovated old theater on the southern edge of downtown Minneapolis, and it expanded its mission to include each season one guest production by a foreign theater company.

Performances are at 8 p.m. Wednesday through Saturday evenings; Sunday times vary, so phone for information. Tickets are $14.50 on Wednesday, Thursday, and Sunday evenings and Saturday matinees; $16.50 on Friday and Saturday evenings.

E.T.C.

Located at Seven Corners, 1430 Washington Ave. S., Minneapolis (tel. 332-6620), near the west-bank campus of the University of Minnesota, Dudley Riggs's Experimental Theatre Company shares a building with Café Expresso, reportedly the Midwest's oldest coffeehouse. There's a full bar in the café and one in the theater and dinner can be brought to your table any night of the week. Stand-up comedy and musical satire are on the bill of fare here.

Like its older sibling, Dudley Riggs's Brave New Workshop, E.T.C. is considered a fine training ground for young performers, with alumni who have included the Flying Karamazov Brothers and former "Saturday Night Live" performers Franken and Davis.

Performances are at 8 p.m. on Wednesday, Thursday, and Friday and at 8 and 10:30 p.m. on Saturday. Prices for dinner theater are $25 on Wednesday, Thursday, and Sunday, $28 on Friday and Saturday. Performance-only prices are $12 on Wednesday, Thursday, and Sunday, $12 to $15 on Friday and Saturday, depending on location.

GUTHRIE THEATER

In 1964 the Tyrone Guthrie Theater, 725 Vineland Pl., Minneapolis (tel. 377-2224), gained worldwide fame as the home of a new classical repertory company, selected by the distinguished director for whom it was named. The fact that Tyrone Guthrie intended to produce classics during his three-year stay at the theater did not imply that these productions would be conventional; in fact, the *Hamlet* he directed during that first season was done in modern dress. The spirit of the production, though, was true to the original; indeed, the topical touches seemed to enhance its universality.

After Guthrie's departure, the theater went through good times and bad under a succession of artistic directors. The original commitment to classics eroded somewhat along the way, but in early 1987 things took a turn for the better, at least in the view of those who had been bemoaning a perceptible shift toward lighter, more "commercial" fare. The newly named and widely admired artistic director, Garland Wright, announced for his first official season an array of classics that qualified in all ways as the kinds of works originally identified with the Guthrie. Theatergoers understood that Wright's production of Molière's *The Misanthrope,* and Livieu Ciulei's guest production of Euripides' *The Bacchae,* would have contemporary resonances, but these works and others on the program were consistent with the original Guthrie commitment.

The move back toward the revitalization of Tyrone Guthrie's original vision has been demonstrated by Wright's commitment toward establishing the acting company as the heart of the organization. Under his impressive leadership, there has been a succession of record-breaking presentations, among them the 1990 Shakespearean cycle that marked the only time in American theater history that *Richard II, Henry IV,* parts I and II, and *Henry V* have been staged by a single professional theater company during a single season.

Whatever your taste in theater entertainment, you'll surely want to include a Guthrie performance in your Twin Cities agenda. This is one of the most famous theaters in the world—I've been questioned about it in Great Britain, on the Continent, and in the Caribbean—and your afternoon or evening is bound to prove memorable.

There are several reasons to arrive early for a Guthrie performance: you'll want to see one of the country's largest public sculpture gardens, just across the street, and to explore the theater itself. Before you enter the auditorium, you'll be surrounded by a tempting array of dining and sipping and shopping choices. At certain times of year you can carry a drink and a snack to the outdoor terrace overlooking Vineland Place. And year-round you can try to find a table in the Aisle 10 section of the lobby, where glass walls provide a view to the outdoors of those who arrive later than you do.

The Guthrie shares an entry lobby with the adjacent Walker Art Center and is just steps away from the Walker's extensive, and often expensive, selection of gifts and souvenirs. The Guthrie's own smaller gift shop carries a variety of theater-related items, and you'll want to check those as well. And once in your seat you'll enjoy looking at the large, handsome complimentary program, which provides interesting and informative background about the production you're about to see. Shortly before the lights dim, you'll hear the trumpeters signaling that the auditorium doors will soon be closed just before the performance gets under way. Performances begin at 7:30 p.m. Tuesday through Thursday, 8 p.m. Friday and

Saturday, and 7 p.m. on Sunday (the theater is dark on Monday). Matinees are usually presented at 1 p.m. on Wednesday and Saturday with an occasional matinee on Sunday, but do call to confirm specific days and times. Ticket prices range from $6 to $34.

ILLUSION THEATRE

Headquartered at the Hennepin Center for the Arts, 528 Hennepin Ave., Minneapolis (tel. 339-4944), this eight-member company, which started in 1974 as a mime troupe, has made a name for itself in two distinctly different arenas. In 1977 Illusion Theatre became the first company in the country to use drama as a means of preventing sexual abuse and interpersonal violence. *Touch,* an original play for children, has been performed throughout the country in schools, churches, and at conferences for community education. So have two other works, *No Easy Answers,* written for adolescents, and *For Adults Only,* designed for grownup audiences. And, most recently, three new plays have been added to the repertoire: *Family,* dealing with relationships among family members, as well as *Amazing Grace* and *The Alphabet of Aids,* both of which deal with HIV/AIDS.

In addition to the touring productions of these plays, the Illusion Theatre maintains a February-through-July Twin Cities season, during which it presents new works and presents productions of lesser-known European scripts.

Illusion productions are staged at the eight-story sandstone Masonic Temple at 6th Street and Hennepin Avenue. Ticket prices are $10 on Thursday and Sunday, $14 on Friday, and $15 on Saturday. All performances are at 8 p.m., except on Sunday when they begin at 7 p.m.

MIXED BLOOD THEATER

This professional theater at 1501 S. 4th St., Minneapolis (tel. 338-6131), was founded in 1976 to produce new works in a color-blind fashion. Mixed Blood has by now received numerous local awards for productions like *The Boys Next Door, A My Name Is Alice,* and *For Colored Girls Who Have Considered Suicide When a Rainbow Is Enuf.* Founder Jack Reuler has also received national awards, none more prestigious perhaps than his selection by *Esquire* in December 1984 as one of those under 40 who were changing the face of America. Reuler was cited not only for Mixed Blood's color-blind casting of all productions, but for his theater's being the largest employer of minority professional actors in the entire country. And most recently, in February 1990, Actors Equity presented Mixed Blood with the Rosetta Le Noire award for its contribution to the universality of the human experience in American theater.

Mixed Blood productions are presented in a 100-year-old firehouse with a large, flexible space where plays can be presented in a proscenium setting, on a thrust stage, or as "theater in the rectangle." It's said that you never know when you walk into Mixed Blood which way you'll be facing. What you do know, though, is that you'll be seeing a top-quality production that's very likely making its area or world premiere here in the Twin Cities. Alumni of this theater include Carl Lumbley, a one-time regular on TV's "Cagney and Lacey," and whose recent TV work includes episodes on "L.A. Law."

Showtime is 8 p.m. on Thursday, Friday, and Sunday; on Saturday there are two performances, at 7 and 9:30 p.m. You'll pay $7.50 on Thursday and Sunday, $10 on Friday, and $12 on Saturday.

OLD LOG THEATER

This popular playhouse, located at 5175 Meadville St., Excelsior (tel. 474-5951), is very much a family affair on the shores of Lake Minnetonka, where since 1941 Don Stolz has been staging Equity productions at one Old Log Theater or another. The small original theater, now used as a scenery shop, was replaced in 1960 by the present Old Log, closer to the water's edge and, with 655 seats, one of the largest theaters in the Twin Cities area.

Comedies are the specialty of this house, and eldest son Tom Stolz has developed through the years into an adept comic actor, notable for his droll deadpan delivery in productions as diverse as *Brighton Beach Memoirs* and *Bedfull of Foreigners*. Other family members make their own contributions behind the scenes and at the front of the house. Jon Stolz is the scenery and lighting designer, Tim Stolz the stage manager. And it's Donny Stolz who will greet you at the box office, of which he's the manager.

Broadway and London comedy and farce are the prevailing fare that's offered here. In fact, British playwright Ray Cooney, whose *Run For Your Wife* enjoyed an extended run in London, was so impressed by the Old Log's production of this hilarious farce that he later gave Stolz the right to produce the world premiere of *Whose Wife Is It Anyway?* several months before this comedy premiered in London. From time to time more serious work has been presented at the Old Log, including admirable productions of *Look Homeward, Angel* and *84 Charing Cross*.

If you're in the Twin Cities during the Easter season, you might want to phone the theater for word on Tom Stolz's annual tour-de-force performance in *The Gospel According to Saint Mark*. But at any time of year a visit to the Old Log will introduce you to the work of the Twin Cities' oldest professional theater company. Shows are at 8:30 p.m. Wednesday through Saturday and at 7:30 p.m. on Sunday. Tickets are $11 for the Saturday performance, $10 on other days.

RED EYE COLLABORATION

The only resident experimental theater company in the Twin Cities, Red Eye Collaboration performs in a 70-seat studio theater in the downtown Minneapolis Warehouse District at 126 N. Washington Ave. (tel. 870-0309). You'll know you've arrived at Red Eye when you see a historic warehouse with a large red neon sign featuring a blue neon fish swimming above it. One of this troupe's greatest successes to date was, conventionally speaking, not a play at all but an "animation"—essentially a prose poem divided among members of a group, each one representing a different aspect of the central animal character.

Four mixed-media productions are staged each year by the Red

Eye Collaboration, along with one work-in-progress series. Tickets for these productions are $10 on Friday and Sunday, $12 on Saturday; on Thursday evenings two people are admitted for $12. All performances are at 8 p.m.

THÉÂTRE DE LA JEUNE LUNE

This unique international ensemble was founded in 1978 by four students, two Twin Citians and two Parisians, who met while studying at the École Jacques-Lecoq in Paris. Their name is taken from lines in a Bertolt Brecht poem: "The young moon holds in its arms for one night the old moon." This symbolic blending of past traditions into modern, dynamic forms has been at once the mission and the method of the company that now calls Minneapolis home. Productions by this constantly interesting group tend to be highly physical and visually exciting, reflecting elements of clowning, farce, mime, and vaudeville. Recent hits include the wild comedy *Yang Zen Froggs in Moon over a Hong Kong Sweatshop* and a production of *Romeo and Juliet* in which the title characters were portrayed as middle-aged.

Although this company has no home of its own, it performs regularly at Hennepin Center for the Arts in downtown Minneapolis and at the Southern Theater in the heart of the west-bank theater district. Tickets for Théâtre de la Jeune Lune productions range from $7 to $17. Call 333-6200 for more information.

THEATER IN THE ROUND

Since 1952 talented Twin Citians have contributed their time and their talents, onstage and behind the scenes, to community-theater productions by Theater in the Round, 245 Cedar Ave., Minneapolis (tel. 333-3010), or TRP as it's known locally. More than half a million theatergoers have attended productions in an old one-story brick building at Seven Corners in the west-bank theater district. Some of the Twin Cities' top directors have worked here with aspiring actors and technicians who have gone on to professional careers in theater, TV, and the movies.

Play selection here is eclectic: the biggest hits to date have been *Equus, Of Thee I Sing, The Mouse Trap, Mrs. Warren's Profession,* and *Cyrano de Bergerac.* Plays by aspiring authors are produced as well. Although arena staging poses special problems for directors, actors, and designers, audiences enjoy the intimacy of the well-staged in-the-round productions for which TRP is known. You'll also enjoy the chance during intermission to browse in the back gallery where works by local artists are displayed.

2. Other Area Theaters

At the **Penumbra Theatre,** 270 N. Dent St., St. Paul (tel. 224-4601), you'll find Minnesota's only black professional theater company. Penumbra has another claim to fame as well; at this writing, it's the only Twin Cities professional troupe to have staged the plays of August Wilson. Their production of this renowned St. Paul playwright's *Fences* won high praises in 1990. It starred Penumbra founder Lou Bellamy. (Wilson's *Fences* is the only play in American theatrical history to have won the Pulitzer Prize, the Tony Award, the New York Theater Critics Award, the Outer Critics Circle Award, and the award of the American Theater Critics Association.) Wilson found at Penumbra a superb staging of his play—no surprise for a company that enjoys high regard not only for the consistently high quality of its productions but also for its unswerving fidelity to its stated mission: "to present artistically excellent productions that address the African-American experience." The fact that St. Paul is home to a distinguished black playwright and a distinguished black theater company has proved a boon to local audiences. Call for information about current productions whenever you're in or near St. Paul. You won't be disappointed.

The success of the **Heart of the Beast Puppet and Mask Theatre** is a perfect example of one good turn begetting another. Established in 1973 with the stated purpose of serving a racially mixed community in one of the oldest business areas in the Twin Cities, this company of artists performed at outdoor sites and in rented theater spaces for nearly 15 years before being asked by the community to take over a neighborhood theater which was notorious as a porno movie house. Now, with a 300-seat playhouse to call their own, Heart of the Beast Puppet and Mask Theatre has increased its audience more than 700%, with family-oriented shows like *La Befana,* based on an Italian folk story, and *Invisible Child,* based on a traditional Swedish tale. Among its adult productions is *The Reapers Tale,* which provides a history of Columbus's arrival in the New World from the Native Americans' point of view. Members of the company, all of whom are trained in puppet and mask performance, also put on an annual festival on the first Sunday of each May. Participants numbered about 8,000 in 1987, 21,000 in 1990. Performances take place at 1500 E. Lake St., Minneapolis (tel. 721-2535). Tickets cost $4 for children from 4 to 12 years old, $7 for adults. Children under 4 are admitted free. (Those willing to usher or barter in some other way are admitted free.)

The **Frank Theatre,** one of the area's youngest theater companies, scored a huge success during the 1990–91 season with *Top Girls,* by British playwright Caryl Churchill.

Founded in August 1989 by director Wendy Knox and actor Bernadette Sullivan, the Frank Theatre quickly established its reputation by staging two hit productions in a row. With *Top Girls,* though, this young company outdid itself, having to twice extend a sold-out run that finally closed leaving a good many disappointed theatergoers unable to get tickets.

At this writing, the Frank Theatre is acquiring rights to other plays and searching for its own space. Who knows what triumphs will have been achieved by the time you arrive? Call 871-8836 or 374-5641 for more current information.

The **Great American Theater,** located in the Weyerhauser Auditorium at St. Paul's magnificent Landmark Center, 75 W. 5th St.

(tel. 292-4323), stages original plays dealing with representative people and important events in Minnesota's past.

One of the oldest community theaters in the area is **Lakeshore Players,** at 4280 Stewart Ave., White Bear Lake (tel. 429-5674), has provided musical comedies and other family entertainment to suburbanities and city folk alike for nearly 40 years. Recent hits include *Dames at Sea* and *The Foreigner.* Six productions are staged here each year. Ticket prices range from $6 to $8, with discounts for children and seniors.

The **Park Square Theatre,** 253 E. 4th St., St. Paul (tel. 291-7005), offers two distinctly different seasons, the main Classic Season and the summertime Festival Season, when new American plays are staged, usually in conjunction with their authors.

The **University of Minnesota Theatre Department**'s four separate stages at the handsome Rarig Center theater complex (tel. 625-4001) consistently present a wide variety of enjoyable entertainment. You'll also enjoy the perennially popular productions aboard the university's Centennial Showboat, when audiences are welcomed aboard for hissing-and-booing summertime productions of 19th-century melodramas.

Local newspapers and magazines carry comprehensive listings of current and upcoming presentations by these and other theater companies.

VII

MUSIC, DANCE, MUSEUMS, AND GALLERIES

1. MUSIC
2. DANCE
3. MUSEUMS
4. GALLERIES

The Twin Cities are rich not only in theater, but in music, art, and dance as well. With two world-class music halls and two famous art museums, it's noteworthy that facilities in Minneapolis and St. Paul complement rather than compete with each other.

Orchestra Hall is an assertively modernistic building; the Ordway Music Theatre has an old-world beauty. The Walker Art Center is famous for its collection of modern art; the Minneapolis Institute of Art is associated primarily with more traditional works.

1. Music

MUSIC HALLS

There are two major ones in the Twin Cities, Orchestra Hall and the Ordway.

Orchestra Hall

As its name implies, Orchestra Hall, 1111 Nicollet Mall, Minneapolis (tel. 371-5656), was built as a home for the internationally acclaimed Minnesota Orchestra. In addition, since it opened in 1974, this 2,300-seat hall, with its acclaimed acoustics, has offered a diversity of programs featuring a range of artists, from Isaac Stern and Itzhak Perlman to Andy Williams and Pearl Bailey. The highly praised purity of sound here results in large part from the remarkable cubelike shapes you'll see set into the ceiling of the auditorium. These hundreds of surfaces disperse sound to every corner of the vast hall. Other measures have been taken as well. Lockers, available without charge in the lobby, serve an acoustical purpose: heavy woolens and furs brought into the auditorium tend to absorb a great deal of the sound produced onstage.

Since 1980 Orchestra Hall has also become identified with one of the Twin Cities' most popular events. The annual Viennese Sommerfest brings guest conductors and performers and very large audiences to Orchestra Hall for programs featuring everything from light classics to orchestral masterworks. There's also a Marktplatz, set up on adjacent Peavey Plaza, where colorful booths display delectable Viennese food and beverages. Dance groups and musical ensembles provide free entertainment, and from time to time, al fresco mid-morning fashion shows and late-night vintage movies are presented too. By the way, the benefits of all this fun extend well into the regular season when Kinder Konzerts are made possible in part by proceeds from the Sommerfest pastry booths.

The Ordway Music Theatre

The exquisite structure of the **Ordway Music Theatre,** 345 Washington St., St. Paul (tel. 224-4222), says a lot about the Twin Cities, where private and corporate generosity have played a prominent part in the quality of life the residents enjoy. After St. Paul's only major downtown performing arts building was closed in 1980 because of structural deterioration, the family of Lucius Ordway offered to pay for plans to be drawn for a new theater. They offered to donate $10 million toward a new music hall if public and private interests in the Twin Cities would match that commitment and that contribution.

Since its triumphant opening on January 1, 1985, the Ordway Music Theatre has been praised not only for the programs it presents, but for the beauty it imparts to the historic Rice Park area of St. Paul. Hailed as "the most contemporary classic theater in the United States," the Ordway's design combines the new and the old —faceted glass walls set into a façade of bricks and copper, and state-of-the-art acoustics in a traditional horseshoe-shaped Main Hall.

Liveried doormen await theatergoers at the entrance to the handsome lobby; a magnificent spiral stairway leads to the Grand Foyer and upper Promenade, both of which offer spectacular views of the city. The spacious lobby provides upholstered couches and window-wall mahogany benches just right for conversation, refreshments, and people-watching.

The 1,800-seat Main Hall and the 315-seat McKnight Theatre have played host to a wide variety of programs by distinguished musicians from the Minnesota Orchestra, the Schubert Club, the St. Paul Chamber Orchestra, and the Minnesota Opera Company. And there have been a succession of notable visiting artists as diverse as Leontyne Price, Mel Torme, and the Ballet Folklórico Nacional de México.

In addition, each year a series of touring Broadway shows appears at the Ordway. Past productions have included *Les Miserables, West Side Story,* and *The Heidi Chronicles.* Prices vary according to production or performance. Students can get special rush-line discounts prior to some performances. Call the ticket office for particulars.

Northrop Auditorium

Northrop Auditorium, on the University of Minnesota's main campus at 84 Church St. S.E., Minneapolis (tel. 624-2345), has been called the grand dame of Twin Cities theaters. Since 1929 Northrop has welcomed performances by major artists and popular touring productions. Companies like the American Ballet Theatre, the Joffrey, the Moiseyev, the National Ballet of China, and the Sakailuku, a brilliant Paris-based Japanese company, have all appeared at the 4,800-seat Northrop Auditorium. International stars including Margot Fonteyn, Mikhail Barishnikov, Twyla Tharp, and Merce Cunningham have performed here too. And most recently, the Soviet Union's Kirov Ballet and the Leningrad Philharmonic Orchestra have thrilled audiences at Northrop Auditorium. Touring Broadway shows make stops here as well from time to time.

MUSICAL AND CONCERT ORGANIZATIONS

In addition to the many local bands and musical groups, there are two major orchestras and an organization sponsoring musical recitals and concerts in the Twin Cities.

The Minnesota Orchestra

The Minnesota Orchestra was born in 1903, the eighth major orchestra to be established in the United States. In 1923 it was heard on crystal radio sets; one year later it became the second major American orchestra to make recordings of its performances. Under the leadership of Eugene Ormandy from 1931 to 1936, the orchestra gained international recognition through its recordings and its concerts abroad.

Dmitri Mitropoulos led his musicians geographically as well as musically from 1937 to 1949, during which time the orchestra made a 34,000-mile tour of the Middle East sponsored by the State Department.

During the 19-year tenure of Stanislaw Skrowaczewski, the Minnesota Orchestra increased in size to 95 musicians and took up residence in its new home at Orchestra Hall. The Minnesota Orchestra performs regularly at St. Paul's Ordway Music Theatre as well, and makes guest appearances throughout the state, the nation, and the world.

Since September 1986 the Minnesota Orchestra has been led by the distinguished conductor Edo de Waart.

St. Paul Chamber Orchestra

The St. Paul Chamber Orchestra, 75 W. 5th St., St. Paul (tel. 291-1144), the nation's only full-time professional chamber orchestra, may be performing at the Ordway Music Theatre while you're here, or you may find them in one of the shopping centers, churches, or school auditoriums that used to welcome them during the homeless years when they were identified with the concept "Music on the Move." The group was originated in 1959 by a group of St. Paulites who decided to find a conductor to head a group of freelance professional musicians who performed educational programs. They eventually established a ten-concert season, went on tour, and gained enough backing to incorporate under the name St. Paul Chamber Orchestra.

By the late seventies the group had undertaken a number of important tours—to 140 American cities and to Western and Eastern Europe and the Soviet Union. During this time they also gained a reputation for regularly combining classical works and world premieres on the same program.

From 1980 to 1987, under the leadership of Pinchas Zukerman, the chamber orchestra hosted a musical *Who's Who,* including Isaac Stern and Misha Dichter. And under Zukerman's leadership the local season expanded to 80 concerts and the St. Paul Chamber Orchestra gained fame as one of the country's best musical groups, with frequent guest appearances at Carnegie Hall, Avery Fisher Hall, and the Kennedy Center.

In 1987 a new leadership concept was announced. Replacing a single director now are the Artistic Commission, consisting of director of music, Christopher Hogwood, principal conductor Hugh Wolff, and creative chair John Harbison. The St. Paul Chamber Orchestra now performs 150 concerts during a 40-week season that extends from September to June. In addition to performing at the Ordway, they take their music to seven metropolitan locations throughout the Twin Cities.

The Schubert Club

Vladimir Horowitz, Isaac Stern, Robert Casadesus, and Beverly Sills are among the artists who've been brought—and brought back again—to St. Paul by the Schubert Club, 301 Landmark Center, St. Paul (tel. 292-3267), founded in 1882 and now one of the oldest musical organizations in the United States. If you're a music lover, you might want to inquire about whether one of the 50 or so recitals they offer each year will be at the Ordway Music Theatre during your stay.

In addition to bringing celebrated artists from throughout the world to perform in the Twin Cities, the Schubert Club, in a spirit of "venturesome conservatism," regularly commissions work from selected composers of recital music. One of these commissions, "From the Diary of Virginia Woolf," by Dominick Argento, won the Pulitzer Prize for Music in 1975. This work was sung by Dame Janet Baker both here in St. Paul and at Carnegie Hall in New York City.

Among the club's other projects has been the establishment and maintenance of a musical museum containing over 75 keyboard instruments dating back to the mid-16th century.

2. Dance

No cities except New York and Washington, D.C., offer a more active professional dance scene than the one you'll find in Minneapolis and St. Paul. Whatever the season, there's likely to be at least one major performance during your stay. Calendars of local and touring dance programs are published weekly in local newspapers and magazines, and a call to the **Minnesota Dance Alliance** (tel. 340-1900) will provide specific information about current and upcoming presentations.

The **O'Shaughnessey Dance Series,** a six-week program offered during the spring of each year, is the only one of its kind in the country. Committed to spotlighting local professional dance companies, it undertakes a major selection process, then presents the annual series in the beautiful and flexible O'Shaughnessey Auditorium at 2004 Randolph Ave., St. Paul (tel. 690-6700), on the campus of the College of St. Catherine, where a "magic ceiling" can turn an imposing 1,800-seat hall into an intimate 600-seat chamber.

Among the local troupes that have appeared in the O'Shaughnessey series have been the **Zorongo Flamenco Dance Theatre,** one of only five professional Spanish Gypsy dance troupes in the country. Their dynamic narrative dramas have earned them high marks at home and in the many cities to which they've toured.

Summerdance, a two-week series sponsored by the Minnesota Dance Alliance in June, also showcases the work of selected local companies and choreographers. In 1987 this festival took place in the intimate McKnight Playhouse at the Ordway Music Theatre (see above). The Minneapolis Children's Theatre (see Chapter VI) and the Hennepin Center for the Arts, 528 Hennepin Ave. (tel. 332-4478), also play host to these programs from time to time.

The **Ethnic Dance Theatre** (tel. 872-0024) has made a national and an international name for itself. Comprised of nearly 50 dancers and musicians, this company travels to distant destinations at home and abroad, from Appalachia in the United States to Uzbekistan in the USSR, learning traditional dances and then using these as the basis for original choreography. A recent premiere piece was researched in the Soviet republic of Tadzhikistan and concerns the legendary Tamara Khanum, the first Muslim dancer in the Soviet Union to risk execution by casting aside her veil while performing in public.

Two other companies may be performing during your stay. **The Nancy Hauser Dance Company,** 1940 Hennepin Ave., Minneapolis (tel. 871-9077), is an accomplished modern-dance troupe that has toured widely with the works of the late Nancy Hauser and her daughter Heidi, now director of the company. The work of other company members and of visiting artists is also performed by the company.

Ballet of the Dolls is a company of professional dancers whose work is primarily a combination of ballet and jazz dance. This inventive troupe evolved from a succession of late-evening spontaneous performances directed by Myron Johnson, who has directed frequently at the Minneapolis Children's Theatre. Since the January 1989 opening of Ruby's Cabaret, 400 Third Ave. N., Minneapolis (tel. 333-1006), this busy performance space has served as a base for Ballet of the Dolls as well as for a variety of other artists. Call for information on what's scheduled during your stay in the Twin Cities. You'll find an ample and healthful buffet table awaiting you at Ruby's with catered items ranging from cookies ($1) to a sandwich or pasta salad ($7). There's also a cash bar.

You'll find the price of tickets to dance performances is remarkably low in the Twin Cities. Prices for touring dance productions range from $8 to $23; for local companies, $5 to $15.

3. Museums

From the major art and science museums to smaller, more specialized collections, the Twin Cities has collections to appeal to all tastes.

MINNEAPOLIS INSTITUTE OF ART

More than 70,000 objects of art representing more than 25,000 years of history await you at the Minneapolis Institute of Art, Third Ave. S. and E. 24th St., Minneapolis (tel. 870-3046). Since the Institute eliminated its general admission charge in September 1989, there's been a remarkable increase in the number of families that come here to see and to learn together at this internationally renowned museum.

Many of today's Twin Cities parents report remembering their own first encounter with the Institute's famous 2,000-year-old mummy. Among other favorites are a fascinating assortment of African masks, a rare collection of Chinese jades, and pre-Columbian gold objects from the Incas.

Faithfully recreated period rooms have long been popular, and so are more recent additions—everything from ethnic galleries to the meticulously restored Purcell-Cutts house, an example of the early 20th-century design movement known as the Prairie School.

Other holdings here include work by Rembrandt and a number of French Impressionists as well as superb examples of contemporary art. A photography collection adds further to the diversity.

Even the exterior of the Institute represents an intriguing blend of periods. On the 24th Street side is the original majestic classic revival structure, which faces Fair Oaks Park, while around the corner, extending past the main entrance, is the contemporary facade, a blend of steel and brick whose color and texture blends gracefully with the original.

If you're here in June, check out the annual June Fete, an extravaganza of fun, food, crafts, and entertainment. Throughout the year, you'll find an interesting schedule of lectures, gallery concerts, and films.

THE WALKER ART CENTER AND THE MINNEAPOLIS SCULPTURE GARDENS

The Walker Art Center, 725 Vineland Place, Minneapolis (tel. 375-7577 or 375-7622), adjoining the Tyrone Guthrie Theatre and facing the Sculpture Garden, is famous for its permanent collection of contemporary art. In addition, some of the most prestigious exhibitions that tour the country make stops at the Walker.

In February 1980, "Picasso: From the Musée Picasso, Paris" brought Picasso's own Picassos to the United States for the first time; these works were later incorporated into the Picasso retrospective at New York's Museum of Modern Art.

The Walker is famed too for the popular presentations it offers under the auspices of its Department of Film and Video and Department of Performing Arts, and as well as for its Education Department.

Gallery hours are 10 a.m. to 8 p.m. Tuesday through Saturday; 11 a.m. to 5 p.m. Sunday. Gallery admission prices are $3 for adults, $2 for students. Admission is free to Walker members and to seniors. And there's free admission to the Walker for everybody each Thursday.

Across Vineland Place, the Minneapolis Sculpture Garden, whose display of artworks and educational activities are managed by the Walker Art Center, has been attracting wide attention since it was dedicated in September 1988. The most extensive garden of its kind in the United States, it's been called the country's finest new outdoor space for displaying sculpture.

Probably the most readily recognizable work here is *Spoonbridge and Cherry,* by Claes Oldenburg and Coosje van Bruggen—a 52-foot-long spoon bearing a cherry that measures 9½ feet in diameter, with a 12-foot stem. This sculptural fountain and reflecting pool stand in honor of William and Mary Weisman, parents of Minneapolis-born philanthropist and art collector Frederick R. Weisman.

The wide variety of 20th-century sculpture on display here includes work by artists Henry Moore, Isamu Noguchi, George Segal, and Jackie Ferrara. California architect Frank Gehry is represented by the dramatic *Standing Glass Fish* in the conservatory, which features horticultural displays throughout the year.

Somewhat to the surprise of many observers, the Sculpture Garden has become a year-round attraction, so do come and see it for yourself, whatever the weather.

THE AMERICAN SWEDISH INSTITUTE

At 2600 Park Ave. in Minneapolis, the American Swedish Institute (tel. 871-4907) is a museum that doesn't have to be entered to be enjoyed. This is a fairytale castle of pale limestone, with arches and turrets, a small balcony, and a tall tower. It's equally grand within: decorative ceilings, intricately designed rugs of Swedish wool, and a glorious stained-glass window copied from a famous and historic Swedish painting.

This magnificent 33-room mansion was donated to the American Swedish Institute by Swan J. Turnblad, who came to this country in 1887 at the age of 8. By the time he was 27 Turnblad had become manager of the *Svenska Amerikanska Posten,* a Swedish-language weekly, and 10 years later he was its owner, having increased circulation from 1,500 to 55,000 in the interim, making it the largest Swedish-language newspaper in America. His general purpose for the Institute, to "foster and preserve Swedish culture in America," has been admirably fulfilled. Artifacts in the mansion demonstrate over 150 years of the Swedish experience in the United States. There are examples in this museum of the items Swedish immigrants brought with them from the old country and examples of works of art created by Swedish and Swedish-American artists.

Museum hours are Tuesday, Thursday, Friday, and Saturday, noon to 8 p.m.; Wednesday and Sunday, 1 to 5 p.m. Admission is $3 for adults, $1 for senior citizens and students under 19. A film program is presented every Sunday at 2 p.m. and musical programs are offered at 3 p.m. on Sunday afternoons during the winter months.

MINNESOTA MUSEUM OF ART

Two historic structures house the Minnesota Museum of Art (tel. 292-4355) in St. Paul: the striking 1931 art deco Jemne Building, St. Peter Street at Kellogg Boulevard, and two blocks away the majestic 1906 Romanesque-style Landmark Center, 5th Street at Market Street.

Holdings at the Jemne include works from the ancient as well as the contemporary world. The most recent additions to the museum's collections of American and non-Western art are exhibited at the Jemne, where the building itself is a treasure, with its original terrazzo floors, brass railings, and lighting.

The museum's temporary exhibition galleries at the Landmark Center include the work of new midwestern artists as well as major exhibitions. At times, touring exhibitions are on display here too. In the fifth-floor gallery known as "Kidspace," children can enjoy a "hands-on" experience with art.

Hours at both museums are Tuesday through Friday from 10:30 a.m. to 4:30 p.m. (on Thursday to 7:30 p.m.), on Saturday and Sunday from 1 to 4:30 p.m. Admission to the museum and to most exhibitions is free.

By the way, there's food for the palate as well as the soul in both buildings of the Minnesota Museum of Art. At the Jemne, one of the best Sunday buffets in either town can be found on the fourth-floor Deco Restaurant overlooking the Mississippi River. And at the Landmark, budget-pleasing soup-and-sandwich lunches are a popular weekday feature.

JAMES FORD BELL MUSEUM OF NATURAL HISTORY

The James Ford Bell Museum of Natural History, at University Avenue and 17th Avenue S.E., Minneapolis (tel. 624-1852), is the oldest museum in the state of Minnesota—and one of the most popular. Located on the Minneapolis campus of the University of Minnesota, this museum is famous for its three-dimensional scenes of Minnesota wildlife, which are works of art in themselves, and which have proved endlessly fascinating to generations of visitors.

Animals and birds in their natural habitats are painstakingly reproduced and displayed here; accompanying legends provide information in a concise and interesting way.

In the popular "Touch and See" room, children can examine for themselves the skins, bones, and skulls of a wide variety of animals, including mammoths and dinosaurs. Among the creatures on hand are stuffed wildlife specimens such as moose, elk, and caribou, as well as Lenny, a live gila monster, which is sometimes kept company by visiting animals from the Como Park Zoo.

Hours are Tuesday through Saturday from 9 a.m. to 5 p.m., on Sunday from 1 to 5 p.m. Ticket prices are $2 for adults, $1 for seniors and children 3 to 16 years old. There's no charge for those under 3 or for University of Minnesota students with a current fee statement and I.D. On Thursdays, admission is free to one and all.

THE CHILDREN'S MUSEUM

Children get to do all sorts of grownup things at the Children's Museum, a hands-on "aware house" at 1217 Bandana Blvd. N. (tel. 644-3818), in St. Paul's historic Bandana Square complex. Here, in a two-story reconverted blacksmith's shop, children can experience for themselves some of the activities they've only observed before coming here. At a DJ desk they can control cassette decks and dancing colored lights. At the telegraph station they can operate Morse code devices that signal simultaneously with a clicker and with blue lights so that deaf children can receive messages of their own. Another top draw here is the crane-and-train exhibit, where children can use an electromagnetic crane to pick up and deposit metal discs. At the Now-and-Then fountain, visitors can compare prices in the 1950s with those of the present. At the bank, children can examine foreign and domestic currency on a light table.

Although the museum is always closed on Monday, hours change from season to season; you can receive the latest update from a recorded message by calling 644-3818. (For more personalized information, call 644-5305.)

GIBBS FARM MUSEUM

This popular living museum at Cleveland and Larpenteur avenues, Falcon Heights, St. Paul (tel. 646-8629), re-creates life on a 7-acre urban-fringe farm at the turn of the century. Costumed guides are on hand to answer questions about the artifacts and activities on this homestead. You'll see how the Gibbs family's home grew from a one-room cabin to a large, comfortable farmhouse complete with parlor, sitting room, kitchen, bathrooms, and more. In a red barn you'll find friendly barnyard animals, and there's a one-room schoolhouse with wooden double-desks, a pump organ, slate boards, and a school bell. Quilting, baking, and blacksmithing are demonstrated, and a slide presentation explains what farming on the fringe of St. Paul was like in those days.

Information about individual programs, which vary from month to month, can be obtained from the Ramsey County Historical Society, 323 Landmark Center, 75 W. 5th St., St. Paul (tel. 222-0701).

The Gibbs Farm is open May 1 through October 31. Hours are Tuesday through Friday, 10 a.m. to 4 p.m.; Saturday during June, July, and August, noon to 4 p.m.; Sunday, noon to 4 p.m. Admission is $2.50 for adults, $2 for seniors, $1 for those 2 to 18 years of age.

The Science Museum of Minnesota

At the entrance of this immensely popular two-building complex at 30 E. 10th St., St. Paul (tel. 221-9454), you'll be greeted by *Iggy,* a 40-foot steel iguana that, appropriately enough, was sculpted by a 16-year-old St. Paul schoolboy. Boys and girls of all ages have an entertaining and educational time at this massive museum, which offers hands-on exhibits dealing with natural history, science, and technology. Members of an acting troupe turn up here and there to bring to life some of the figures who have played a part in the development of this area.

The East Building holds *Our Minnesota,* a permanent exhibit featuring a 12-by-14-foot map of the state that permits visitors to walk or crawl across forests, marked in green; croplands, marked in gold; mines, represented by taconite pellets; and lakes—an expanse of blue plastic representing "sky-blue waters."

The Hall of Paleontology features the dinosaur lab, in which visitors can watch fossils being cleaned, identified, and assembled.

The West Building contains the Hall of Anthropology, the Physics and Technology gallery, and the Collections Exhibit (miscellaneous artifacts from the collection) as well as a succession of traveling exhibits.

And then there's the **Omnitheater,** whose screen is a tilted dome, 76 feet in diameter, that puts viewers right into the center of adventures dealing with every time and every place.

Hours for the exhibit halls and the Omnitheater differ according to season. Call 221-9454 for information.

Prices for the exhibit halls only are $4 for adults, $3 for those 65 and older or 12 and under.

Call 221-9400 for information about prices for the Omnitheater alone and for Omnitheater-Museum combination tickets.

4. Galleries

Night turns into day and staid city streets take on a festive air on the Saturday nights every six weeks or so when openings at more than a dozen galleries in the Warehouse District of Minneapolis attract many hundreds of artists, patrons, and passersby. (Estimates vary, but reliable word has it that more than 2,000 first-nighters typically turn out for these events.) Whatever the season, you'll find gallery-goers strolling from one historic building to another to get their first glimpse of works that range widely in form, style, and price. Some viewers come to buy, some to browse, and some just for the fun of it. After the works have been studied and the plastic wine glasses discarded, it's time to repair to the New French Cafe or Faegre's Bar and Restaurant or Cafe Brenda or some other nearby gathering place for discussions and disputes on the paintings and sculpture and other art forms that were introduced that evening.

Actually, the people-watching is an important part of the evening's fun. As one gallery director puts it, "You see every kind of clothing from ripped-out jeans and T-shirts to $70,000 fur coats. It's as mixed as Minneapolis is." And so are the works on display. It's their sheer variety that accounts for the coordination of these openings. Like so many other elements in the Twin Cities, these galleries complement rather than compete with one another. Each has its own niche, its own clientele, and its own unique appeal to the sophisticated gallery-goer and to the neophyte. The concentration of so many galleries within a few city blocks makes this a delightful destination for visiting art fanciers.

Most galleries are open from 11 a.m. to 4 p.m. Tuesday through Saturday, and by appointment. Some remain open Thursday evening until 8 p.m. Do phone to confirm hours.

IN THE WYMAN BUILDING

The Wyman Building, at 400 First Ave. N., houses nearly a dozen galleries, which have combined into a loosely formed co-op. Here are a few of them:

Thomas Barry Fine Arts, Suite 304 (tel. 338-3656), offers contemporary American work, including photography, prints, drawings, paintings, and sculpture. Artists include Don Gahr, Lynn Geesaman, Bruce Charlesworth, and Ken Moylan.

Peter M. David Gallery, Suite 236 (tel. 339-1825), shows the drawings, prints, paintings, photography, and sculpture of contemporary American and British artists. Midwestern artists represented here include Cynthia Starkweather, William Weege, and Mark Rediske.

Flanders Contemporary Art, on the first floor of the Wyman Building (tel. 344-1700), features museum-quality contemporary painting, drawing, and sculpture by nationally and internationally known American and European artists, among them Eric Fischl, Nancy Graves, and Tom Holland.

McGallery, Suite 332 (tel. 339-1480), is an avant-garde fine-art gallery offering works in a variety of forms—painting, sculpture, and glass and ceramics, among others. Paul Benson, Sheldon Hage, Jean Murakami, and Barbra Nei are among the artists represented here.

NEARBY MINNEAPOLIS WAREHOUSE DISTRICT GALLERIES

Other galleries in the district, all within easy walking distance of one another, include the following:

Artbanque, Suite 150, 300 First Ave. N., Minneapolis (tel. 342-9300), is one of the largest galleries in the Twin Cities, and one of the most diverse. The work of promising young unknowns can be found here, and so, twice a year, at investment art shows, can the works of giants like Rembrandt, Picasso, and Moore.

Thomson Gallery, 321 Second Ave. N., Minneapolis (tel. 338-7734), offers contemporary drawings, paintings, prints, photography, and sculpture by such artists as Philip Larson, Lance Kiland, Steven Sorman, and Tom Rose. Much of the work shown here is of museum quality.

Warm Gallery, 414 First Ave. N., Minneapolis (tel. 332-5672), offers a wide variety of work, much of it related to the concerns of feminists. The Women's Art Registry of Minnesota, more than a decade old, is the country's oldest nonprofit collective of women artists. Members, who share the responsibilities of directing this gallery, include artists Harriet Bart, Carol Lee Chase, and Jean Murakami.

The **Forum Gallery,** 119 N. 4th St, Minneapolis (tel. 333-1825), emphasizes sculpture, including the work of Philip Rickey and William Mayer. You'll also find large oils by Stephen Erickson here.

ST. PAUL GALLERIES

Meanwhile, over in St. Paul there's the **Suzanne Kohn Gallery,** 1690 Grand Ave. (tel. 699-0477). Regional painters are featured here, and if you don't see what you want on the walls of this small gallery, you're welcome to go downstairs for a look through the works stored there. After nearly a quarter of a century as a gallery owner, Suzanne Kohn still favors beauty of subject and expression in art. Among those she represents are established Midwestern artists like Jerry Rudquist, as well as regional artists like Tom Maakestad and Steven Carpenter. Suzanne Kohn also has a gallery in Minneapolis at the International Design Center, 100 2nd Ave. N. (tel. 341-3441). Exhibits change here monthly.

Art Resources, 494 Jackson St., St. Paul (tel. 222-4431), features the work of Midwestern artists, with over 6,000 pieces of original art, ranging from the abstract expressionism of Bernel Bayliss and Steve Wolff to classical realist oils by Chris Copeland and Bill Murray.

The work of late-19th-century and early-20th-century regional artists is featured at **Kramer Gallery,** 229 E. 6th St., St. Paul (tel. 228-1301). Other American and European painters of that period are shown here as well, along with turn-of-the-century Native American art and artifacts. Among the famous painters represented here are Alexis Fournier, who left St. Paul to study with Barbizon masters in France, and Nichola Brewer, another notable turn-of-the-century painter of the Barbizon school. You're also likely to find work by regional impressionists George Ames Aldrich and Alfred Janssen, as well as western works by John Fery, Edgar Payne, and Frank Hoffman.

If you're interested in bringing top-quality crafts back from your visit to Minnesota, you might try the **Raymond Avenue Gallery,** 761 Raymond Ave., St. Paul (tel. 644-9200). You'll find baskets, jewelry, and more here, as well as the nationally known pottery of Warren MacKenzie.

VIII

TWIN CITIES NIGHTSPOTS

1. LIVE MUSIC, DANCE HALLS, AND PUBS
2. COMEDY CLUBS

Exciting entertainment can be found in late-night clubs all around these towns, although the term "late-night" is used advisedly. By early morning—1 a.m. Monday through Saturday and midnight on Sunday, to be exact—our chariots turn back into pumpkins as nightclub doors close and lights go out. Don't worry though, you'll find lots to see and do and still get a good night's sleep before rising to another full day of activities here in Minneapolis and St. Paul.

Rock-and-roll, jazz, and comedy clubs are great favorites hereabouts, with some of the country's foremost performers appearing on stages in nightclubs that are themselves often worth writing home about.

1. Live Music, Dance Halls, and Pubs

Glam Slam, at 110 N. 5th St., Minneapolis (338-3383), has been since its September 1990 opening the only Twin Cities nightclub offering in-person performances by Prince and other celebrated Paisley Park recording artists. And, thanks to another exclusive Glam Slam agreement, this is the only place you'll hear unreleased material produced at Paisley Park, Prince's widely admired state-of-the-art recording complex.

The second-floor private area at Glam Slam is reserved for members only, but don't fret. There's plenty to enjoy on the main floor of this 20,000-sq.-foot nightclub, which features disc jockeys brought in from notable nightspots throughout the world. Located in Minneapolis's Warehouse District, Glam Slam is open five nights a week, Tuesday through Saturday.

A cavernous converted bus depot serves as the site of one of Minneapolis's largest, busiest, and most famous nightspots. The

1,200-seat **First Avenue Club,** 701 First Ave. N., Minneapolis (tel. 338-8388), is familiar to movie-goers around the world as the setting for Prince's movie *Purple Rain.*

There's recorded music for dancing four times each week at First Avenue, where hi-tech sound and lights provide a noisy and exciting atmosphere.

On Mondays and Wednesdays, live national and international acts are presented here, in styles ranging from pop to metal to jazz. Tuesday, Thursday, and Friday through Sunday are dance nights, with music ranging from rhythm-and-blues to the newest progressive dance music.

While some promising unknowns play First Avenue from time to time, the usual launching pad for new talent is the adjoining **7th Street Entry,** 701 First Ave. N., Minneapolis (tel. 338-8388), which is open seven nights a week and features at least three live bands each night. Formerly a storage area, this room has become the club in which publicists try to book their young clients, hoping to catch the eye of scouts who've made this a regular stop in their search for new talent. All First Avenue customers have access as well to 7th Street Entry. There's a separate cover charge for each place on Thursday, Friday, and Saturday, and it varies. You'll find drinks of all kinds here, but no drink specials, because First Avenue is here primarily to sell entertainment, not refreshments. Its small kitchen serves only snacks like nachos and pizzas. It's food for the ears— and strong ears at that—which you'll find featured at First Avenue and at 7th Street Entry. Phone 332-1775 for daily recorded information about performances. If you'd rather speak to a real person, call 338-8388 Monday through Friday from noon to 5 p.m.

Just a few blocks away, you'll find **The Fine Line Music Cafe,** 318 First Ave. N., Minneapolis (tel. 338-8100). Unlike thematic nightclubs that limit themselves to one musical niche or another— jazz, rock and roll, or blues, for example—this is a "showcase room," which, according to owner Joel Conner, means the Fine Line is free to put any kind of music onstage, so long as it's of a high quality.

Groups performing here have included Bonedaddies, a Cajun group from New Orleans; Zvuki Mu, rock-and-rollers from the Soviet Union; and bellAmitri, a group that brought their pop rock to the Twin Cities from Scotland.

Situated in the Warehouse District of downtown Minneapolis, the Fine Line somehow manages an aura of intimacy while accommodating some 460 patrons at small tables on two levels of their storefront space.

The eclectic dinner menu, with prices ranging from $6 to $14, includes a lot of fish, pasta, and chicken, as well as a wide variety of appetizers and drinks.

It's well to call before coming to the Fine Line, to see whether the musical fare being offered is likely to suit your taste. No need to take that precaution for the Sunday brunches, though, because the "Gospel Brunch" here has become a longstanding tradition with many Twin Cities families and friends. You'll pay $11.50 for the Gospel Brunch if you're 9 or older; $6.50 if you're under 9. Brunch hours change seasonally, so you'd better phone. Evening hours at the Fine Line are Monday through Friday 5 p.m. until 1 a.m., Saturday and Sunday 6 p.m. until 1 a.m.

Jazz enthusiasts claim that our local clubs rank among the best in the country. The **Dakota Bar and Grill,** at Bandana Square, 1021 E. Bandana Blvd., St. Paul (tel. 642-1442), offers live jazz seven nights a week, with groups ranging from 3-piece combos to 17-piece big bands. During recent months, the following world-class performers have appeared here: pianists McCoy Tyner and Ahmad Jamal, singers Carmen McRae, Betty Carter, and Joe Williams, trumpeter Freddie Hubbard, and drummer Art Blakey. The Twin Cities' finest local jazz musicians appear here regularly as well.

Musicians booked to appear at the Ordway or other large halls in town frequently end up here to enjoy the late-night entertainment, which lasts until 1 a.m. seven nights a week.

Cover charges vary according to the entertainment being offered, so call for specific information. And see Chapter IV of this guide for word about the fine dining that awaits you at the Dakota Bar and Grill.

If you want specific information about the jazz entertainment being offered during your stay in the Twin Cities, call **Jazzline** (tel. 633-0329), a service of the Twin Cities Jazz Society. They provide a lengthy rundown on the artists appearing throughout the Twin Cities at clubs, bars, restaurants, hotels, parks, plazas, and even on local radio. During the summer months, much of the jazz hereabouts is performed outdoors.

Interested in other types of music? At the popular suburban **Rupert's Nightclub,** 5410 Wayzata Blvd., St. Louis Park (tel. 544-3550), 10 musicians and 6 singers entertain Tuesday through Saturday nights. This huge three-tiered club offers a wide range of entertainment, from rock to pop, jazz, and R&B. The diversity of its offerings probably accounts for the diversity of the crowds. You'll encounter people of all ages gathered here, dressed in styles from the most formal to the most casual. One exception, though: if you want to wear jeans or tennis shoes, better check with the management first. Reportedly that's the only kind of garb unwelcome at Rupert's. Many of the people here look as though they've just arrived from the office, and that may be true because a popular happy hour, weekdays from 5 to 7 p.m., features a tasty variety of complimentary appetizers. They seem a perfect prelude to an evening in the club. Hours here are 4:30 p.m. to 1 a.m. on Tuesday, 5 p.m. to 1 a.m. on Wednesday, Thursday, and Friday, and 7:00 p.m. to 1 a.m. on Saturday. Rupert's is closed Sunday.

On Tuesday nights, ladies get in free. From 5 to 7 p.m. on Tuesday and Friday nights there's complimentary champagne for ladies, along with a complimentary buffet table.

At the **New Riverside Café,** 329 Cedar Ave. S., Minneapolis (tel. 333-4814), you'll hear a variety of music by Twin Cities bands and vocalists. In this 20-year-old west-bank collective, where the owners also serve as managers and maintenance staff, the often first-rate musicians are paid by tips from patrons and a meal from the café. You'll find the work of local artists mounted on the wall here as well. "The Riv" is a vegetarian, alcohol-free restaurant with a reputation for tasty food in a wholesome environment. Check it out. Music entertainment begins at 7:30 p.m. Tuesday through Thursday and at 9 p.m. Friday and Saturday, and lasts until 11 p.m. on weekdays, until midnight on Saturday.

At **O'Gara's Bar and Grill,** 164 N. Snelling, St. Paul (tel. 644-3333), you'll find a complex that's far outgrown the pub founded in March 1941 by James Freeman O'Gara of County Sligo. Originally serving food and liquor to locals who helped manufacture World War II munitions hereabouts, O'Gara's has expanded since those early days and now boasts a game room (which was formerly a barber shop run by the father of "Peanuts" creator Charles Schultz). Nowadays you can enjoy music in O'Gara's piano bar and listen to a variety of bands in the Garage (Friday and Saturday 7:30 p.m. to 1 a.m.). Food and drink are served in the expanded dining and drinking areas. Students, professors, and white-collar types mix affably here with the blue-collar regulars.

At **Sweeney's Saloon,** 96 N. Dale St., St. Paul (tel. 221-9157), you'll find a boisterous place with a large selection of beers, to say nothing of daily food specials that really are special. Thirteen tap beers include a few brewed in New Ulm, Minnesota. The saloon is open from 11 a.m. to 1 a.m. seven days a week.

At **Fitzgerald's** in St. Paul's Galtier Plaza, on Sibley Street between 5th and 6th avenues (tel. 297-6787), you'll find a pub with an open contemporary air; window walls offer a lovely view of Mears Park below. Featured here is a wide variety of Scotches and cognacs, after-dinner cordials, and premium imported and domestic wines. It's popular for lunches with local businesspeople. Dinner is served starting at 5 p.m. seven days a week. Mesquite-grilled fresh fish are a specialty. You'll also find here a wide variety of steak and chicken entrées, as well as pasta and salads.

Fitzgerald's comes to life late at night, when it's frequented by out-of-towners staying at nearby hotels with skyway access to Fitzgerald's until closing time. This is also a popular place for after-theater audiences. The bar is open 11 a.m. to 1 a.m. Monday through Saturday, 11 a.m. to midnight Sunday.

Over at 788 Grand Ave., St. Paul (tel. 227-7328), the popular **Grand Central** features live music and dancing Wednesday through Sunday each week. Deejays offer top 40 hits each evening from 9 p.m. until 1 a.m. Things really get lively from 10 or 10:30 p.m. on. There's a variety of imported beers to add to the merriment.

If you're a jazz enthusiast in town on a Friday or Saturday evening, do consider the **Emporium of Jazz Restaurant and Lounge,** 1351 Sibley Memorial Highway, Mendota (tel. 452-1830), located across the Mississippi River from the International Airport. The Emporium is open from 8 p.m. to 1 a.m. with a cover charge that varies according to the musicians playing.

You'll see and hear a variety of jazz artists here each week from Wednesday through Sunday, including Stan Hall and his jazz band, frequently featuring famed pianist Butch Thompson.

Back in downtown Minneapolis, you'll want to check out the **Pacific Club,** 10 S. 5th St. (tel. 339-6100 or 339-6206). This nightspot gained instant popularity with its lavish happy hour from 4 p.m. to 7:30 p.m. Monday through Friday. The big draw for the hundreds of downtowners who flock here after work each day is the buffet with more than 10 selections, from appetizers to desserts— all for a single $1 charge. And when the bountiful buffet tables come down, the high-energy music and dancing get underway. There's a $2 cover charge after 7:30 p.m. from Tuesday to Thursday, a $4 cover after 7:30 p.m. on Friday and after 8:30 p.m. on Saturday. Only those 21 years of age or older are admitted.

On the ground floor of Riverplace, the trendy shopping and entertainment complex on the shores of the Mississippi River, you'll find **J. Cousineau's,** at 15 Main St. S.E., Minneapolis (tel. 623-3632), a popular pub with a large outdoor patio. It's famous for its enormous half-yard and full-yard ale glasses, reproductions of the glasses used in England during the 17th and 18th centuries. After quaffing your selection, feel free to purchase the one-foot glass at $29.95, half-yard glass at $35.75, or the full-yard at $59.95. (Less hearty or less thirsty souls can imbibe from smaller vessels. Steins and tankards are available for the likes of them.)

On the strip in Bloomington, you'll find other nightspots including the **Cattle Company,** 4470 W. 78th St. Circle (tel. 835-1225), with deejays on hand seven nights a week from 8 p.m. to 1 a.m. (Sunday until midnight). A wide mix of dance music, from the fifties and sixties to the current Top 40, is featured here.

Finally, in a class by itself, is **Champps Sports Bar and Gourmet Hamburger Grill,** at three locations: 2431 W. 7th St., at Sibley Plaza in St. Paul (tel. 698-5050), 66th and Lyndale Avenue S. in Richfield's Market Plaza shopping center (tel. 861-3333), and 1641 Plymouth Road, Minnetonka, in the Bonaventure shopping center (tel. 546-3333). People of all ages, sizes, backgrounds, and temperaments mix merrily amidst six large TV screens showing, of course, sports events. When visiting the Twin Cities, sports celebrities from out of town head for Champps, and local sports figures congregate here as well. The atmosphere is jovial, food and drink prices are moderate. Known as "one of the top six sports bars in the nation," Champps is always busy, bustling and, to a degree, blasé. A note on the menu says it all: "If your order doesn't arrive in 5 minutes, you'll be served in 9 minutes, . . . or maybe 12 . . . Relax . . . " Patrons seem to do just that.

2. Comedy Clubs

Comedy clubs are an important part of the after-hours scene here in the Twin Cities. In fact, Twin Cities comedy clubs have become something of a one-man show thanks to Scott Hanson, a local impresario whose own credits as a comic include local performances at the Guthrie Theatre and at Riverfest. On the national scene, he's opened for celebrities including Jay Leno, Roseanne Barr, Rodney Dangerfield, and another Twin Citian, Louis Anderson.

More recently, though, Hanson has developed a series of comedy "galleries" throughout the Twin Cities area. There's a $10 admission charge to each, and, unless otherwise noted below, the phone number for each is the same: tel. 331-JOKE.

Comedy Gallery Riverplace, 25 Main St. S.E., Minneapolis, offers performances by comics you may have seen on national TV. Headliners including Jake Johannsen, Robert Schimmel, and Susan Norfleet. Shows are presented at 8 p.m. Sunday through Thursday, at 8 and 10:30 p.m. on Friday and Saturday.

At the **Comedy Gallery Uptown,** 2911 Hennepin Ave. S., Minneapolis, in the Williams Pub complex, the emphasis is on local talent. In fact, on Monday night, you're welcome to sign up for an opportunity to show off your own comedic skills on the open stage. Performances are Sunday through Thursday at 8 p.m., 8 and 10:30 p.m. on Friday and Saturday.

The same schedule applies at Scott Hanson's **Rib Tickler,** 716 N. 1st St., Minneapolis, where women comics, local and national, are featured.

At **Comedy Gallery East,** located at Day's Inn, Maplewood Mall, 1780 County Road D, Maplewood, performances by regional comics take place on weekends only, Friday and Saturday nights at 8 and 10:30 p.m.

The newest comedy gallery of all is located at St. Paul's Galtier Plaza, 5th and Jackson streets.

SPORTS AND RECREATION

Whatever the season, Twin Citians turn out in large, enthusiastic numbers to watch and participate in a wide variety of sporting events. With four major-league teams to support, fans find excitement and fun in superb sports facilities like the Metrodome in Minneapolis and the Civic Center in St. Paul. During the past few years they've enjoyed thoroughbred horseracing at suburban Canterbury Downs as well.

But Twin Citians don't spend all their time watching sporting events. They're participants too. What else would you expect in cities that pride themselves on their remarkable abundance of parks and lakes? Delightful walking and jogging, boating and swimming, golf and tennis, and a variety of wintertime activities enhance the quality of life hereabouts for residents who call St. Paul and Minneapolis home and for visitors who call the Twin Cities a great place to enjoy top-notch sports and recreation.

1. Spectator Sports

BIG-LEAGUE TEAMS

Minneapolis and St. Paul are big-league towns. With four professional sports teams to their credit, the Twin Cities are unique in the diversity of sports competition that they offer and the state-of-the-art facilities that are provided for them.

Home clubs include the **Minnesota Vikings** football team, **Minnesota Twins** baseball team, **Minnesota North Stars** hockey team, and the **Minnesota Timberwolves** basketball team. Tickets to Viking games are $23 for any seat, and can be obtained by writing to 500 11th Ave. S., Minneapolis (333-8828). Twins tickets range in price from $3 to $11. Write to 501 Chicago Ave. S., Minneapolis (375-1366). Timberwolves tickets range from $5.50 to $25. For specific information call 989-5151 or write Timberwolves Ticket Office, 500 City Place, 730 Hennepin Ave., Minneapolis.

As to sports facilities, consider that in downtown St. Paul each March, at the **Civic Center,** Kellogg and 7th Streets (tel. 224-7403), nearly a quarter of a million spectators come from everywhere to attend the Minnesota State High School League wrestling, basketball, and hockey tournaments. And that in suburban Bloomington, the **Metropolitan Sports Center,** 7901 Cedar Ave. (tel. 853-9310), plays host to fans who turn out for ever-popular North Star hockey.

Over in downtown Minneapolis, 1990 saw the opening of the brand-new **Timberwolves Arena,** designed to accommodate a wide variety of sports, musical, cultural, and family-entertainment events. Located in downtown Minneapolis at 1st Avenue North between 6th and 7th streets, this large and handsome complex is just two blocks away from the business district and a few blocks away from all the major highways that serve the area. (Parking for arena events, in two garages that connect to the arena via a skyway, costs $1.50.)

You'll find all manner of amenities, including giant, high-resolution color replay scoreboards and color monitors throughout the concourses, plus more restrooms and concession stands than at any other stadium in the country. (You want facts? How about 1 bathroom stall for every 45 patrons here, compared to the average 1 to 175 nationwide? As for concession areas—there are twice as many here as the average number elsewhere, which may or may not be good news.)

Certainly if you're looking for a health facility during your stay, you'll want to consider the Arena Health Club, with its racquetball, squash, and full-size basketball courts as well as a 75-foot-long swimming pool and a seven-lap-per-mile running/walking track. There are three aerobics studios here as well, among many other attractions. Clearly professional athletes won't be the only physically fit folks to be seen in the Timberwolves Arena.

But the **Hubert H. Humphrey Metrodome,** 5th Street and Chicago Avenue, Minneapolis (tel. 375-1116), is the area's most famous sports installation. Opened in 1982, this massive facility—it accommodates 55,000 baseball fans or 62,000 football fans—was really built with you in mind. Visitors enjoy knowing for certain that the baseball game they've come to see won't be rained out and that wintry blasts won't make their football viewing uncomfortable. Only the locals look back longingly on the pre-Metrodome days when tailgate parties, held in the vast suburban parking lot, were part of the fun to be found at outdoor Metropolitan Stadium on the Bloomington strip. In its downtown location on the eastern edge of Minneapolis, the Metrodome has no facilities for the convivial get-togethers that were virtually a ritual in these parts.

For better or worse, though—and you'll get lots of eloquent arguments on both sides—then was then and now is now, and there's a lot to be said for the comfort and convenience that's been engineered into the massive domed stadium.

Here are some of the plusses: The Metrodome is the world's first rectangular domed stadium, so the sightlines are particularly good. The domed ceiling is constructed of translucent material that lets in natural light; the claustrophobia that afflicts fans in other indoor facilities has been avoided here. And there are some technological wonders: a pitcher's mound that appears and disappears at the flip of a switch; a seating system that converts, in practically no time, from football to baseball and back again; and a main scoreboard above left-center field that transmits multiple messages and instant replays (auxiliary boards, strategically placed above first and third base and above right-center field, keep you in touch at all times with messages from the sophisticated scoreboard control room).

Games at the Metrodome tend to be well attended, and, especially if it's a Viking game you've got in mind, it's well to order your tickets in advance.

CANTERBURY DOWNS

After initial skepticism concerning the notion of thoroughbred horse racing in wholesome Minnesota, the "sport of kings" has recently turned out to be just what the commoners were waiting for. Since 1985, when Canterbury Downs first opened its gates at 901 County Road 83 in south-suburban Shakopee (tel. 445-7223), racing fans of all kinds and all ages have been turning out in surprising numbers. Horseracing is by now a big part of summertime fun for folks you might not expect to find at a racetrack.

Busloads of senior citizens can be seen arriving every Sunday, when there's no charge for those 60 years of age and older. Moms, dads, and the kids park nearby, then unload their station wagons and proceed to haul gear and provisions over to the trackside picnic area for their day at the races. Gas grills are available for those who like their picnic fare sizzling hot.

On nearly 400 acres, this facility includes not only stables, starting gates, and paddocks but also playgrounds where the youngest members of the family can amuse themselves and one another while their elders set out the good things to eat on picnic tables protected by canvas tents. Concession stands nearby can provide anything that somehow didn't get packed up and brought along. Parimutuel windows are conveniently close as well.

Actually, the whole day at Canterbury Downs can be spent in Shire Square, in the shadow of the grandstand and close to the railing, which many find the best place for watching the races. Up in the grandstands you'll find most of the 300 mutuel windows that have been conveniently placed on every level of the rambling three-story facility. You'll also find some of the more than 150 closed-circuit TV monitors that keep the action in full view should bettors be delayed in getting back to their seats.

Trackside bench seats are available without extra charge as part of the $3 price of general admission, and lawn chairs are welcome on the apron that separates the grandstand from the track railing.

For $5 you can reserve a seat in either the open-air or the glassed-in section of the grandstand. Reservations must be made by mail or in person. A reserved seat in the Clubhouse can be yours for $7.50. There's no admission charge for youngsters 17 and under, but they must be accompanied by their parents. You'll pay $2 for general parking, $4 for preferred parking, or $6 for valet parking.

All the trappings of any first-class racetrack are here at Canterbury Downs. Before each race begins you can size up the horses in the paddocks garden, get a closer look at them as they parade around the European-style walking ring, and then feel the pressure as the starting gates open to the announcer's cry, "And they're off!"

Reportedly, the most commonly placed bets are $2, so you can have an exciting time for about the same investment as you'd make in many other kinds of mass entertainment. The secret, of course, is to allow yourself no more money at the betting windows than you've set aside for betting before you get to the track.

The Canterbury Downs racing season usually runs from the last week of April to the first week of October. Post time for the first race is 7:15 p.m. Wednesday through Friday (racing until about 10:30 p.m.) and 1:30 p.m. on Saturday, Sunday, and holidays (racing until about 6 p.m.). Gates open at 6 p.m. on weekdays, at noon on weekends and holidays.

Getting to Canterbury Downs

Your hotel or motel may have bus transportation available to the track. If you prefer to drive out yourself, you'll find the going easy, but you should get an early start because the traffic tends to be heavy on weekends and holidays. Here are alternative routes from both Twin Cities.

From Minneapolis: Take I-35W south to Hwy. 13 and then proceed west; Hwy. 13 becomes Hwy. 101 before you complete the 5-mile stretch to the Canterbury exits. Or you can take I-494 west to Hwy. 169, then proceed south to Shakopee and go east on Hwy. 101 to the Canterbury exits.

From St. Paul: Take I-35E south to County Rd. 42 in Burnsville, then proceed west 11 miles to Canterbury Rd. and turn north to Canterbury Downs. Or take Cedar Avenue south to Hwy. 13 and proceed west; Hwy. 13 will become Hwy. 101 as you drive the 5 miles to the Canterbury Downs exits.

---

2. Tennis and Golf

Of course Twin Citians don't spend all their time watching sporting events—they're participants too.

TENNIS

The popularity of tennis in St. Paul and Minneapolis has grown during recent years, along with the growing number of indoor tennis courts. Now it's no longer necessary to pack away the racket when outdoor courts close for the season.

Private Clubs

Several local clubs offer guest rates to out-of-town visitors and offer discounts to those who can identify themselves as members of clubs affiliated with the International Racquet Sports Association of America (IRSA).

The tennis club visited by most out-of-towners is likely to be one of the five major facilities operated by **Northwest Racquet, Swim, & Health Clubs**, at 14600 Burnhaven Rd., Burnsville (tel. 435-7127); 6701 W. 78th St., Bloomington (tel. 835-3113); 1001 W. 98th St., Bloomington (tel. 884-1612); 4001 Lake Breeze Ave. N., Brooklyn Center (tel. 535-3571); and 5525 Cedar Lake Rd., St. Louis Park (tel. 546-6554). In addition to tennis courts, you'll find such features as swimming pools, running tracks, Nautilus and Universal weight equipment, and free-weight and aerobics rooms. The $15 guest fee admission charge for out-of-towners ($10 for those with an IRSA membership card) entitles visitors to full use of the club facilities. Hours are 5:45 a.m. to midnight, seven days a week.

The **Eagan Athletic Club,** 3330 Pilot Knob Rd., Eagan (tel. 454-8790), offers indoor tennis along with a variety of other activities, including swimming, racquetball, aerobics, cardiovascular equipment, Nautilus, whirlpool, and sauna. The admission fee of $5.30 entitles guests to use the club's assorted facilities. Tennis-court time costs $8 per hour per court. Tennis-ball machines are available at no extra charge. The club is open Monday through Thursday 6 a.m. to 11 p.m., Friday 6 a.m. to 10 p.m., Saturday and Sunday, 8 a.m. to 8 p.m.

There's no visitors' admission charge at the indoor courts of the **Nicollet Tennis Center,** 4005 Nicollet Ave., Minneapolis (tel. 825-6844). This privately leased installation stands on city-owned parkland and is therefore open to the public without charge. Court fees here vary according to time of year, with prices lower during outdoor-tennis months. From April 30 to September 1, you'll pay $8.40 per hour. The charge during the rest of the year is $11.40 per hour. The Nicollet Tennis Center is open seven days a week. Located in Martin Luther King Park, these well-maintained courts are among the most popular in the cities.

Public Courts

The seasonal fee scale at the Nicollet Tennis Center reflects the fact that when Twin Citians are able to play tennis outdoors, they tend to do so—and why not? With more than 200 free courts available, many located in picturesque parkland settings, it's no wonder that tennis is so popular an outdoor recreation in St. Paul and Minneapolis.

With more than 100 of these tennis courts located throughout the city of St. Paul, it would be impossible to list them here, but at **Phalen Park** you'll find popular courts at Johnson Parkway and Maryland Avenue, in a particularly beautiful location adjacent to Lake Phalen. Tennis play is on a first-come, first-served basis; posted signs urge that court time be limited to one hour if others are waiting. Tennis courts here are lit after dark, thanks to a control box that stops functioning at 11 p.m. In Minneapolis, only the Nicollet Tennis Center offers lighted courts.

Among the most beautifully located and popular courts in the Twin Cities are the ones you'll find in Minneapolis's **Kenwood Park,** at the north end of Lake of the Isles. The most centrally located Minneapolis courts may be the ones in **Loring Park,** at Hennepin Avenue and Harmon Place. On the edge of downtown Minneapolis, these courts have a view of Loring Lake and are only a footbridge away from the Guthrie Theater/Walker Art Center complex. For **information about municipal courts,** call the Park Board (tel. 348-2226 for courts in Minneapolis, 292-7400 for courts in St. Paul).

GOLF

There are more par-3 courses in the Twin Cities than in any other metropolitan area in the country, and visitors are often surprised not only by the number of busy courses in the area, but also by the excellent condition of the public greens. If golf is your game, here are a few courses for you to consider.

Private Clubs

The **Majestic Oaks Golf Course,** 701 Bunker Lake Blvd., Ham Lake (tel. 755-2142)—privately owned but open to the public—was rated among the top 50 American public golf courses by *Golf Digest.* Rates are $8.50 for 9 holes, $17 for 18 holes. Carts are available at $10 for the 9-hole course, $20 for the 18-hole course, and clubs can be rented for $4 (9 holes) or $7 (18 holes).

The **Braemar Golf Course,** 6364 Dewey Hill Rd., Edina (tel. 941-2072), has hosted many national tournaments, and recently converted its par-3 course into an executive 9-hole course. Rates are $6.25 for 9 holes. Rental carts cost $9 for 9 holes; club rental is $5.

Municipal Courses

The following are three of the area's best 18-hole municipal golf courses. Facilities include clubhouses, food service, lockers, and showers.

The **Francis A. Gross Golf Course** is at 2201 St. Anthony Blvd., Minneapolis (tel. 789-2542). Rates are $9.50 for 9 holes, $12 for 18 holes. Carts are available at $10.50 for 9 holes, $18 for 18 holes, and clubs can be rented at $6 for 9 or 18 holes.

At the **Meadowbrook Golf Course,** 300 Meadowbrook Rd., Hopkins (tel. 929-2077), rates are $9.50 for 9 holes and $12 for 18 holes. Rental carts are available at $10.50 for 9 holes, $18 for 18 holes, and clubs can be rented for $6 (18 holes), $3 (nine holes).

The **Hiawatha Golf Course,** 4553 Longfellow Ave. S., Minneapolis (tel. 724-7715), charges $9.50 for 9 holes, $12 for 18 holes. Carts are rented at $10.50 for 9 holes, $18 for 18 holes, and clubs are available for $6 (18 holes), $3 (nine holes).

In addition, the 18-hole public course in St. Paul's **Como Park** was completely renovated in 1986, and the 9-hole Como Park course remains one of the best around. Phone 488-7291 for information.

Brand-new is the **Edinburgh USA** golf course in Brooklyn Park, 8600 Edinbrook Crossing (tel. 424-7060). Green fees are $22.

---

3. In the City and Suburban Parks

Golf is extremely popular in the superb public parks that the Twin Cities boast, but golf is only a small part of what these parks have to offer in the way of recreation.

PARK ACTIVITIES

For walkers, joggers, and runners, there are more than 38 miles of designated bituminous parkland trails, and for bicyclists, 36 miles of bike paths. If you didn't bring your bike along, you can rent one, and if you like, a sailboat, canoe, fishing boat, or windsurfer as well. During the winter you'll find ice skating, snowshoeing, snowtubing, sledding, and skiing. In fact, those golf courses that prove so popular during the spring, summer, and fall, serve in winter as popular cross-country skiing sites.

Each of the Twin Cities' parks deserves a chapter of its own, but there's room here for just a mention of the fun to be found in some of them.

Call for further **information** about all the activities in local parks (tel. 348-2243 in Minneapolis, 488-7291 in St. Paul).

Water Sports

Whether they're gliding through Minneapolis's picturesque chain of lakes, skimming the expanses of St. Paul's lovely Lake Phalen, or winding through Minnehaha Creek, boats of all kinds are an everyday sight in many Twin Cities neighborhoods. If you want to go **canoeing,** you can literally paddle your way through these towns. For example, canoeists can start out in Minnetonka, then follow Minnehaha Creek from Gray's Bay through suburban Hopkins, St. Louis Park, and Edina, and then go on to a spot not far from the Mississippi River in Minneapolis. **AARCEE Recreational Rental,** 2900 Lyndale Ave. S., Minneapolis (tel. 827-5746), rents 15-foot Coleman canoes for $25 a day and 17-foot aluminum canoes for $30 a day, including life jackets, paddles, and car-top carriers. Some hardy sportsmen make the round trip in one outing; others arrange for a car to be waiting for them when they reach the end of the route.

Shorter outings are popular at Cedar Lake in Minneapolis, and canoes and rowboats can be rented at **Lake Calhoun** for $4.50 an hour (cash only). A particularly popular course here leads canoeists through the chain of lakes that extends from Lake Calhoun to Lake of the Isles and then to Cedar Lake. In St. Paul, you can canoe or row on **Lake Phalen** for $4.50 per hour with a $25 deposit and photo I.D.

Bright-hued sailboats are a familiar part of the summertime scenery in Minneapolis and St. Paul, where the next best thing to **sailing** is watching the graceful boats making their colorful way through local lakes. Sailboat races are a weekend event each summer at **Lake Nokomis,** at Cedar Avenue and 50th Street in South Minneapolis, but more leisurely boaters are welcome to enjoy the facilities as well. In fact, this is one of the three Minneapolis lakes designated for sailing; the other two are **Lake Harriet,** at Lake Harriet Parkway and William Berry Road, and **Lake Calhoun,** at 3000 E. Calhoun Parkway, off Lake Street.

If you'd like to try your own hand at sailing, or even **windsurfing** on one of the Twin Cities' most beautiful public lakes, head again for **Lake Phalen.** You'll reach the lake from an entrance at Wheelock Parkway and Arcade Street (Hwy. 61), or Maryland Avenue and Johnson Parkway. Awaiting you there at the boathouse will be sailboats and windsurfing boards for rent at $9.50 for the first hour and $6 for every hour thereafter. (A $25 deposit and a photo ID are required for rentals.) Hours are 10 a.m. to sundown.

Suburban **Lake Minnetonka,** the largest freshwater lake in the metropolitan area, is another favorite spot for sailing. In fact, this lake has been known for centuries as a uniquely beautiful recreational area. Dakota Indians favored it long before wealthy southerners traveled up the Mississippi River to spend their summers here. With the advent of the railroad, summer resorts began to appear. One of them, the Lafayette Hotel, built by railroad magnate James J. Hill, was among the most popular before it fell victim to fire; occupying that lakeside site today is the Lafayette Country Club. The more than 200 miles of shoreline around Lake Minnetonka is the site of some of the loveliest homes in Minnesota, while the lake plays host to some of the biggest and best recreational craft.

Want something to show for your day on the water? For **fishing,** try the lagoon in St. Paul's ever-popular Lake Phalen. You'll pay $4.50 to rent a fishing boat for the first hour, plus $2.50 for each additional hour (there's a $25 deposit on all boats, and you'll need a photo I.D.).

For more passive boating, you might enjoy a ride on an old paddlewheeler, the *Queen of the Lakes,* which will take you on a leisurely ride around Lake Harriet in about 25 minutes. The charge is $2 per person.

I'll end this rundown with the most basic water sport of all: **swimming.** In St. Paul, **Phalen Park** offers a lovely sandy beach, adjacent to walking and jogging paths and other park facilities. In Minneapolis, try the beach at **Cedar Lake. Thomas Beach,** at the south end of Lake Calhoun, is a favorite with Twin Cities visitors too. In suburban Eden Prairie, you'll find the popular **Round Lake Park** north of Hwy. 5 and west of Hwy. 4. And in northwest Bloomington, you'll enjoy **Bush Lake.** Exit onto Bush Lake Road from I-494, proceed south for about 1½ miles, and there you are.

Winter Sports

Here in the Twin Cities, the same lovely lakes and golf courses that provide so much fun during summer months become wintertime playgrounds for skiers, skaters, snowtubers, and other hale and hearty folks.

For serious **skiing,** experienced downhill skiers often head north to Duluth's Spirit Mountain during the winter (see Chapter XII, "Twin Cities Getaways"), but for beginning downhill skiers and for absolutely all cross-country skiers, there's a lot of fun to be had right here in the twin towns. At **Como Park** in St. Paul there's downhill skiing, with a ski lift and a chalet featuring light food service. In **Wirth Park,** snow machines are ready to help nature along whenever that turns out to be necessary. Cross-country skiing has long been popular here, but another lovely Twin Cities setting remains something of a secret. At **Crosby Farm Park,** with an entrance off Shepherd Road and Mississippi River Boulevard, cross-country skiers can imagine they're off somewhere in the remote wilderness as they traverse the trails under a canopy of trees, amid shrublined paths—truly an idyllic setting.

One of the big surprises of the past couple of winters was the enthusiastic response to **snowtubing** at Wirth Park, where "Winter at Wirth," a comprehensive program of snow-related activities, has attracted people from throughout the Twin Cities. Adults pay $3 daily, children $1 for an innertube that will whirl round and round even as they're sliding uncontrollably down the snowy hill.

You'll see **ice skating** on virtually all city and suburban lakes, at most of which warming houses provide a welcome and considerate touch.

SUBURBAN PARKS

By the way, don't overlook the many activities to be enjoyed in suburban parks. For example, you'll find skiing galore at Bloomington's **Hyland Hills** at 8800 Chalet Rd. (tel. 835-4604). Nine downhill runs serve skiers of different abilities; three triple-chair lifts and four rope tows will get you back up so you can start down all over again. The snow-making equipment there keeps the skiing prime, with or without the cooperation of nature. Ski packages including boots and poles are available at a total of $12. Lift tickets range from $6 to $14. Seniors can ski for half price at any time, and preschoolers under 3 ski free. The area is lighted for picturesque night skiing too.

WENDING YOUR WAY THROUGH THE PARKS

And then there's the always-popular recreation of walking or jogging or running through the parks of Minneapolis and St. Paul. Each park has its own distinctive attractions, and you'll glimpse them firsthand as you follow their foot and bicycle paths through some of the loveliest settings in any city anywhere. Since this is all new to you, you may find yourself straying from the straight and narrow, taking time to explore more closely some of the picturesque places that you pass.

Lake Harriet, 42nd Street West and Lake Harriet Parkway, is famous hereabouts for its exquisite flower gardens, an All-American Rose Selection test bed foremost among them. But there's a beautiful iris garden here too, as well as special areas for seasonal and perennial flowers. And across the street is the fascinating Lake Harriet Rock Garden, which was reconstructed in 1984–85, more than 50 years after it was first created on the site. It includes a "peace garden" with rocks from Nagasaki, Japan.

In **Wirth Park,** the largest in the Minneapolis park system, you'll see the Eloise Butler Wildflower Garden and Bird Sanctuary. This 20-acre garden features plants native to Minnesota. Exhibits of prairie and woodland plant life are labeled. The serenity of these gardens is enjoyed by an incredible variety of birds that add their own delightful dimension to this lovely setting, just minutes away from busy downtown Minneapolis.

Como Park is the largest park in St. Paul and reportedly the most popular in the entire Twin Cities area. Most frequently visited is its free zoo, which welcomes between 850,000 and 1,000,000 visitors a year. Another stellar attraction is the Como Park Conservatory, an enclosed structure where plants from all over the world are exhibited year round. Many's the wedding that's been conducted here in the most exquisite setting imaginable. Built at the turn of the century, the Conservatory features a succession of flower shows and other events that draw visitors in very great numbers. The recently renovated 18-hole golf course now boasts a brand-new clubhouse, and down by the lake there's a popular pavilion where plays and concerts are presented.

Lake Como is a year-round attraction, of course, with canoes and paddleboats for rent during the summer and both ice-skating and speed-skating programs available during the winter months. Landscaped and lighted bike and walking paths are much used by visitors. Baseball diamonds, swimming pools, and picnic pavilions are busy places too. An amusement area with miniature-golf course, merry-go-round, occasional pony rides, and other delights for the young and the young at heart is located at Como Park.

THE MINNESOTA ZOO

At the Minnesota Zoo, 12101 Johnny Cake Ridge Rd., Apple Valley (tel. 432-9000), the terrain has been carefully created to resemble the hilly grasslands and woodlands of the wild animals that now make their home here. What may be the world's most remarkable cross-country skiing takes place in the Minnesota Zoo, where, for the price of admission—$4 for adults, $2 for seniors, $1.50 for ages 6 through 16, plus $1 per car for parking, $5 per van—you glide within full view of camels, Siberian tigers, Asiatic wild horses, moose, snow monkeys, musk oxen, red pandas, and more.

The Minnesota Zoo is, of course, a year-round recreation attraction for Twin Citians and visitors to these parts. It's open Monday through Saturday from 10 a.m. to 6 p.m., 10 a.m. through 8 p.m. Sundays. Six separate "trails" offer education so entertainingly that you won't even realize how much you've learned until you've left the 480-acre site, approximately half an hour from downtown Minneapolis and St. Paul.

The **Tropics Trail** is one of the most exotic areas of the zoo, an indoor oasis of plants and animals from far-away tropical areas. This is the largest structure in the zoo, with more than 650 animals and

15,000 plants of 500 different varieties—a fascinating environment in which crowds move slowly and thoughtfully through paths alive with the sounds of rushing water and fluttering birds.

The **Minnesota Trail** features animals indigenous to these parts, but they're more clearly visible and accessible here than in the wild, of course. A beaver pond, one of the highlights of this extraordinary zoo, provides amazing evidence of the inborn engineering know-how of these industrious creatures. Other native Minnesotans in indoor, outdoor, daylight, and nocturnal settings include otters, lynx, weasels, and an assortment of creatures hailing from Minnesota's lakes, prairies, and forests.

The **Discovery Trail** will introduce you to some unlikely new friends. Visited with a tarantula lately? Or a sea star? You'll have the opportunity for close encounters with these and other unusual beings in the **Zoo Lab.** And you'll be able to watch an intriguing bird show, ride a camel or an elephant, pet a goat, and enjoy other hands-on experiences in one of the most deservedly popular of all the areas here.

On the three-quarter-mile **Northern Trail,** you'll be surrounded by northern types like tigers, Asian lions, coyotes, musk oxen, camels, wild horses, and moose. And you'll get to meet what may be your first-ever pronghorn, a graceful antelope look-alike.

The **Sky Trail** is an option you can enjoy for an additional $2 per passenger (children under 5 ride free). This monorail weaves in and out of hills and lakelands as you view wild terrain and listen to "nature narratives" provided by knowledgeable guides.

Getting to the Zoo

To reach the Minnesota Zoo from Minneapolis by car, take the Cedar Avenue Expressway south to Apple Valley, then follow the signs directing you to the zoo. From St. Paul, take I-35E to the Cedar Avenue Expressway and follow the directions above.

On weekends and on the third Tuesday of every month you can take the no. 57 bus from any bus stop on Marquette Street in downtown Minneapolis. Buses leave at 9:30 and 11:05 a.m., and return back downtown from the zoo at 1:20 and 3 p.m. Fares are $1.50 for adults, 70¢ for children 6 through 17; kids under 6 ride free.

PARKS ENTERTAINMENT

There is a wide range of entertainment available in the area's parks. Let me give you an idea of what will be available to you if you're in the Twin Cities during the summer months. Much of what's being offered each activity-filled season comes as a surprise to locals as well as to visitors.

At **Nicollet Island Park,** adjacent to historic St. Anthony Falls, you'll find a **picnic area** on a large deck overlooking the Mississippi River. Not far from the bridge that connects the island to Riverplace, the **Durkee Atwood Building,** a historic industrial structure, serves as a large picnic building in case of inclement weather.

Boom Island Park, connected to Nicollet Island by a railroad bridge, was dedicated during the summer of 1987 and opened officially in the summer of 1988. It offers a boat-launching dock into the Mississippi. Picnic tables are available here too.

As for outdoor summertime entertainment, a glimpse of the past offers a glimpse at the future. During June, July, and August 1990, for example, **Nicollet Island** offered **instrumental music** seven nights a week by groups as diverse as the Latin Jazz Combo and the Minneapolis Pops Orchestra, the singing Sweet Adelines and the Minnesota Dance Alliance. On Sunday, July 22, there was a fireworks salute to the Aquatennial celebration. (Fireworks were set off on July 4, too.)

At **Lake Harriet,** during the summer of 1990 you could have heard the St. Anthony Civic Orchestra, the Linden Hills Chamber Players, and the Goodtime Gospel Quartet, among many many other talented groups.

And at Lake Harriet, Loring Park, Powderhorn Park, and Boom Island, among others, you'd have been delighted by perennially popular **theater companies.** The Comedy Troupe offered *Off the Wall and Into the Frying Pan,* the Minnesota Shakespeare Company presented *Julius Caesar* and *Twelfth Night,* the Commedia Theatre offered 3 tales for children, the Outcast Players Theatre offered *Spreading the News,* a comedy by Irish playwright Lady Gregory, and a troupe called En Garde Unlimited! performed swashbuckling swordplay.

Of course, this isn't nearly all that you'll find by way of sports and recreation in the Twin Cities, but it's enough to prove that there's truly something for every taste. What's most exciting about it all is the opportunity to expand your taste by trying new forms of entertainment, thanks to the wide diversity available.

TWIN CITIES SHOPPING

1. SOUTHDALE
2. OTHER SHOPPING CENTERS
3. CHOICE SHOPPING NEIGHBORHOODS
4. SHOPPING MISCELLANY

An American Revolution got under way in the Twin Cities back in October 1956, when the country's first fully enclosed, climate-controlled suburban shopping mall—Southdale—opened its doors to a somewhat skeptical public.

1. Southdale

There were lots of unanswered questions at the time. Would there really be enough business in the quiet community of Edina to support two of the Twin Cities' largest department stores? At Southdale, the Twin Cities' version of Macy's and Gimbels became the first competing department stores in America ever to locate under one roof. In addition to these blockbusters, 64 specialty shops had leased space in the center. Well and good, but after the initial novelty wore off, would customers revert to their long-established shopping patterns, leaving the mall a fully enclosed, climate-controlled suburban ghost town?

Not a bit of it! Today, more than 30 years after that grand opening, Dayton's and Carson Pirie Scott face each other across Southdale's busy courtyard, while since 1972 a third department store, J. C. Penney, has been doing a brisk business elsewhere in the center. And the 64 specialty shops that seemed such a phenomenal number in 1956 will have grown to 190 by August 1992.

Located at 66th Street and France Avenue in the southern Minneapolis suburb of Edina, Southdale is south of crosstown Hwy. 62, north of I-494, and between I-35W and Hwy. 100. In addition to the three big-name department stores—Dayton's, Carson's, and J. C. Penney—Southdale houses nationally known shops like Peck and Peck, Eddie Bauer, Ann Taylor, Gantos, and Florsheim. But what may interest you more are the dozens of specialty shops with less-familiar names that feature fine apparel, jewelry, toys, mementoes, and more. You'll also find a self-service post office here, along with a Northwest Airlines ticket office, and two one-hour photo-processing shops.

Southdale's success has been contagious. The undeveloped land that surrounded its 84-acre site now houses a wide variety of medical, commercial, and governmental agencies. Southdale Medical Center and Fairview Southdale Hospital stand just one block away, across busy 66th Street. Southdale Square offers its own shopping features nearby. And a powerful magnet, the bountifully stocked Southdale-Hennepin Area Library of Edina, with its extensive book and audio-visual holdings, is within a short walking distance. So are some of the Twin Cities' most desirable condominium apartment complexes.

One of Southdale's greatest claims to fame is the manner in which it has integrated itself into the surrounding community. For example, at 7:30 a.m. Monday through Saturday, and at 10:30 a.m. on Sunday, long before the shops open for business, members of the Southdale Walking Program arrive to track their course along designated routes. At 8:30 a.m. on the fourth Tuesday of each month, doctors and other medical personnel from Fairview Southdale Hospital conduct seminars in the Southdale Community Room on subjects of local concern—exercise, diet, cancer awareness, stress reduction, etc.

At other times the center plays host to book fairs, musical programs, symphony balls, and demonstrations of every kind (phone 925-7885 for information).

It's been said that shopping centers are today's version of yesterday's town square. Southdale, the granddaddy of all of America's shopping malls, is that and more. Maybe because it was for so long the only mall of its kind here, a whole generation of shoppers grew up wearing the clothes and playing with the toys that came from Southdale. For these and many other Twin Citians, Southdale remains to this day simply the most natural, most comfortable place to go shopping.

For these and many other Twin Citians, Dayton's department store at Southdale had become almost synonymous with the center as a whole. That's why its closing in August 1990 came as something of a shock. But any sense of loss was short-lived, because two days later a splendid new Dayton's opened right next door at 66th Street and France Ave. S. in a strikingly beautiful four-story building.

The greatly enlarged new space made possible a variety of welcome innovations here, including a full-service Estee Lauder Spa (See Chapter XII, "Twin Cities Getaways"), complimentary coat checking, and a drive-through parcel-pickup area accommodating six cars at one time.

Serving as a backdrop to the dramatic display of top-quality merchandise throughout the elegant Southdale Dayton's are striking works of art, including three allegorical murals executed by Evergreen, a New York-based painting studio (the studio's Twin-Cities-born staff artist Dean Kalomas returned home to participate in this assignment). In one of the lovely murals, an assemblage of winged figures, accented in gold leaf and silver, hover over the second-floor perfume department. On the dome ceiling that's visible from all four floors of the store, Neptune rises from the sea while Apollo races against the setting sun.

And what's become of the old familiar Dayton's? It's been put to good use as the home of some 50 specialty shops that add further interest and variety to the one-and-only Southdale.

---

2. Other Shopping Centers

Southdale may be the oldest of the malls, but there are by now nearly 200 other shopping centers hereabouts. And while it's impossible, of course, to tell you about all of them, here are a few of the many popular places that Twin Citians have to choose from.

Shopping hours generally are 10 a.m. to 9 p.m. Monday through Friday, 9:30 a.m. to 6 p.m. on Saturday, and noon to 5 p.m. on Sunday. During holiday periods, shopping hours are usually extended.

GALLERIA

Located at 69th Street and France Avenue, a block south of Southdale (tel. 925-4321), is a fashionable upscale center with 60 shops and restaurants, many of which are run by the people who own them. The setting is picturesque, with lush greenery, soft lighting, and cobblestone walkways. You'll find stores specializing in handbags, books, swimwear, furs, cookwear, dolls, gourmet foods, pottery, and a great deal more. When Galleria advertises a sale, *run* do not walk. At other times, be advised that prices—and quality—tend to be high, although as one entrepreneur recently pointed out, you can buy a $9 sweater here as well as a $30,000 mink coat.

RIDGEDALE

Located on Hwy. 12 (Wayzata Boulevard), one mile east of I-494 in the western suburb of Minnetonka (tel. 541-4864), Ridgedale first opened in August 1974 with two anchor department stores, Dayton's and Donaldsons. Five months later J.C. Penney and Sears moved in as well. A graceful fountain stands among palm trees in the skylit center court. Four sections extend in a pinwheel pattern that contains more than 130 specialty shops representing national and local retailers. A sidewalk café is one of the 11 restaurants and snackbars here. Unlike many other suburban malls, Ridgedale contains a Woolworth's variety store.

A program sponsored by Methodist Hospital and Ridgedale Center enables "morning milers" to walk year round without concern for the weather. The center opens its doors to walkers at 7 a.m. Monday through Saturday and at 9 a.m. on Sunday.

BONAVENTURE

This small, picturesque shopping center (tel. 925-4321) is located adjacent to Ridgedale at Plymouth Road and Hwy. 12 (Wayzata Boulevard). There's no anchor department store at Bonaventure, but there is one of Leeann Chin's phenomenally popular Chinese buffets, and that may be just as good. Whatever the reason, this beautifully designed mall is a popular place, with its 40 specialty shops clustered around a fountain and glass elevator.

There's a high concentration of women's fashions and accessories here, along with shops that feature classic and contemporary furnishings, toys, gifts, and artwork. Another attraction here is the summer dining in the garden court.

BANDANA SQUARE

Situated north of I-94, between Snelling Avenue and Lexington, not far from Como Park and the State Fair Grounds, Bandana Square (tel. 642-1509) is an interesting blend of the old and the new. The buildings that house this St. Paul collection of specialty shops, eating places, and recreational areas are listed on the National Register of Historic Places. That's because these were previously the Como Shops, where Burlington Northern Railroad coaches and locomotives were maintained at the turn of the century, the period when railroading was a dominant force in the Midwest. Exposed beams, skylights, and even railroad tracks are reminders of those times, and serve as an interesting setting for more than 30 retail and dining places, and for the ambitious and highly appropriate project of the Twin City Model Railroad Club. In their own section of the upper level of Bandana Square, railroad-club members are re-creating the railroading era of long ago with what eventually will be 1,800 feet of track, accommodating four main lines on which ten model trains can travel at one time. This is, in fact, a popular parking place for fathers and their young, while the women of Twin Cities families make the rounds of shops that feature fashions, furnishings, and gifts, many of them appropriate souvenirs of Minnesota.

Outdoor dining and band concerts are popular warm-weather attractions at Bandana Square, and so is the nearby Children's Museum, in a historic building that used to be a blacksmith shop.

CALHOUN SQUARE

In the trendy Uptown section of Minneapolis (also known as "Yuptown"), you'll find Calhoun Square at the corner of Hennepin Avenue and Lake Street (tel. 824-1240). This is a bustling two-story center where the shopping, dining, and people-watching are among the best anywhere. If the weather's warm, try for a sidewalk table outside **Figlio's,** the popular Italian restaurant recommended in Chapter IV. During recent years there's been a picturesque influx of punkers in this area. Expect to see everything from mohawks to multicolored hairdos.

There are three galleries here featuring works of local artists, one of the cities' best bookstores, **Odegard Books** (tel. 825-0336), and more than 70 other shops and restaurants, including the **Ediner** (an upscale "diner") (tel. 822-6011) and **Tony Roma's** (tel. 824-RIBS).

---

3. Choice Shopping Neighborhoods

GRAND AVENUE

This specialty shopping and ethnic dining area in St. Paul has gained enormous popularity during recent years with young up-wardly mobile professional types much like the ones who inhabit the Uptown area of Minneapolis. Turn-of-the-century residences abound here, many of them now serving as condominiums, town houses, and rental apartments.

How specialized are the specialty shops on Grand Avenue? Well, you'll find the **Balloon Bunch** here at 638 Grand Ave. (tel. 292-0289), where you can order balloons sent out singly or by the dozen(s). Or you can come in and pick out the balloon of your choice from a variety of sizes and colors.

You probably won't be in town long enough to need the **Wedding Shop,** 1196 Grand Ave. (tel. 298-1144), but many local folks find this one-stop service invaluable, with absolutely everything taken care of, starting with the invitations.

One of the Twin Cities' favorite markets is here on Grand Avenue too: **Crocus Hill Market,** 674 Grand Ave. (tel. 228-1761), with grocery shelves on one side and a meat showcase on the other. Rolling ladders date back to 1900. This might be the place to find some picnic provisions before an afternoon or evening at one of St. Paul's delightful parks.

If you'd rather dine out at one of Grand Avenue's many popular restaurants, try the informal **Café Latte** at 850 Grand Ave. (tel. 224-5983). Café Latte is famous for made-from-scratch soups, breads, sandwiches, salads, and desserts. And if it's Greek food you favor, the **Acropol** awaits at 748 Grand Ave. (tel. 298-0151), one of the most popular dining spots in either town.

There are two popular **shopping malls** on Grand Avenue: Victoria Crossing, 857 Grand Avenue, and Milton Mall at Milton and Grand. That's where you'll find shops like **Old Mexico Shop** (tel. 293-3907), with lovely imports from across the Rio Grande, and the **Coat of Many Colors,** at 1666 Grand Ave. (tel. 690-5255), with some of the most unusual clothing around.

Whether or not you actually buy anything during your visit to Grand Avenue, the browsing is bound to be memorable.

DOWNTOWN MINNEAPOLIS

The Conservatory at 808 Nicollet Mall, Minneapolis, (tel. 332-4649), is a remarkable new shopping center opened in the fall of 1987, and chances are you've never seen anything quite like it.

Designed as a "20th-century public square," the Conservatory incorporates the activity outside the block-long building with the activity within. Passersby on the picturesque Nicollet Mall can glimpse two dramatic four-story glass atriums, two gracefully winding staircases, an abundance of decorative trees, a ground-floor dining court, and more. And at the same time, of course, the activity taking place on the Nicollet Mall is visible to those within.

Custom-made for the site it occupies, the Conservatory is consciously designed to contrast with suburban malls, which generally would look out, if they could, on hundreds of cars in crowded parking lots. But here the decorative Nicollet Mall serves as a living mural for those looking out through the rose-colored glass walls of the Conservatory.

Connected by skyway and by underground "serpentine" to Dayton's, one of the city's premiere department stores, the Conservatory offers enticing wares of its own. Among the upscale retailers located here is the fabulous **F.A.O. Schwarz** toy store, a veritable wonderland for children and their elders. Also present are the **Sharper Image,** a shop filled with wondrous electronic gadgetry, and the **Nature Company** with unique gifts for you and those you left at home. A local firm that chose to locate at the Conservatory is **Frost and Bud,** a specialty gift shop well known to shoppers in fashionable Wayzata on Lake Minnetonka. What souvenirs you'll discover here! Want to take home a set of bocce balls, a sundial, or a personalized birdhouse? The Conservatory can offer you these—and a whole lot more.

The opening of the Conservatory added to the diversity of fine shops already located in downtown Minneapolis in nearby **City Center** (tel. 372-1234) and the **IDS Crystal Court** (tel. 372-1660). Here are some others.

It's been nearly 90 years since **Dayton's** department store first began doing business under that name at 7th Street and Nicollet Avenue in downtown Minneapolis. The store that first opened on that site in 1902 was named Goodfellow's, but a year later George Draper Dayton bought the business and named it Dayton Dry Goods Co. In 1910 the name was changed to the Dayton Company and now there are 37 Dayton's stores in all. But none does as much business as the one that started it all.

During the past months, Dayton's has embarked on a program of remodeling and enlarging a number of its stores, including the ones in suburban Edina, Burnsville Center, and Roseville. And by fall 1991 work will be completed on restoring the downtown store to its original appearance. The ornamental railing and cornice of the original structure store will be rebuilt, for example. But the interior of the downtown Dayton's will undoubtedly remain as up-to-the-minute as any store in the country. If you can't find what you're looking for at one Dayton's, chances are it's waiting to be sent to you from one of the others. And if none of the Dayton's stores has what you're looking for, better reconsider whether you really want it after all.

Carson Pirie Scott, on the Nicollet Mall across 6th Street from Dayton's, is a relative newcomer to the Twin Cities, but it's become a favorite with many of us who'd shopped for a very long time at Donaldson's, the department store that originally occupied the sites that now bear Carson's name. The quality here is high, the selection wide, the service attentive, and the prices competitive. With stores in both downtown Minneapolis and downtown St. Paul and in many suburban areas, Carson's has quickly become an integral part of the shopping scene here in the Twin Cities.

Gaviidae Common, on 6th Street, directly across the Nicollet Mall from Carson Pirie Scott, is an elegant downtown shopping complex whose list of tenants reads like a retailing who's who: Burberry's of London, Rodier of Paris, Laurel of Munich, Cactus of Montreal, Lillie Rubin of Florida, Brentano's of Connecticut, Westminster Lace and Eddie Bauer of Washington, Ann Klein and Saks Fifth Avenue of New York. Their presence here indicates a real commitment to the Twin Cities and, in fact, to Minnesota as a whole. In fact, the name "Gaviidae"—Latin for "loon"—pays tribute to the state bird of Minnesota. And a 20-foot wood and metal loon emerging from a pool of water provides a focal point for the magnificent five-level atrium here. Topping the atrium is a barrel-vault ceiling 42 feet in diameter, representing a northern starry sky. (Specially designed lighting illuminates the painted ceiling at night; natural light, entering through a skylight, provides illumination during the day.)

You'll see for yourself that Gaviidae Common is a distinguished addition to the achievements of famed architect Cesar Pelli. And you'll understand why we Twin Citians are so pleased to have it here.

DOWNTOWN ST. PAUL

St. Paul has its own array of fine shops at **Town Court, Town Square,** and **Carriage Hill,** where savvy shoppers find a lot to choose from.

---

4. Shopping Miscellany

Bargain hunters have their own special places, some of them already known beyond these borders. There's **Loehmann's** in suburban Bloomington (tel. 835-2510) for discount designer fashions, and the **Burlington Coat Factory** in St. Louis Park (tel. 929-6850) for a lot more than coats. You'll find a very wide variety of clothing for the whole family here, with periodic arrivals of ultrasuede apparel at very good prices.

A SPECIAL SUPERMARKET

You won't want to leave the Twin Cities without a visit to **Byerly's,** 3777 Park Center Blvd. in suburban St. Louis Park (tel. 929-2100), one of the world's most unusual supermarkets and, in fact, a self-contained shopping center par excellence.

Retailers from throughout the world travel to the Twin Cities regularly to tour the flagship of Don Byerly's local chain of nine supermarkets. What's all the fuss about? When you've seen one super-market, haven't you seen them all? Not quite. In contrast with the usual supermarket, which carries 15,000 to 18,000 items, Byerly's carries over 25,000. And that includes everything from catsup for 25¢ to mustard for $25 (it's a French Dijon packaged in a ceramic jar, in case you're curious). That's not the only import here of course. There are some very special items in the Gift Gallery, where collectibles are available at prices ranging from $10 for small hand-carved wooden animals to $75,000 for a gold-plated six-foot-tall bird cage. Laliques and Hummels are sold here too; so are imported women's accessories by Judith Leiber, whose snakeskin belts go for $50 to $300.

Services as well as goods are available at Byerly's. Particularly popular is the on-site cooking school, with classes in everything from ethnic to microwave to couples' cooking. Other services include the opportunity to consult with representatives of the Hummel factory, who arrive from Germany about once each year for a week of demonstrations, with time out to appraise Hummel pieces that customers may already own.

News of these and other classes and services is published in the in-house publication called *Byerly's Bag*. Each month 75,000 of these are printed and left on racks near the entrances of the stores. They go fast.

How this all got started could hardly be a shorter, simpler story. Don Byerly decided in the late 1960s to find out what people liked and didn't like about shopping—and then to do something about it. Hence the 24-hour day at Byerly's, a store that's open at everybody's convenience. And hence the understated but very considerate touches: low lighting, wide carpeted aisles, on-site restaurants, and on-site delicatessens and salad bars for quick and easy food to go.

In 1990, Don Byerly retired from involvement in the running of his stores, but shoppers aren't likely to notice any difference because members of senior management have taken over day-to-day operation of Byerly's supermarkets.

Whether you're seeking supplies for a lakeside picnic or a souvenir to take home from this visit to the Twin Cities, chances are you'll find just the thing at Byerly's. If not, mention it to a member of the staff. It'll be here by the time you come back.

THE WORLD TOMORROW

And now for a few words about a future addition to Twin Cities shopping—three words, actually, "Mall of America." Scheduled to open in suburban Bloomington in the fall of 1992, this mammoth complex will, we're told, take its place at once as the largest integrated retail and entertainment complex in the entire country with 1,000 hotel rooms, 8 department stores, 400 specialty shops, a family theme park, and a saltwater aquarium.

There'll reportedly be over 12,000 parking spaces available here, all of them free, so folks like you from distant places can more easily come see the Mall of America for yourselves. Construction is well underway, just as some of today's most celebrated Twin Cities sites and sights were still on the drawing board when the last edition of this guide went to press—Gavidae Common, the Conservatory, and the Sculpture Garden to name just three. All of these have, in a short time, become prominent parts of life hereabouts, so why not the Mall of America? Wait and see.

BOOKS

No Twin Cities shopping chapter would be complete without mention of our abundance of bookstores. We have the distinction of being home to the first-ever **B. Dalton Bookseller,** which opened in suburban Edina back in 1966 and changed the face of American bookselling forever. There are by now nearly two dozen B. Dalton Booksellers in this area. Add to that eight **Waldenbooks** stores and you'll see that people hereabouts do a lot of reading.

But independent bookstores are popular and successful in these parts as well. The **Hungry Mind,** 1648 Grand Ave., St. Paul (tel. 699-0587), boasts an extraordinary selection of books and a relaxed ambience featuring easy chairs and couches. Table of Contents, a recently opened café, shares these premises with Hungry Mind, so there's more than food for thought to be found here. Try coffee, pastries, and three meals a day.

Two other busy independents, **Odegard Books,** 3001 Hennepin Ave. (tel. 825-0336), and **Orr Books,** 3043 Hennepin Ave. (tel. 823-2408), are located just a few doors apart in Minneapolis's Uptown area. (There are two more Odegard stores in the area, one in suburban Edina and one in International Market Square in downtown Minneapolis.) You'll also find a great selection of children's books at **Red Balloon,** 891 Grand Ave. (tel. 224-8320), St. Paul.

Finally, just to remind you that this is cutting-edge territory, in September 1990, **Barnes & Noble** opened the first of its projected "superstore" bookstores in Roseville, a Twin Cities suburb.

This list is admitted incomplete, but it should be enough to give you some idea of the diversity of offerings among the booksellers of this area.

FESTIVALS AND FAIRS

What's so amazing about the fairs and festivals in Minneapolis and St. Paul is the number that are recordbreakers of one kind or another.

The Minneapolis Aquatennial, for example, is the largest summertime civic celebration in the United States. And the St. Paul Winter Carnival ranks first among the nation's annual salutes to winter.

The Minnesota State Fair, after more than 100 years, is still the largest 12-day fair in the United States, and after nearly 20 years, the Renaissance Festival is the country's largest.

Taste of Minnesota, born in 1983, is still a fledgling, but it, too, is well on its way to establishing its own national records.

Whatever the season, the fairs and festivals in the Twin Cities are perennially popular with home folks and visitors alike. You'll enjoy them too.

1. The Minnesota State Fair

For more than 100 years the annual Minnesota State Fairs have been identified with the city of St. Paul, but it wasn't always thus. These gala end-of-summer get-togethers began as territorial fairs that brought mid-19th-century farm families together to display their prize products and to enjoy final festivities before the long, cold winter set in.

The first official Minnesota State Fair was held in 1859, one year after Minnesota was named a state. For the next 25 years this annual event was moved from city to city until the Minnesota Agricultural Society, governing body of the Minnesota State Fair, began considering suggestions that a single permanent site be found.

Not surprisingly, it was the two largest and most influential cities, Minneapolis and St. Paul, that ended as finalists in the ensuing competition. A fierce battle burst out between the Twin Cities and finally the issue was brought to the legislature, where oratory flourished while action stalled.

But back in those simpler times it was possible for the Ramsey County Board of Commissioners to hold a secret meeting with the State Agricultural Society and to make them an offer they couldn't refuse: St. Paul was willing to make a gift of its 200-acre Poor Farm to the society as a permanent home for the Minnesota State Fair. Of course the cost of maintaining the Poor Farm had become something of a burden, and many of the city fathers welcomed the chance to be rid of this nonproductive land that lay more than two miles from downtown, but these considerations apparently didn't come up during the discussions.

The Agricultural Society accepted St. Paul's offer without great objection from Minneapolis. After all, the Poor Farm was about equidistant from both downtowns, so if Minneapolis wasn't going to get the State Fair within its own city limits, neither was St. Paul—not then, at least.

By now St. Paul has expanded to the very edge of the State Fair site, as those early St. Paul commissioners must have expected it would. What they couldn't have expected is that one century later this would be the largest 12-day state fair in the country, and the model for all other festivals of its kind. Unlike most other fair sites, these grounds now extend over nearly 300 acres of well-kept lawns and trees, with large, spacious permanent buildings on paved streets that offer easy access to a great array of activities. And the fairgrounds offer a varied program of events, not just at fair time but all year round.

Although any Minnesota schoolchild can tell you that the State Fair takes place at the end of summer, just before school vacation ends, had you visited the Twin Cities during the spring and summer of 1990, you could have attended a number of events at the fairgrounds. In May, a country-art show and sale were among the activities there; in June there was a national screen printers' sale; and in July a variety of Olympic Festival equestrian events were conducted.

Many of the events at the Minnesota State Fair are, of course, farm related, and involve the judging of crops and livestock, but many others are of more interest to nonfarmers, including those innocents who take it for granted that produce grows in supermarkets. For fair-goers of this type, the live entertainment in the Grandstand is probably one of the greatest attractions.

One of the very biggest changes in the activities at the Minnesota State Fair came about with the turn-of-the-century introduction of gas lighting. Now it was possible to extend events beyond daylight hours. Fireworks, vaudeville, and other forms of evening entertainment became an important part of the program then, and remain so to this day.

There are four stages on the fairgrounds, with daily free shows offering everything from comedy to mime to music to variety shows. And for an extra charge, the Grandstand features a galaxy of nationally known entertainers. Past performers include a who's who of contemporary entertainment: Bob Hope, Rodney Dangerfield, John Denver, Willie Nelson, Tom Jones, Charley Pride, Ronnie Milsap, and the Oak Ridge Boys, among many others.

But the most consistently popular attractions at the fair are exhibits. More than $400,000 in cash prizes lures entrants in a wide variety of competitions. The largest juried art show in the state takes place here each year, with winning works exhibited in the Fine Arts Building during the fair. Prizewinning works of needlecraft and carpentry are displayed in the Creative Activities Building, while outstanding school projects and technological exhibits can be seen in the Education Building.

One of the best-attended exhibitions during the past 50 years has been the one established by the Department of Natural Resources, which maintains a display of state minerals and animals in a giant log cabin.

Food is an important part of fair-going, of course—not only the hot dogs, french fries, snowcones, "Tom Thumb" minidonuts, and other goodies you get at busy concession stands, but the down-home meals available at dining halls staffed by various churches, where you can get a full dinner at very nominal cost. Many fair-goers bring their own picnic baskets along and take advantage of picnic facilities on the grounds.

The midway is a must, of course, and you won't want to miss the marching bands, floats, and parades that pass by. If you prefer viewing motor sports, you'll enjoy the auto races or the truck-and-tractor pulls. And, of course, rodeos and horse shows are always well attended.

Maybe by now you're getting the idea that there's a lot to be seen and done at the Minnesota State Fair, but it's important to remember that first and foremost this is an event that salutes the agriculture of Minnesota. Take time to visit some of the prize-winning examples of the work being done by present and future farmers of Minnesota. They'll remind you how much we owe to an industry that's too often taken for granted.

The Minnesota State Fair is held midway between the downtowns of St. Paul and Minneapolis; take I-94 from either city to the Snelling Avenue exit and go north about half a mile. The festivities take place around the end of August and the very beginning of September, ending each year on Labor Day. It's traditionally regarded as the official end of summer in Minnesota. Admission to the fair is $4 for those 13 to 64 years old, $2.50 for children 5 to 12. There's no entrance charge for children under 5. Those 65 and over pay

$2.50. Parking anywhere on the grounds is free. For information, phone 612/642-2200.

2. The St. Paul Winter Carnival

The oldest winter carnival in the United States came into being back in 1886, after a New York newspaperman published stories about his visit to the bone-chilling wasteland of wintry Minnesota. Far from dignifying these reports with a defense of the local climate, St. Paulites chose to organize a celebration of the fun to be found amid the snow and ice.

From this defiant beginning, the St. Paul Winter Carnival has grown into an exuberant 12-day annual festival that features more than 100 events including parades, snowtubing, hot-air-balloon rides, ice-carving contests, treasure hunts, and assorted team sports, from volleyball and touch football in the snow to softball, "snow golf," and auto racing on ice. The specific dates of the frosty gala vary from year to year, but it takes place roughly from the end of January through early February. Phone 612/297-6953 for carnival information.

Among the 1989 St. Paul Winter Carnival events that drew the largest crowds were a softball tournament played on the ice that involved 200 teams from throughout the nation. Then there was the kite-flying festival, in which over 3,000 people flew kites that had been provided to them free of charge. (Members of the Minnesota Kite Society turned up for this event as well, to demonstrate large elaborate kites, including some that looked like birds flying synchronized maneuvers.)

Not all Winter Carnival events take place outdoors. In the massive St. Paul Civic Center you'll find a four-day event that's come to be called the carnival's "Indoor Fun Fair." A midway offers varied attractions including Ferris wheels and tilt-a-wheels and games of skill and chance, while in Lifestyle Lane browsers can examine a variety of products and services, with demonstrations of everything from computers to chiropractic. And if you're so inclined, you can have your hair cut in the latest fashion. Adults pay $6 to enter the Civic Center for this event; children 10 and under are free.

Nearby, at the Roy Wilkins Auditorium, named for the St. Paulite who served as longtime head of the National Association for the Advancement of Colored People, musical entertainment is featured, much of it provided by notable local performers. One locally based artist created something of a stir when he made an unscheduled appearance in 1989. Prince apparently enjoyed what he saw, and remained long enough to greet his fans.

Much of the merriment associated with the Winter Carnival centers around a mythology that's grown up to occupy center stage: the story of arch-enemies King Boreas and Vulcanus, God of Fire. Long ago, it seems, King Boreas, the monarch of the ice and snow, discovered a winter paradise called Minnesota. He made this lovely land his winter playground, but Vulcanus, God of Fire and arch-foe of Boreas, set out to melt the snow and ice that were needed for the joyous winter carnival presided over by Boreas and his lovely Queen of the Snows.

Finally, after 10 days of frosty frolic, interrupted from time to time by the mischief-making of Vulcanus and his followers, the Queen prevailed upon Boreas to return to Olympus for a while until the developing warmth of spring and summer passed, and winter fun returned again.

Each year a prominent citizen of St. Paul is chosen to represent King Boreas, while candidates from St. Paul neighborhoods and companies vie to become Queen of the Snows. These royal figures rule over the myriad festivities and then set out to visit other festivals across the country and as far away as London. The announcement and coronation of King Boreas is a highlight of each year's Winter Carnival, and so is the selection of the queen. Then there are the machinations of Vulcanus and his red-clad followers, who roar through the city in fire engines when they're not bursting into elegant balls and banquets to leave a spot of soot on the faces of women who fail to elude them.

It's estimated that 1.5 million people take part in the Winter Carnival each year, either as participants or as observers. Ice skaters glide across an illuminated rink in Rice Park, while dedicated nonskaters have a fine time watching the creation of exquisite snow-and-ice sculptures.

Two big parades draw enthusiastic crowds to downtown St. Paul during Winter Festival Week. The King Boreas Grand Day Parade weaves its way through the city accompanied by marching units and colorful floats. Each year a different national celebrity is chosen to serve as Grand Marshall of the parade; after a succession of TV and movie stars, the selection in 1986 was a group composed of Snoopy, Charlie Brown, Linus, and Lucy, all of them related to famed cartoonist Charles Schulz who is himself a native of the Twin Cities.

Vulcan's Victory Torchlight Parade takes place on the final Saturday night of the carnival, which ends with a spectacular fireworks display that concludes the festivities until the next year.

---

3. The Minneapolis Aquatennial

As St. Paul's Winter Carnival celebrates the wintertime fun to be enjoyed in the Twin Cities, the Minneapolis Aquatennial salutes the water-related activities that make summer such a festive time in Minnesota.

The fun gets underway during the third week in July each year with the downtown Grand Day Parade that features the antics of AquaJesters, an assemblage of 70 solid citizens who go into hiding once a year behind the traditional makeup and costumes of clowns. With more than 40 crowd-pleasing years to their credit, these zanies proceed by foot or skates or on bikes or other means of locomotion, delighting kids and their elders, many of whom bring along folding chairs for a comfortable view of the floats, bands, and marching groups.

A sampling of events during the 1990 festivities will give you an idea of the kinds of events that have led to the perennial popularity of this largest of American summer civic festivals.

Family Fun Day is a free ice-cream-and-cake social held on Nicollet Island on the edge of downtown Minneapolis. Musicians, mimes, jugglers, and other entertainers are on hand, and so are arts-and-crafts booths for grownups, and games and contests for children.

The enormously popular **Youth Fishing Clinic** at Lake Calhoun provides children with free tackle and bait, and with instructions from fishing experts on how to keep that big one from getting away.

The **Community Band concerts** give families the chance to enjoy together performances by local musicians performing in the accoustically acclaimed bandshell on the shores of beautiful Lake Harriet.

Elsewhere on Lake Calhoun, the **Sand Castle Sculpture Competition** divides beach sand into plots for teams of up to six people. Some of the castles and shapes and structures are remarkable, constructed with only the use of pails and wood and water.

The **Nicollet Mall Art Fair** generally offers more substantial artifacts—works of blown glass and batik, paintings and sculpture, and other forms displayed by craftspeople from across the nation.

And then there are the ever-popular **boating events—** everything from sailboards to sailboats to rowboats to the annual milk carton boat races, in which imagination and milk cartons come together, with frequently hilarious results.

And all of it comes to a rousing conclusion each year with a dazzling display of fireworks set off in downtown Minneapolis.

For **information** on Aquatennial events, call The Connection (a local advertiser-supported service) at 612/922-9000.

---

4. The Renaissance Festival

Have you been back to the 17th century recently? Thousands of Midwesterners have traveled back in time since 1971, starting season for the annual Renaissance Festival. By now this is the largest such festival in the country in terms of attendance and number of activities. It's also the largest in area—125 acres of farmland about four miles southwest of suburban Shakopee on Hwy. 169.

You'll be greeted at the banner-bedecked gates by costumed peasants, royals, and members of every social class in between. And you'll find more than 150 booths selling everything from pottery and jewelry to furniture and flowering plants.

When hunger pangs begin to gnaw, you can choose from a grand array of edibles, the most popular of which are enormous turkey legs which may or may not resemble food favorites of that day.

Visitors find themselves mingling with a variety of acrobats, magicians, jugglers, and jousters, and on seven separate stages there's nonstop entertainment by talented comics, musicians, and singers.

You'll see dancers here of all kinds—Scottish country dancers, morris dancers, belly dancers. Yes, belly dancers are indeed on hand, as they reportedly were in England after the Crusaders returned home from their journey to recover the Holy Land for the faithful. While in the Middle East, these Crusaders encountered a wholly unfamiliar and exotic culture and brought back with them intriguing mementoes and tales of novel activities, some of which caught on at home.

Arabic numbers went over well in the West. So did falconry, a sport involving the use of specially trained hunting hawks. And so did a new kind of dancing by entertainers adept at moving muscles proper Britons didn't even know they had.

Actually we don't get to meet very many proper Britons at the Renaissance Festival. Most are bawdy Brits who engage in loud harangues with one another and even with modern-day passersby.

There seems to be a parade in progress nearly all the time, in addition to demonstrations and competitions that include such unlikely contests as human chess matches: living forms on a giant chess board, moving from one square to another on direction from wily chess masters.

The American Bus Association recently named Minnesota's Renaissance Festival among the top 100 events in North America, but visitors, performers, and craftspeople from all over the United States didn't need to be told that; they've been making their way here, summer after summer, since the very start of it all. There's truly never a dull moment at this annual celebration that helps wind up the summer season in a very merry way.

The Renaissance Festival takes place on weekends from mid-August through late September each year. Gates open at 9 a.m. on Saturday and Sunday and close at 7 p.m. Admission at the gate is $12 for adults, $5 for children 6 to 12. There's no charge for children 5 and under.

---

5. Taste of Minnesota

The youngest and most surprising major festival in Minnesota dates back to 1983, when members of the St. Paul Downtown Council came up with an unlikely proposal—a Fourth of July celebration featuring food and fun in the shadow of the beautiful Minnesota State Capitol. It wasn't the setting of this proposed fête that was so surprising—it was the timing. Fourth of July weekend is traditionally the time when roads leading out of the cities are clogged with folks on their way "to the lake." (Somehow locals expect you to know which one of the more than 10,000 Minnesota lakes they're referring to.) Who'd be left to come to a festival in St. Paul? It seemed an impractical idea at best, but the planners went ahead anyway, on the premise that there must be plenty of people without a lake to call their own. How nice for them if the capital city played host on our national holiday in a truly spectacular setting, when the weather's at its warm and sunny best.

The planners gambled that hundreds of people would be attracted by the prospect of browsing through dozens of crafts booths and would enjoy the chance to buy sample-size portions of specialties from the Twin Cities' most famous restaurants. An added attraction was free musical entertainment every day and evening, culminating in a Fourth of July appearance by the Minnesota Orchestra, whose performance in front of the State Capitol Building would conclude with a spectacular fireworks display.

The gamble paid off in a very big way. Nearly 250,000 people now come to the beautifully landscaped capitol approach during the Fourth of July weekend to enjoy a down-home celebration that gets more popular year after year. Restaurants vie for the privilege of preparing and selling their samples on the premises in exchange for tickets that are purchased at booths throughout the grounds. Save your cash for the jewelry, leather goods, woodworking, pottery, metalwork, and other crafts you'll find here. To pay for food, you hand over the requisite number of 25¢ tickets from the $5 block you bought earlier at one of the booths on the grounds.

What kind of food will you find at Taste of Minnesota? Everything from gyro sandwiches to barbecued ribs to chicken nuggets on skewers to corn on the cob to cookies and cakes and soft drinks and wine and snowcones and Häagen-Dazs. And much of this is consumed by celebrants sitting on manicured lawns under graceful branches, watching performances on stages set up at strategic locations throughout the grounds. A main stage in front of the capitol steps features different types of music each day: jazz and contemporary, oldtime rock and roll, country, and finally classical, via the stirring strains of the Minnesota Orchestra.

Children have an area and program of their own, and the number of beaming little faces with flowers, butterflies, and other colorful designs painted on them leaves no question as to which activity they enjoy the most.

What's best about Taste of Minnesota is that there's no aftertaste of commercialism here. You can spend a delightful day or evening enjoying the surroundings and the entertainment without spending a penny. And that's particularly nice on this particular holiday. It shouldn't cost money to celebrate our country's birthday and our own good fortune in living here.

TWIN CITIES GETAWAYS

There's so much to see and do in the Twin Cities that you could spend your entire Minnesota stay just getting acquainted with Minneapolis and St. Paul. If time permits, though, you might want to see for yourself some of the places that lure local folks out of town for weekend excursions. Actually, historic Stillwater is close enough for a one-day shopping and dining getaway. Rochester, home of the famous Mayo Clinic, is close enough for a 90-minute drive, a bit of sightseeing, and a return on the same day. For the Rivertown rambles, though, or a visit to Duluth, you'll probably want to set aside at least one night, maybe more. In any case, these excursions will give you an idea of the diversity to be found in marvelous Minnesota.

1. Stillwater

This is where it all began. It was on August 28, 1848, that 61 delegates gathered in Stillwater to draft a petition asking Congress and President James J. Polk for the "early organization of the Territory of Minnesota." On March 3 of the following year, under the sponsorship of Sen. Stephen A. Douglas, the bill was passed, and the rest, as they say, is history.

Nestled in the picturesque St. Croix River Valley, Stillwater today is as readily reached by boat as by car, and during the summertime pleasure craft from throughout Minnesota and nearby

Wisconsin, just across the St. Croix River, occupy the docks that are located a block or two from the city's main street. The St. Croix River has been an important factor in Stillwater's commercial and recreational well-being since the early 19th century, when logs from the area's bountiful forests were floated down the river to distant lumber mills and markets. In 1904, though, the supply that had seemed virtually inexhaustible finally ran out, as the last log drive marked the exhaustion of the forests and the end of this lucrative industry. The spirit of 19th-century Stillwater lives again today, however, thanks to an ambitious restoration program that got under way during the 1970s, when aged brick and limestone structures were carefully renovated and transformed into tourist attractions.

ATTRACTIONS

As you approach Stillwater on Hwy. 36, you'll pass one of the area's most popular destinations. Turn left on Manning Avenue North (Hwy. 15) and you'll find **Aamodt's Apple Farm,** 6428 Manning Ave. N. (tel. 439-3127), a 180-acre orchard with its own processing plant, gift shops, bakery, and lunchroom. A large carving of Johnny Appleseed stands in the renovated 1800s barn, where visitors munch contentedly on apple goodies—apple-cheese soup, apple salad, and most popular of all, giant apple-oatmeal cookies. And of course they're washing it all down with tasty apple cider.

Antique scythes, rakes, wooden shovels, and corn planters hang from the wooden joists that extend from the floor to the beamed ceiling. Apple-related antiques are for sale in the gift shop, but the most popular purchases are of the apples that are grown and processed on these premises. Try the popular Haralson, an oldtime Minnesota apple noted for its tart crispness. At this writing, Aamodt's is open from August to March, with cross-country skiing available through 30 km of groomed, tracked trails. (Call from the Twin Cities to check on the hours.) If you're lucky enough to be here in spring, enjoy the visual and aromatic pleasure of apple-blossom time at Aamodt's.

Once you get to town, your first stop should be the **Stillwater Chamber of Commerce,** 423 S. Main St. (tel. 612/439-7700). You'll find maps here, along with brochures about minitours, lodgings, antiques, and other information of interest.

There's a diversity of outdoor fun to be found at such Stillwater picnic sites as **Pioneer Park,** on a bluff at 2nd Street overlooking the scenic St. Croix River, and **Lowell Park,** two blocks east of Main Street, which borders downtown from north to south. In the large amphitheater at Pioneer Park, musical events are held all summer, and during the town's annual spectacular, Lumberjack Days, local talent shows are presented too.

At Lowell Park during **Lumberjack Days**—customarily held the third weekend of July—you'll be able to watch a variety of lumber-related activities, including log-rolling, tree-climbing, and cross-chop-sawing demonstrations by professional lumberjacks. On Sunday the festivities end with a grand parade that features march-

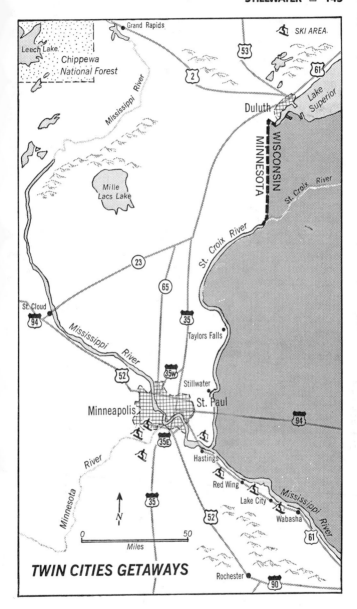

TWIN CITIES GETAWAYS

ing and musical groups from all over the state. Downtown store windows are customarily decorated with historical artifacts during Lumberjack Days.

On July 19, 1987, the **Minnesota Zephyr** made its inaugural run from the old depot at 601 N. Main St. and promptly became one of Stillwater's most popular dining and sight-seeing attractions. Passengers board these meticulously restored 1949 dining cars for a three-hour "travel back in time" that carries them through some of the most beautiful landscape in Minnesota. You'll pass the meandering St. Croix River on one side and picturesque limestone river bluffs on the other, then make your way through forests in which maple, ash, oak, walnut, white birch, and other state trees abound. An abundance of sumac, wildflowers, and lacy ferns cover the forest floor.

The taped dinner music and the authentic decor will put you so much in mind of the late 1940s that you may find yourself startled to see an occasional '80s automobile whizzing by or idling near the railroad track, waiting for the *Zephyr* to pass by. (The entire journey proceeds at about five miles per hour and takes about 3¼ hours.)

The delightful four-course dinner service begins with chicken-and-wild-rice soup, followed by green salad, and your choice of prime rib; flounder stuffed with lobster and crab; or rock game hen, served with vegetable, starch, and hot bread sticks. Finally, there's excellent cheesecake, along with coffee or tea. You can have pre- and post-dinner libations brought to your table, or you can enjoy them in one of the beautifully restored Vista-Dome club cars, each with its own bar.

The cost of this visit to the past is $47.50 per guest, with one glass of wine included in the price of the meal; cocktails and gratuity are not included.

For reservations and further information, call 430-3000, a local phone call from Minneapolis and St. Paul.

SHOPPING

Browsing and buying, popular pastimes in Stillwater, are especially enjoyable because so many of the stores are located in historic structures. On Main Street you'll find an assemblage of fine specialty shops in a complex called the **Grand Garage and Gallery,** 324 S. Main St. This was the Stillwater Motors Building when it first opened in the 1880s. Now among its occupants is the charming **Kmitch Girls Shop** (tel. 430-1827), which features not only dolls, but a delightful collection of cats, dogs, and teddy bears as well. At the **Brick Alley Mall,** 423 S. Main St., two 19th-century structures, separated by an old alley, have been connected by an enclosed walkway. Here, among other interesting shops, you'll find the **Brick Alley Bookstore** (tel. 439-0266), which has a wide-ranging collection of publications.

Elsewhere in town, **Tamarack House Galleries,** 236 S. Main St. (tel. 439-9393), attracts art collectors from throughout the Midwest, while sweater and outerwear collectors have a fine time in another restored building, where the **Winona Knitting Mills Factory Outlet,** 215 S. Main St. (tel. 430-1711), offers a wide selection of apparel at prices about 30% to 50% lower than in department and specialty shops. (The only items that aren't made in America are the genuine Icelandic sweaters, jackets, and accessories available here.) At the other end of Main Street you'll find a collectors' delight, **Staples Mill Antiques,** 410 N. Main St. (tel. 439-8674), a complex that accommodates more than 30 dealers and craftspeople in a converted 19th-century sawmill. And at the **Old Post Office Shops,** 220 E. Myrtle St. (tel. 430-1431), across from the famous Lowell Inn, you can browse at a variety of shops for gifts, many of them handcrafted, to bring back home as souvenirs.

WHERE TO STAY

The **Lowell Inn,** 102 N. 2nd St., Stillwater, MN 55082 (tel. 612/439-1100), offers by far the most famous accommodations in Stillwater. A beautiful three-story structure with large white columns, arched windows, and a comfortably furnished veranda, it offers 21 lovely guest rooms. This "Mount Vernon of the West" was opened in 1930 by a handsome and enterprising theatrical couple, Arthur and Nelle Palmer, whose experiences on tour had taught them a thing or two about how hotels should be run. They envisaged an elegant establishment offering impeccable service, and their Lowell Inn has more than fulfilled that dream. Today their son, Art, his wife, Maureen, and a third generation of hoteliers are carrying the tradition forward. Sumptuously furnished with a mixture of French provincial and Victorian reproductions and antiques, these romantic rooms are much in demand by couples who find this the perfect place for an anniversary celebration. Others favor the Lowell Inn as a relaxed and elegant getaway. In fact the demand is so great that you might have trouble getting a room here, so do call ahead for reservations. Rates range from $95 to $169 per night depending on the room's size, location, and accoutrements. Four of the rooms have Jacuzzis (presumably these don't date back to the 18th century); one room has its own adjoining living room, and one boasts a shower-in-the-round, with fixtures imported from Italy.

Just minutes away from Stillwater, about 15 miles south on Hwy. 95, you'll find the delightful **Afton House,** 3291 S. St. Croix Trail, Afton, MN 55001 (tel. 612/436-8883). On the banks of the St. Croix River, the inn's 12 guest rooms have been furnished individually with antiques that include trundle beds, clipper chairs, and English armoires. Four of the rooms have small private balconies, with a larger one available to all guests. Rates range from $47 to $125 during the winter, $55 to $130 during the summer. Rollaways are available at $8.

At the **Stillwater Inn Motel,** 1750 W. Frontage Rd., Stillwater, MN 55082 (tel. 612/430-1300), you'll find more modest but very pleasant accommodations ranging in price from $40 to $76. All prices include a free Continental breakfast.

WHERE TO DINE

A block off Main Street, overlooking the St. Croix River, you can while away your time at the **Freight House Restaurant,** 435 S. Water St. (tel. 439-5718). This building, listed on the National Register of Historic Places, was once occupied by an old railroad company, and the large picture windows that now provide diners with a panoramic view of the St. Croix River were guillotine doors back when lumber and mill products were being shipped nationwide from this terminal. Prices here are moderate, with a lunch of a salad, sandwich, or hamburger going for about $6. Barbecued ribs at $13 remain a long-time favorite for dinner, with other à la carte entrées ranging from $7 to $13. Wintertime hours, usually from November 1 to March 1, are 11 a.m. to 4 p.m. for lunch, 4 to 10 p.m. for dinner Friday and Saturday, and 11 a.m. to 8 p.m. on Sunday, with the lunch menu in effect the entire time. During the rest of the year, hours are 11 a.m. to 10 p.m. Sunday through Thursday, 11 a.m. to 11 p.m. Friday and Saturday.

Vittorio's, 402 S. Main St. (tel. 439-3588), features tasty northern Italian food in a large restaurant with four dining rooms and a lounge where a 19th-century brewery stood. In fact, if you dine in the most elegant room of all, the Blue Grotto, you can look through a window in the original limestone wall and see part of a network of storage caves that were dug during the early 1840s. Popular dinner entrées, served here with antipasto salad and garlic toast, include ravioli carne (meat-filled pasta prepared with the house red sauce) at $12.95, and pollo alla cacciatore (chicken sautéed in wine, and served with a portion of baked canelloni rossi) at $15.95. In the front dining room, you can enjoy a wide variety of homemade pizza and pasta specialties ranging from spaghetti with white sauce ($5.95) to a large Vittorio's special pizza, topped with a mixture of cheese, sausage, pepperoni, green olives, green pepper, and onion ($18). Open for lunch from 11 a.m. to 3 p.m. daily; for dinner from 3 to 11 p.m. Sunday through Thursday, to midnight on Friday and Saturday.

In what was in the 1860s a general store, **Brine's Old Fashioned Meats,** at 219 S. Main St. (tel. 439-7556), offers first-floor grocery shopping with informal dining on the second floor. Old-world delicatessen items, along with hamburgers and milkshakes, are the specialties of the house.

But the most celebrated dining in Stillwater is still to be found at the **Lowell Inn,** 102 N. 2nd St. (tel. 439-1100), which attracts diners from throughout the state. In the comfortable cocktail lounge you can await your table in one of the three dining rooms. The George Washington Room is elegant, with its Capi di Monte porcelain, Sheffield silver, Dresden china, and antique sideboards. In the Matterhorn Room, notable for its acid-etched stained-glass windows, you'll find authentic Swiss carvings dominated by a formidable life-size carved eagle. And in the Garden Room, with its indoor trout pool, you can eat your entrée just a little while after you fish for it. The Matterhorn Room features a beef-and-shrimp fondue dinner with a European wine-tasting for $92 per couple; the George Washington Room and the Garden Room have the same varied American menu, with dinner ranging from $20 for sautéed chicken livers to $30 for lobster tail. Lunch and dinner hours vary from room to room, so phone ahead for specifics and reservations.

Just minutes away from downtown Stillwater, the **Afton House,** 3291 S. St. Croix Trail, in Afton (tel. 436-8883), with three dining rooms of its own, is accessible by road and by river. Close enough to the Twin Cities to make it a special dinner destination, this beautiful inn, now on the National Register of Historic Places, caters to a wide variety of patrons throughout the year. Skiers from nearby Afton Alps make this a mandatory stop during the winter months. And during the summer boaters tie up at the on-site dock.

Look for the unique carvings throughout the dining rooms and bar, done by the late Elmo "The Builder" Erickson, whose talent and sense of humor are best expressed in the Erickson Room, where you get an underwater view of the world, with the legs and bare feet of a fisherman extending downward from the ceiling while a wary fish swims by.

Proprietor-manager Gordy Jarvis had been a chef at a number of fine Twin Cities restaurants before he and his wife, Kathy, bought the Afton House in 1976. Lunch and dinner are available here. In the elegant Wheel Room, dinner favorites include steak Diane garnished with fresh vegetables, and poached salmon served with champagne sauce. Dinner prices range from $11 to $18; for lunch your tab will be somewhere around $3 to $7. The Catfish Salon features a variety of burgers, sandwiches, and two much-requested soup selections: a thick, rich seafood chowder and a savory chili. Lunch is served in the Catfish Room Monday through Saturday from 11:30 a.m. to 2:30 p.m. Dinner is served in the Wheel Room seven nights a week, from 5:30 to 9 p.m. Monday through Thursday; 5 to 10 p.m. Friday and Saturday; and 4:30 to 9 p.m. Sunday. Sunday brunch is served from 10 a.m. to 2 p.m.

---

2. Taylors Falls

For a view of the St. Croix River Valley, follow Hwy. 95 from Stillwater. Drive past lush farmlands, magnificent bluffs, and dramatic waterways until you reach Taylors Falls, nestled on the northern end of 900-acre Interstate Park, which extends from one side of the St. Croix to the other and includes within its scope the towns of St. Croix Falls, Wisconsin, and Taylors Falls, Minnesota. (This was the first interstate park ever established in the United States.)

ATTRACTIONS

Taylors Falls is famous for its hiking, camping, boating, and swimming, as well as for the catfish, smallmouth bass, northerns, and walleyes to be caught here. But perhaps this area's greatest claim to fame derives from potholes and log jams, reputedly the largest in the world. You can see for yourself an enormous pothole more than 60 feet deep that was created out of volcanic rock during the meltdown of ancient glaciers. No remnants of the great Taylors Falls log jam remains, but the memory lingers on of those months in 1886 when lack of rain made it impossible for logging companies to float white pine downriver to the sawmills at Osceola. Huge piles of logs accumulated on the riverbanks, and finally, when heavy rains did begin to fall, there was a mad dash by loggers to get the wood on its way. Unfortunately, though, the St. Croix River narrows and then bends just below Taylors Falls; that's where a log jam developed that eventually reached a height of 30 feet and a length of more than two miles. It took until the following spring for the jam to be completely cleared, long enough for it to have become a tourist attraction in its own day and a legend in ours.

Another tie with the past is Taylors Falls' famous **historic residential area** where 19th-century homes and churches have been carefully preserved. One of them might be of special interest to you.

WHERE TO STAY

The **Taylors Falls Jail,** 102 Government Rd., Taylors Falls, MN 55084 (tel. 612/465-3112), now a unique two-story guesthouse, started life as the lockup for unruly locals and still has bars on its windows, but in recent years it's welcomed some very estimable citizens indeed. The jail's outside appearance was restored after consultation with the Historic Preservation Office of the Minnesota Historical Society. Its interior has been turned into a comfortably furnished living room, well-equipped modern kitchen and bathroom, and a loft bedroom far cosier than anything oldtime prisoners ever enjoyed. In fact, at certain times of year you'll need a reservation to spend the night in jail. Taylors Falls Jail rates are $100 for one night, $70 a night for two nights or more. In the neighboring Schottmuller Building, an old saloon now known as the Cave, rates are $110 per night, $75 per night for two nights or more. The third floor of the building rents for $90 a night, $65 per night for two nights or more.

In all three accommodations provisions are left for you in the refrigerator so that you can do your own cooking at your convenience.

A pleasant, economical, and centrally located alternative to the hoosegow can be found at the **Springs Inn,** one block west of the junction of Hwys. 8 and 95 (P.O. Box 11) Taylors Falls, MN 55084 (tel. 612/465-6565), which features a popular hot tub and Jacuzzi, housed in an adjoining geodesic dome. Basic rates here range from $32 for a room with one double bed to $38 for a studio kitchenette. There's a $4 surcharge on weekends, a $5 surcharge for a roll-away, and a $3 surcharge for a crib.

---

3. New Prague

Whether you're getting away for a day or a weekend or longer, you'll do well to consider nearby New Prague, located just 35 miles southwest of the Twin Cities. Here you'll find the remarkable **Schumacher's New Prague Hotel,** which has been featured in such national magazines as *Gourmet, Good Housekeeping,* and *Better Homes and Gardens* and in newspapers in cities as distant as New York and Los Angeles. The hotel was designed by famed architect Cass Gilbert, whose other work includes Minnesota's state capitol in St. Paul, the U.S. Supreme Court Building in Washington, D.C., and the Woolworth Building and George Washington Bridge in New York City. A favorite getaway for Minnesotans with an event to celebrate, the New Prague is as famous for its cuisine as for its accommodations. Innkeeper and head chef John Schumacher and his wife Kathleen have worked together on an extensive bilingual menu in English and Czechoslovakian. John, who graduated with high honors from the Culinary Institute of America, has included a wide variety of authentic Bavarian dishes in his breakfast, lunch, and dinner menues, featuring everything from paprikash to wienerschnitzel to the house specialty, Czechoslovakian roast duck. Kathleen Schumacher, a registered dietitian, has introduced to the menu a "healthy heart" section of her own, including dishes which are at once delicious and low in fat and cholesterol. Everything here is prepared to order from scratch, so such special dietary requirements pose no problem. Reservations are required at this popular restaurant where guests come from long distances for what is by now nearly legendary hospitality. Lunchtime prices range from $4 to $10 for sandwiches to $11 to $18 for entrées served with your choice of accompaniments, which include dumplings, homemade sauerkraut, German potato salad, and the vegetable of the day. Dinner, served with hot or cold soup, German salad plate, choice of two Bavarian side dishes, and homemade kolache and rye roll, will cost from $19 for boneless breast of chicken to $26 for "hunter's feast" including quail, rabbit, and pheasant.

There are 11 guest rooms on the hotel's second floor; each has been named for a month of the year and decorated in a manner consistent with that month and its season. Czech glasswork and Bavarian folk art enhance the accommodations here. So do the antique wall sconces and chandeliers. Nearby attractions include golf, tennis, cross country skiing, biking, canoeing, and, of course, shopping.

A visit to **Sponsel's Minnesota Harvest Apple Orchard** in nearby Jordan is a good bet too. There's a wonderful array of fruit to be picked from the tree or from the bin. There's also an assortment of other attractions, including an animal farm and hiking trails and, from time to time, helicopter rides. Call 492-2785 or 492-3169 for news on what's underway when you're in these parts. Minnesota Harvest's hours vary according to the season: in July, August, September, and October hours are 9 a.m. to 7 p.m. Monday through Thursday and 9 a.m. to 8 p.m. Friday, Saturday, and Sunday; in November and December hours are 9 a.m. to 6 p.m. daily; January and February hours are 9 a.m. to 5 p.m. Friday, Saturday, and Sunday only.

4. Rochester

Rochester, Minnesota, about 80 miles south of the Twin Cities, may be the most cosmopolitan community of its size in the entire country. That's because nearly a quarter of a million visitors from throughout the world arrive here each year to visit the famous Mayo Clinic.

The pleasant drive to Rochester from the Twin Cities takes you along Hwy. 52 through some of the state's loveliest rolling countryside and luxuriant farmland. If you'd prefer to leave the driving to Greyhound (tel. 612/371-3311 for information), the fare each way for the two-hour trip will be about $10. Northwest Airlines (tel. 612/726-1234) has a 30-minute flight from the Twin Cities to Rochester, with prices ranging from $52 to $135 each way.

THE MAYO CLINIC

With a staff of more than 800 physicians, surgeons, and medical scientists, in addition to 1,500 medical trainees and more than 5,000 paramedical personnel, the Mayo Clinic, 200 1st St. S.W. (tel. 507/284-2511), is the largest and probably the most prestigious group medical practice in the world. It also maintains the largest graduate school of medicine in the world, with an international student body that adds further to the cosmopolitan atmosphere in Rochester.

How did so famous a medical complex happen to develop in a small Midwestern city? The story began back in 1883, when a devastating tornado struck this obscure farming community, leaving 26 people dead and the entire northern part of the town demolished.

Dr. William Worral Mayo was a local English-born physician who had practiced in Rochester for 20 years, after first coming here as an examining surgeon for the Union Army Enrollment Board. After the tornado struck, he worked with other Rochester doctors and with the nuns from the Convent of Saint Francis to treat the injured, but their efforts were severely hampered by the lack of adequate medical facilities.

Shortly after the disaster, the mother superior at the convent suggested to Dr. Mayo that he head the medical staff of a hospital which the sisters were planning to build and maintain. At first reluctant, Dr. Mayo agreed, although he knew that hospitals then were frightening to the public, who viewed them as places where people went to die. Physicians were leery of hospitals too, it seems. When St. Mary's Hospital was opened in 1889, other local doctors refused to associate with it, leaving Dr. Mayo and his two physician sons, Will and Charlie, to serve as the entire medical staff.

Both Drs. Will and Charlie had been trained in the antiseptic methods introduced by Joseph Lister, and both began to practice the relatively new field of surgery as staff members of St. Mary's Hospital. Word soon got around that patients suffering from chronic ailments like ulcers, appendicitis, and gallstones were being made well again, quickly and permanently, by these young physicians.

Even as patients in Minnesota helped spread the word about Drs. Will and Charlie Mayo, physicians from around the country and even from Europe began coming to Rochester to see for themselves the kind of work that the young Mayos had described at medical meetings and had written about in medical journals.

By the mid-1890s their growing practice made it necessary for the Drs. Mayo to enlarge their medical staff, and by 1914 they opened a building that they called the Mayo Clinic. The group medical practice they established then was unique in that it provided for a sharing of knowledge among a group of medical specialists for the purpose of promoting more comprehensive care for patients. That remains the practice and the purpose of the Mayo Clinic to this day.

WHERE TO STAY

Should you decide to stay the night in Rochester, you'll have a wide choice of accommodations in this city that prides itself on making visitors feel at home.

Some of the most famous names in the world have been registered at Rochester's 720-room **Kahler Hotel,** 20 Second Ave. S.W., Rochester, MN 55902 (tel. 507/282-2581, or toll free 800/533-1655). Elegant enough for the most festive of getaways, this hotel serves primarily as a comfortable home away from home for those who have come to Rochester to visit the Mayo Clinic.

Accommodations here are comfortable and cheery, nearby medical facilities notwithstanding. Rates range from $54 for a room for one with one double bed to $78 to $120 for a room for two with two double beds. Suites are available for $350 to $900 a night. (It was presumably a suite that was occupied by the Saudi Arabian princess who lived at the Kahler for nearly a year.) Along with fine restaurants (see my dining recommendations) and shops, the Kahler offers a domed recreation center with swimming pool, sauna, and whirlpool.

The Mayo Clinic and the Kahler Hotel are very careful to protect the privacy of the hotel's visitors to Rochester, but word does get around town when celebrities like Lady Bird Johnson, Bill Cosby, or Jim Nabors check in. And then there was the genial old gentleman whose daily greeting to fellow patrons in the Kahler Coffee Shop was, "Hi. I'm Johnny Carson's father." And he was.

Another property with connections to the Mayo Clinic is the more modest 142-room **Clinic View Inn,** 9 Third Ave. N.W., Rochester, MN 55901 (tel. 507/289-8646). Rates here range from $53 to $63 for rooms with private baths; for accommodations that include kitchenettes, you'll pay $70 for a single, $80 for a double, with a $10 charge for each additional person.

A very welcome addition to available accommodations in Rochester is the city's very first bed-and-breakfast. Located just three blocks from the Mayo Clinic, the **Canterbury Inn,** 723 2nd St. S.W., Rochester MN 55902 (tel. 507/289-5553), is a restored three-story Victorian home that offers four double-bedded guest rooms, each of which has a private bath with both shower and tub. A fireplace for wintertime guests and a cool, shady porch for summertime visitors provide a cozy atmosphere, as do the abundance of turn-of-the-century furnishings. Adding to the warmth is the gracious welcome you'll receive from proprietors Mary Martin and Jeffrey Van Sant. Word is spreading too about the gourmet cooking at the Canterbury Inn. Breakfast is likely to include such items as wild-rice waffles, Norwegian fruit soup, Grand Marnier French toast, or fresh pears poached in sherry, and it is served either downstairs in the comfortable dining room or upstairs in the guests' own rooms. King-size, queen-size, and twin beds are available. Rates are $75 per day double occupancy, $60 per day single.

WHERE TO DINE

You won't find a more elegant setting for a memorable dinner than the famous **Elizabethan Room** at the Kahler Hotel, 20 Second

Ave., S.W. (tel. 282-2581). The coats-of-arms on dark paneled walls, the stained-glass panels, red velvet hangings, and large, double-tiered wrought-iron chandeliers give a majestic ambience to this handsome room. A romantic air is provided by the Elizabethan Strings, strolling violinists who make a lovely musical contribution to your dining pleasure. The irresistible blend of impeccable service and fine fare—for example, breast of chicken at $14.50 or rack of lamb for two at $39—make for a terrific evening out. The Elizabethan Room is open for lunch Monday through Friday from 11:30 a.m. to 2 p.m., and for dinner Monday through Friday from 5:30 to 9 p.m., on Saturday from 6 to 10 p.m.; Sunday brunch is on from 10 a.m. to 2:30 p.m.

The adjoining Lord Essex Room is a perfect complement to the Elizabethan Room. Similar in decor but smaller in size, the Lord Essex Room provides a delightfully intimate setting. Primarily a cocktail lounge, the Lord Essex becomes a small dining room during the Elizabethan Room's elaborate Sunday brunch. Overflow brunchers are directed to the Lord Essex Room, a very pleasant alternative indeed!

If you're interested in another cocktail lounge, try the Kahler's Penthouse, a delightful retreat where you can sink into overstuffed chairs amid towering plants and enjoy a commanding view of the city. And there's a third bar down on street level, the Greenhouse, with a terrarium, an aquarium, an oversize TV screen, and 2,000 hanging plants, all of them for sale.

No Rochester dining spot is better known than **Michaels.** Centrally located at 15 S. Broadway (tel. 941-9828), this family restaurant was started in 1951. Now six times larger than it was then, Michaels somehow manages to retain an air of intimacy and cordiality. But there's a cosmopolitan touch here as well. Although the decor in most of the rooms will remind you of an old English country home, one area, the Harkala Room, is decidedly Greek, as is the Pappas family that owns and runs Michaels. A section of the menu includes Greek dishes, but primarily this is an American steak-and-seafood spot. The food will please you, and so will the tab. Luncheon prices are in the $6 to $8 range, dinners run from $12 to $23. The wine list is extensive and excellent. Lunch is served from 11 a.m. to 3 p.m. Monday through Saturday; dinner is served from 3 to 9 p.m. Monday through Thursday and Sunday, and from 3 to 10 p.m. on Saturday. Michaels serves a buffet-style brunch for $5.95 on Sunday from 10 a.m. to 2 p.m.

Another well-known family restaurant in these parts is **Wong's Cafe,** 4 Third St. S.W. (tel. 282-7514 or 282-7545). Now being run by second-generation owners, brothers Michael and Dennis Wong and their cousin Steve Wong, this restaurant was opened in 1952 by Ben and Mae Wong and Neil and Poya Wong. It was in 1982 that the second generation took over and two years later moved the restaurant into a remodeled 100-year-old bank building. (Just 50 feet from where the original restaurant stood, the "new" Wong's Cafe increased its seating capacity from 150 to 240.) Although American dishes occupy a prominent place on the menu seven days a week, Wong's is probably best known for its Chinese cuisine, particularly for such dishes as the ever-popular moo goo gai (sweet and sour chicken with pork-fried rice). Children have their own menu here, on place mats that also feature games and puzzles. Breakfast is served from 6 to 10:30 a.m. Monday through Saturday, with lunch from 11 a.m. to 4 p.m. and dinner from 4 to 9:30 p.m. Sunday hours are 11 a.m. to 9 p.m. Reservations are recommended for groups of 5 or more.

WHAT TO SEE AND DO

Many of the tourist attractions in Rochester are related to the **Mayo Clinic,** a complex of buildings that extends over a seven-block area of downtown Rochester. Free tours of the impressive clinic facilities are available from 10 a.m. to 2 p.m. Monday through Friday.

The **Mayo Medical Museum,** open free to the public, offers a variety of films and videotapes as well as exhibits that enable visitors to examine the human body and its functions, to learn about some of the illnesses and injuries that pose a threat around the world, and to become acquainted with some of the methods by which the medical profession deals with these problems. Hours are Monday through Friday from 9 a.m. to 9 p.m., Saturday 9 a.m. to 5 p.m., and Sunday from 1 to 5 p.m.

Perhaps the most beloved local attraction in downtown Rochester is the **Rochester Carillon,** in the tower of the Plummer Building. This set of 56 stationary bells of various sizes, sounded with levers pressed by a carillonneur's fist, was bought by Dr. Will Mayo during a trip to Europe in the 1920s. With a range of 4½ octaves, it's the most complete carillon in North America. Concerts are offered at 7 p.m. on Monday and at noon on Wednesday and Friday. Additional recitals are held on holidays and for special events.

Mayowood, the splendid home of two generations of the Mayo family, was built in 1911 by Dr. Charles H. Mayo. He and his wife, Edith, brought up four daughters and two sons in this large, gracious home. Later, Dr. Charles (Chuck) W. Mayo, his wife, Alice, and their four sons and two daughters resided here. Perched on 3,000 acres overlooking the Zumbro River Valley, Mayowood has welcomed such famous figures as Helen Keller, Franklin D. Roosevelt, and Adlai Stevenson. Over 38 rooms are furnished in American, English, French, Spanish, and Italian antiques. There is also less imposing evidence of the personal tastes of the family to whom Mayowood was not a showplace but a home. The only way to get to Mayowood is via an Olmstead County Historical Society shuttle bus; phone 282-9447 for information concerning tours.

Another popular home tour is offered at the **Plummer House,** 1091 Plummer Lane (tel. 281-6182), once the residence of Dr. Henry Plummer. Dr. Plummer joined the Mayo Clinic staff in 1901, and he is credited with having devised the pneumatic tube and the clinic's remarkable communication and recordkeeping systems. When he and his family moved into this Tudor-style mansion in 1924, they were the first in the area to make use of natural gas and the first to have burglar alarms. It's still notable for its exquisite rose garden and for its 11 acres of parkland, open to the public throughout the year from sunrise to sunset. House tours are available June through August on Wednesday from 1 to 7 p.m. The cost is $1.50 per adult and $1.00 per child or student; children under 5 are admitted without charge.

Perhaps the unlikeliest of all clinic-related attractions in Rochester are the hordes of giant **Canadian geese** that winter here each year. They were first attracted by a flock of 12 brethren donated by a grateful patient in 1947 and released in Silver Lake Park, at North Broadway and 13th Street. The following year, Rochester's new power plant began using Silver Lake for cooling water, with the result that the lake remained free of ice throughout the winter. The Canadian geese stayed on that winter—and ever since. Now numbering in the tens of thousands, these amiable birds are welcomed in Rochester by human friends of all ages, who bring them breadcrumbs, popcorn, and other goodies. Silver Lake Park has more than geese to offer, though. Paddleboats and canoes can be rented during the warmer months, and picnicking is popular then too.

Other outdoor activities can be enjoyed on the city's six 18-hole golf courses and 30 outdoor tennis courts. There's a popular nine-mile nature trail here as well. For **sports information,** phone 289-7414.

Cultural attractions in Rochester include the fine **Rochester Art Center,** 320 E. Center St. (tel. 282-8629), open Tuesday through Saturday from 10 a.m. to 5 p.m., and the highly regarded **Rochester Symphony Orchestra,** 109 City Hall, 200 First Ave. S.W. (tel. 285-8976).

---

5. Mantorville

About 65 miles south of the Twin Cities and 20 minutes west of Rochester, you'll find the historic town of Mantorville, whose entire 12-block downtown area is listed on the National Register of Historic Places. Limestone quarries were this town's claim to fame during the 19th century, and a great many important buildings throughout the country are constructed of "Mantorville stone," among them St. Mary's Hospital in Rochester. The Dodge County Courthouse, Minnesota's oldest operating courthouse, is also made of local limestone.

Among the historically significant buildings to be visited here are a 19th-century one-room schoolhouse, a recently restored log house (one of the earliest buildings in town), and the **Grand Old Mansion,** 501 Clay St., Mantorville (507/635-3231), an imposing Victorian building that serves today as a bed-and-breakfast remarkable not only for its fine cuisine but for its original woodwork, its hand-carved staircase, and the many antiques with which it's been furnished by owner/hostess Irene Selker. Rates range from $30 for a double-bed room with shared bath to $53 per couple for accommodations in a remodeled schoolhouse. (There's an $8 charge for each additional person.)

WHERE TO DINE

Perhaps the most frequently visited old building in Mantorville is **Hubbell House,** Hwy. 57, Mantorville (tel. 507/ 635-2331), an old country inn established in 1854 and today one of the state's most famous restaurants. Its guests have included Senator Horace Greeley, best remembered for his advice "Go west, young man. Go west . . ." Alexander Ramsey, Minnesota's first U.S. senator, dined here as well. So, more recently, did a variety of other luminaries, including circus impresario John Ringling North, Gen. Dwight D. Eisenhower, baseball great Mickey Mantle, and movie star Fred MacMurray. Facsimiles of their signatures and those of more than a dozen other famous guests decorate the place mats that have become popular as souvenirs.

Many Twin Citians drive down regularly for dinner at Hubbell House, where the elegant decor in no way detracts from the casual, comfortable atmosphere. The chateaubriand served here is justly famous. It's also reasonably priced; served with appetizer or soup, salad, vegetable, and potato, the price is $28. Jumbo shrimp slowly broiled and served over pasta and walleye pike almondine (both $13) are other dinner specialties. Luncheons represent a particularly attractive buy, with entrées, served with potato, vegetable or salad, and beverage, at prices ranging from $5 for stuffed pork chop to $7 for a pasta seafood salad. Reservations are always recommended. Hubbell House is open for lunch Tuesday through Saturday from 11:15 a.m. to 2 p.m., for dinner from 5 to 10 p.m. Sunday hours are 11:30 a.m. to 10 p.m.

---

6. River Towns

Follow the Mississippi south from the Twin Cities and you'll find a succession of quaint river towns that retain much of the architecture and atmosphere of bygone days.

Combine the historical interest of this area with the natural beauty of the surrounding Hiawatha Valley, add the unique attractions each community has to offer, and you'll see why Hastings, Red Wing, Lake City, and Wabasha are popular Twin Cities getaways for a day, an evening, a weekend, or longer.

HASTINGS

Just 25 miles from the Twin Cities, Hastings was one of the earliest river towns in Minnesota. A trading post was established here as early as 1833, and the town was incorporated in 1857. Three rivers—the Mississippi, the St. Croix, and the Vermillion—made Hastings readily accessible to other markets, and the spectacular Vermillion waterfalls provided power for the mills that made this one of the great wheat centers of the Northwest.

Attractions

Today, there are 61 buildings in Hastings that have been listed on the National Register of Historic Places. The newest of these is a contemporary work by Frank Lloyd Wright, who in 1957–1959 built the dramatic **Fasbender Medical Clinic** at the southeast corner of Hwy. 55 and Pine Street. Situated on land that blends into an adjacent park, the clinic, which is largely submerged in the ground, is readily identified by its folded roof.

As part of the National Trust program known as "Main Street," all of downtown Hastings has been designated a historic district. See the helpful **Hastings Chamber of Commerce,** at 220 Sibley St. (tel. 612/437-6775), for a handy guide to your own walking tour of these fascinating buildings, foremost among them the **Le Duc-Simmons Mansion,** 1629 Vermillion St. (Hwy. 61). This imposing limestone structure, with its pointed arched windows, high tower, and intricate scrollwork, dates back to 1856.

The **Alexis Bailly Vineyard,** 18200 Kirby Ave. (tel. 437-1413), was founded in 1973 and has since won more than a dozen awards from Wineries Unlimited, an international competition involving wineries all over the United States and Canada. From June through October the winery is open to the public from noon to 5 p.m. Friday through Sunday. And in fact individuals and small groups are welcome to walk through the vineyards and to sample and purchase wines anytime during working hours. By the way, it was the original Alexis Bailly who selected the site for the trading post that would one day develop into the town of Hastings.

The **Carpenter St. Croix Valley Nature Center,** 12805 St. Croix Trail (tel. 437-4359), conducts a number of programs, including the rehabilitation of raptors (birds of prey such as bald eagles and hawks), the banding of birds, and the maintenance of orchards. It also organizes maple syruping in the spring, organic gardening in the summer, and animal tracking in the winter. The center is open to the public on the first and third Sunday of the month.

Food and Lodging

Perhaps the best-known restaurant in Hastings is the **Mississippi Belle,** 101 E. 2nd St. (tel. 437-5694), a replica of the side-wheel packet steamers that traveled the Mississippi during the golden era of riverboats, from 1855 to 1875. A perennially popular dinner entrée here is baked seafood au gratin, which combines shrimp, scallops, crabmeat, and lobster in a sherry sauce. A smaller version is available at lunchtime as well. Oven-fried chicken, broiled center-cut pork chops, and Port of Hastings steak (a boneless New York cut) are among the items that have made Mississippi Belle a drawing card. The pies here are legendary, with lemon angel, sour cream raisin, and southern pecan pies among the delicious offerings.

Lunches, served daily from 11 a.m. to 2:30 p.m., are in the $5 to $6 price range; dinners, served Tuesday through Saturday from 4:30 to 9 p.m., run $8 to $16, and Sunday dinners, served from 11 a.m. to 6 p.m., cost $8.45.

An overnight suggestion, **Thorwood Bed and Breakfast,** at 649 W. 3rd St., Hastings, MN 55033 (tel. 612/437-3297), is a re-converted 1880 mansion that's been turned into a delightful accommodation by Pam and Dick Thorsen. There are eight rooms here, some with fireplaces, all with private bath, some with whirlpools, and each with its own distinctive decor. Breakfast, brought to your door in an oversize basket, includes oven omelets, warm pastries, sausages, muffins, coffee or tea, and juice. Reservations are recommended. Prices range from $69 to $150.

A new B&B, also owned by the Thorsens, is **Rosewood,** 621 Ramsey St., Hastings, MN 55033 (tel. 612/437-3297).

RED WING

As you continue your Rivertown ramble southward from the Twin Cities, you'll find Red Wing, a town whose beginnings date back to 1680, when Father Hennepin founded an Indian village here. The town was later named in honor of the area's Sioux Indian chiefs, whose emblem was a swan's wing that had been dyed red. In 1837 white settlers came to Red Wing, and by the 1870s it had become a primary wheat market.

As railroads assumed a greater role in the transportation of products, Red Wing's importance as a shipping center began to diminish, even as the town's manufacture of two products, pottery and shoes, began to draw widespread attention.

Attractions

The Minnesota Stoneware Company, which began production in the late 1800s and eventually became known as Red Wing Pottery, made use of local raw materials and soon established a national reputation. In 1967, after nearly a century of operation, the company closed its plant as the result of a prolonged and bitter labor dispute. But the historic factory and salesroom have been turned into a major tourist attraction. At **Red Wing Pottery Sales,** 1995 W. Main St. (tel. 338-3562), you'll be able to find some remaining pieces of the original Red Wing pottery, along with collectibles from around the world. You can also browse among a variety of country items, and in the candy section you'll find such old-fashioned sweets as homemade fudge.

Winona Mills, 1902 W. Main St. (tel. 338-5738), one of a statewide network of factory outlet stores, offers a wide assortment of high-quality, reasonably priced apparel, all of it made in the United States, with one notable exception—the genuine Icelandic sweaters, which sell for much lower prices here than elsewhere.

And then there's **Loons and Ladyslippers,** 1890 W. Main St. (tel. 388-9418), a delightful shop where you'll find a miscellany of gifts, crafts, and collectibles, all of them related in some way to Minnesota, whose official bird is the loon and whose official flower is the ladyslipper.

At nearby **Pottery Place,** you'll find a two-level mall containing factory outlets, specialty shops, and restaurants.

Where to Stay

After making a national name for itself as the manufacturer of fine leather products, the Red Wing Shoe Company took a step in an entirely different direction in 1977, when it bought the 100-year-old **St. James Hotel,** 406 Main St., Red Wing, MN 55066 (tel.

612/388-2846). Meticulous restoration has turned this into one of the state's proudest examples of respect for historical significance and tasteful adaptation to contemporary needs.

With exacting attention to detail, the 60 original guest rooms were reduced to 41 in order to accommodate private modern baths and facilities. Each room is individually decorated with period wallpaper, period pieces, and coordinated handmade down quilts. In a discreet bow to modernity, handcrafted Victorian wardrobes open to reveal television sets. Delightful examples of Victorian workmanship have been displayed throughout the corridors. Accommodations range from $65 to $120 per room for two.

Where to Dine

Only an hour from the Twin Cities, Red Wing and the St. James Hotel are close enough for an afternoon or overnight getaway, close enough even for a lunch or dinner date. **Port of Red Wing,** the St. James's major restaurant, retains its original limestone walls and a variety of period antiques, which have been put to ingenious use. The original safe-deposit vault, for example, serves now as a fine wine cellar. Port of Red Wing offers a traditional American menu, with specials every evening. Complete dinners run from $16 to $20; lunch, $5 to $7. Lunch is served Monday through Saturday, 11 a.m. to 2 p.m., dinner every night from 5 to 9:30 p.m. Another popular gathering place at the St. James is **Jimmy's Pub,** which offers not only a fine fifth-story view of the city, but a warm, friendly ambience, enhanced by antique stained-glass panels, old English hunting scenes in antique frames over the oak bar, and upholstered armchairs facing the massive fireplace. Jimmy's Pub should really be called Jimmy's Bar—no food is served in this otherwise hospitable room. But you can get a bite at breakfast or lunchtime at the delightful **Veranda Coffee Shop,** with its lovely view of the Mississippi. You have your choice here of a table in the cheery informal dining room or on the adjoining enclosed porch.

LAKE CITY

Picturesque bluffs overlook Hwy. 61 as you approach Lake City, situated on Lake Pepin, the widest expanse on the Mississippi River. Lake City takes pride in the fact that the sport of waterskiing was invented here back in 1922, when 18-year-old Ralph Samuelson steamed and then bent into shape two pine boards. His theory was that if people could ski on snow, they could also ski on water, and the corroboration of that theory put Lake City on the map and enabled millions of men, women, and children throughout the world to ski, if not walk, on water.

This small city features a variety of activities that center on its major claim to fame, the largest **marina** on the Mississippi River. Following a recent expansion, 625 sailboats can now be docked here while a 90-foot breakwater enables others to fish from three 60-foot fishing platforms. Northerns, walleyes, crappies, and bass are among the varieties most often caught in these waters. But fish are not the only wildlife that draws tourists to Lake City. There are also the majestic **bald eagles** that have made their home in the bluffs overlooking Hwy. 61. These imposing birds can be seen from time to time swooping down onto the open water for food, and as the season progresses they do their ice fishing on the shoreline before it, too, freezes over.

WABASHA

You'll be visiting the oldest city in Minnesota when you arrive in Wabasha. Named for Indian Chief Wapashaw, a peacemaker during the Sioux Indian uprising of 1862, Wabasha was by the 1880s a center of lumbering, milling, and boatbuilding. Many of the buildings of that period, constructed of local materials, still stand today. In fact, Wabasha's entire downtown business district has been placed on the National Register of Historic Places.

There are two **marinas** here, offering 400 open slips and 200 closed slips, and the **city dock** provides launching to the public as well. Many sailors take advantage of the shuttle service provided at the docks by the Anderson House, the state's oldest operating hotel.

Food and Lodging

Run by the members of the same family since it first opened in 1896, the **Anderson House,** 333 N. Main St., Wabasha, MN 55981 (tel. 612/565-4524), has received national TV, magazine, and newspaper coverage as the Minnesota hotel which gives new meaning to the term "cat house." Here guests can reserve a complimentary overnight cat when they register for a room; a feline, its food, and even a litter box will be delivered to their door that evening. Daytime visits can also be arranged—usually at naptime for children or their elders.

There are other homey touches at the Anderson House as well. Home-baked cookies are available in a large jar on the front desk 24 hours a day. Heated bricks are provided for those who opt for that sort of bed-warmer. Guests with the sniffles are only one phone call to the desk away from having a mustard plaster delivered to the door. And those who remember to leave their shoes outside the door at night will find them there brightly shined the next morning. Rates are $49 to $75 for single and double rooms with bath; $40–$50 for rooms without bath, $85 to $95 for suites.

But the Anderson House is as famous for its home cooking as it is for its overnight services. Grandma Ida Hoffman Anderson brought her Pennsylvania Dutch recipes from Lancaster, Pennsylvania, at the turn of the century, and the family has been using them ever since. Today Ida's granddaughter Jeanne Hall and Jeanne's son John share the operation of the Anderson House. They've also shared authorship of a number of cookbooks for those who want to try their hand at the kind of fare that's been described as not only the best, but the biggest: cinnamon and praline breakfast rolls at the Anderson House are massive, and so is the selection of home-baked breads and rolls that waitresses bring to your table at dinnertime.

Entrées include Dutch oven steak, Pennsylvania Dutch beef rolls, and batter-fried cod, as well as such standbys as roast turkey and dressing, baked ham, and barbecued ribs. And then there's the Friday-night seafood buffet, an all-you-can-eat selection of seafood gumbo, shrimp, deep-fried pike, crab sections, oven-baked cod and white fish, along with potato and vegetable and, of course, the bread tray, all for $6.

Never mind that the river recreation is top-notch in Wabasha. The Anderson House itself is reason enough to visit this historic river town.

---

7. Duluth

About halfway between the Twin Cities and the Canadian border is Duluth, third largest of the state's cities, but second to none in its importance as an international inland port. Ships from all over the world arrive and depart each day from April to December, imparting a truly cosmopolitan air to this northern Minnesota city.

Like Minneapolis and St. Paul, Duluth is linked to a "twin"—in this case one that resides in a different state. Superior, Wisconsin, and Duluth, Minnesota, have always shared a natural harbor on Lake Superior, the huge inland sea that Henry Wadsworth Longfellow immortalized in 1855 as the birthplace of Hiawatha: "By the shores of Gitche Gumee, By the shining big-sea water. . . ."

Like any siblings, these cities have disagreed at times, most memorably perhaps one April weekend in 1871, after Duluth had decided to do something about the 6½-mile sandbar, Minnesota Point, around which its fishing ships had to travel before reaching open water. The city of Superior enjoyed a natural advantage because Wisconsin Point, less than 3 miles long, gave its boats readier access to the lake.

On this April day in 1871, Duluth officials authorized the digging of an artificial channel through Minnesota Point. A steam shovel had already started work when Superior officials contacted Washington, D.C., with a request that the excavation be halted. Word reached Duluth on a Friday afternoon that an army engineer was on his way with an injunction to halt the excavation. By the time he actually arrived early on Monday, the entire town had bent to the task, working ceaselessly throughout the weekend and finishing the entryway in time for a little tugboat, *Fero,* to toot its way through while Duluthians cheered.

In 1873 the federal government assumed control of the canal and the harbor, and ten years later named it the Duluth-Superior Harbor. Today an aerial lift bridge oversees the nearly 40 million tons of domestic and international cargo that passes through each year.

These international ships carry grain to Europe and beyond, while long, flat-bottomed ore boats take on taconite for shipment to cities in the American east. And of course the presence here of ships from all over the world has become a prime tourist attraction for the city of Duluth. There are other attractions as well.

ATTRACTIONS

One of the "musts" in any visit to Duluth is a drive along **Skyline Parkway,** a 26-mile strip of city that hugs the crest of a hillside at the western end of town. Day or night, winter or summer, this is a beautiful drive, looking out on Lake Superior, St. Louis Bay, and many residential areas. Part of the route goes through another sight-seeing attraction, **Hawks Ridge Nature Reserve,** a place where birdwatchers gather each fall to watch the migratory flights of hawks and eagles.

At the other end of town, **Spirit Mountain** (tel. toll free 800/247-0146) has been bringing ever-increasing numbers of skiers to Duluth during the past decade to enjoy such innovations as the 444 Express, a chair lift that raises four skiers in a bubble-domed quad to a height of 4,000 feet in just four minutes. The first of its kind in Minnesota, the 444 Express is one of only three or four similar lifts in the entire country. Work is constantly under way not only on lengthening and improving existing runs, but also on developing programs for individual skiers and families. One of the most notable events at Spirit Mountain takes place each New Year's Eve when instructors and members of the ski patrol lead a torchlight parade down the slopes before fireworks erupt into the cold, clear winter sky.

One of the long-range development plans here is to extend runs as far as the **Lake Superior Zoological Garden,** at Seventh Avenue West and Grand Avenue (Hwy. 23), which boasts more than 500 animals from around the world, including a variety of "night animals" that recently took up residence in their own newly constructed nocturnal building. Another popular spot here is the **Children's Zoo Contact Building,** where children, under staff supervision, are invited to touch and pet a variety of animals. Admission to the zoo from April 15 to October 15 is $1.50 for adults, 75¢ for children 6 to 12. Zoo hours during this period are 9 a.m. to 6 p.m. seven days a week. There's no entrance fee during the rest of the year, when the zoo is open from 9 a.m. to 4 p.m. Closed Thanksgiving, Christmas, and New Year's Day. For further information, phone 624-1502.

Another favorite sight-seeing attraction, for children and grownups alike, is the **Depot,** 506 W. Michigan St. (tel. 727-8025). An interesting series of exhibits and museums leads visitors through two centuries of local history, with an early stop at the Immigrants' Waiting Room. Elsewhere along the way, children enjoy the two-story walk-through Habitat Tree, and visitors of all ages admire the wonderful mid-19th-century collection of Ojibwa Indian portraits by Eastman Johnson. Elsewhere at the Depot you'll find a fascinating assortment of antique trains, dolls, and furnishings. Open daily from 10 a.m. to 5 p.m. during the summer months, Monday through Saturday from 10 a.m. to 5 p.m. and on Sunday from 1 to 5 p.m. during the winter.

And then there's **Glensheen,** a most popular attraction during the past several years, but maybe for the wrong reason. This magnificent mansion, at 3300 London Rd. (Hwy. 61 North), was donated by the wealthy Congdon family to the University of Minnesota at Duluth and stands in the lakeside neighborhood where logging and mining barons built lavish homes nearly a century ago. The much-publicized murder in this mansion of a member of the Congdon family and the subsequent trial and acquittal of an adopted daughter may have something to do with the renewed interest in the property, but tourists should know in advance that the Junior League docents who lead the tours avoid any reference whatever to the crime—so don't visit Glensheen on that account. If, on the other hand, you'd like to see for yourself a dazzling array of exquisite architecture, interior design, art, and horticulture, you'll find your visit to this 39-room Jacobean manor house one of the highlights of your visit to Duluth. Call 724-8863 for recorded information regarding hours, tours, and admission charges, or 724-8864 for reservations and additional information.

For information about other attractions, call or write the **Duluth Convention and Visitors Bureau Information Center,** Fifth Avenue West and the Waterfront, Duluth, MN 55802 (tel. 218/722-6024, or toll free 800/862-1172 in Minnesota).

ACCOMMODATIONS

Theoretically, you could make a one-day excursion to Duluth, but since the drive takes about three hours each way, I strongly suggest that you plan to spend the night. There's a lot to see and do in this lovely city. There's also a lot of choice so far as accommodations are concerned, everything from small independent motels to large, nationally known hotels. And there's one very special bed-and-breakfast spot that has gained statewide recognition and admiration, although it's only been open to the public since 1983, and just for limited periods each year at that.

The Mansion, 3600 London Rd., Duluth, MN 55804 (tel. 218/724-0739), located just two doors away from Glensheen, was from 1928 to 1932 the ten-bedroom home of another member of the Congdon family, Marjorie Congdon Dudley, and her husband, Harry C. Dudley. Accommodations here are named for the color of the rooms and the view they command. Rates range from $75 to $195 per night.

A hearty country breakfast, served in the formal dining room, is included in the rates. So is access to the oak-paneled library, the pine-paneled living room, and the sun porch and dining room. As of this writing the Mansion is open to overnight guests only from Memorial Day to October 15 and most winter weekends, with certain other periods available by special arrangement. For the doctor's family that runs it, this beautiful and gracious home has become a labor of love, and you'll find all manner of delightful reasons to come back again.

Another notable overnight can be found at **Fitger's Inn,** 600 E. Superior St., Duluth, MN 55802 (tel. 218/722-8826, or toll free 800/726-2982). Listed on the National Register of Historic Places, this restored 19th-century structure offers 48 individually styled rooms, some of them with a view of Lake Superior, some with original stone walls from the days when the building served as a famous Duluth brewery. Rates range from $85 to $105 for individual rooms and $135 to $260 for deluxe suites.

Less expensive but very comfortable accommodations are available at the **Edgewater Inn,** with two locations: Edgewater West, at 2211 London Rd., Duluth, MN 55804 (tel. 218/728-5141), and Edgewater East, 2330 London Rd., Duluth, MN 55804 (tel. 218/728-3601). Rates for a room with Continental breakfast delivered to your door range from $65 to $71 in-season (May 22 through September 22) and $51 to $57 off-season. The more expensive rooms, not surprisingly, are those that look out on Lake Superior. Edgewater East, the original lakeside complex, faces Edgewater West, located on the other side of busy London Road. A new lakeside building has rooms for $89 to $98.

You'll find an interesting variation on the usual increased desirability of lake-view rooms at the **Holiday Inn**, 207 W. Superior St., Duluth, MN 55802 (tel. 218/722-1202, or toll free 800/232-0070). Here, during the autumn, when many Twin Citians drive up to see the splendid fall colors in Duluth, the hillside rooms, which are less expensive than lakeside ones, are considered more desirable because you look out on a living mural of bright fall colors. Rates at the Holiday Inn vary according to the season. Summer rates range from $83.50 to $91.50, with suites available at $290.

WHERE TO DINE

There are some really wonderful and famous restaurants in Duluth. I'll give you a quick introduction to a few of them.

Grandma's Saloon and Deli, 522 Lake Ave. S. (tel. 727-4192), is something of an institution throughout the state, not so much because of its food, which is very good, or its decor, which is very imaginative, but because of its marathon, which is very famous and getting more so year after year. In 1977 Grandma's agreed to sponsor a North Shore run that attracted about 150 participants. One decade later the same route from Two Harbours to Duluth attracted 8,000-plus runners. By now there's a pre-race $5 all-you-can-eat spaghetti fest to fortify the runners with carbohydrates, and $50,000 worth of prize money awaiting the winners. Please note that Grandma's Marathon, which attracts runners from throughout the country, is the only race on record that ends at a bar. Tents, bands, and vendors with balloons, T-shirts, and other memorabilia are also on hand for the occasion.

Oh yes, the food and decor. You'll find absolutely everything hanging on the wall or from the ceiling at Grandma's. That means antique neon signs, stained-glass windows, brass beds and cribs, and even a stuffed black bear (the one, supposedly, that ran into the Hotel Duluth some years ago and thereby achieved immortality). The food is Italian-American—equal proportions of each, actually—and all of it well prepared and reasonable in cost. Pasta ranges from $4 to $10; steaks, from $7 to $15. Grandma's is open daily, 11:30 a.m. to 11 p.m. during winter months, 11 a.m. to 11 p.m. during the summer.

The family-owned **Pickwick,** 508 E. Superior St. (tel. 727-8901), has been serving fine food at reasonable prices since 1914. The decor here is 19th-century German, the cuisine is primarily American, and the beer is imported from a number of European countries. Lunch items range from $1.75 to $7.50. Dinner features T-bone steak, broiled or fried walleye pike, and more, ranging from $4.95 to $28.50. The Pickwick is open Monday through Saturday from 11 a.m. to 1 a.m. It's closed on Sunday.

The service will make you think of an earlier, more gracious time; so will the across-the-board senior citizens' 10% discount, which may account for the somewhat advanced average age here. Or the explanation may be that older folks know value when they run into it and return because of it. At any rate, the Pickwick is a beautiful, unique, and very popular Duluth tradition.

The **Chinese Lantern,** 402 W. 1st St. (tel. 722-7486), was the first Cantonese restaurant in Duluth when it opened in 1965. By now, as photos on the walls attest, diners have included Bob Hope, Loretta Lynn, Pearl Bailey, Barry Manilow, and Tom Jones. The only restaurant north of Minneapolis to be listed in *Who's Who of American Restaurants,* the Chinese Lantern is owned by Wing Y. Huie, whose family fled China in the mid-1930s. His father, Joe Huie, ran a famous 24-hour Duluth café for many years; he claimed that it was open all day and all night because he'd lost the key. He questioned Wing's decision to offer Chinese cuisine to a primarily blue-collar clientele, but lived long enough to admit with enormous pride that his son's judgment in that regard was better than his own. Prices here range from $7 for beef chop suey to $28 for broiled lobster. After dinner, climb the stairs to the second-story **Brass Phoenix Night Club,** another gamble that paid off handsomely for the enterprising Wing Huie. The Chinese Lantern is open weekdays from 11 a.m. to 11 p.m., Saturday from 11 a.m. to 12:30 a.m., and Sunday from noon to 10 p.m.

---

8. Hinckley

Hinckley, Minnesota, has three bona fide claims to fame. First, this is the site of a distinguished museum that memorializes the famous 1894 Hinckley firestorm, second only to the Great Chicago Fire in terms of total destructiveness. Located in a train depot that's listed on the National Register of Historic Places, this museum allows visitors to examine the turn-of-the-century waiting rooms (one for women and one for men), the beanery and freight room, and the depot agent's five-room apartment, furnished with late Victorian antiques. A large diorama shows the town of Hinckley and local landmarks, including the river, where logs were floated to the local lumber mill, and the gravel pit, where many Hinckley residents sought and found safety as the firestorm swept through the town. A slide show, presented hourly, tells more about Hinckley before, during, and after the fire. Admission to the museum is $2 for adults, $1.50 for senior citizens 62 and older and for children 13 to 18. Children 6 through 12 pay 50¢, and those 5 and under accompanied by an adult are admitted free.

Hinckley's second claim to fame is **Mission Creek,** an authentic Indian-village theme park where thousands of visitors each summer see historical demonstrations of the hunting, fishing, and trapping techniques of Minnesota Indians. The construction of wigwams, lodge houses, and birch-bark canoes is also demonstrated. (Maybe just a tad less authentic are the three gunfights that take place each day and the costumed personnel of **Froggy's,** the saloon where you can order a buffalo burger, a sarsaparilla, or, if you're so inclined, a glass of beer or wine. From Memorial Day to Labor Day, Mission Creek is open seven days a week. Tickets are $5 for children from 3 to 15 and seniors over the age of 60. Adults pay $7. Weekend prices are $2 higher. The price of admission includes a ride on a steam locomotive dating back to 1926, reportedly the only such working locomotive in the country today.

To many many Minnesotans, though, the name "Hinckley" for the past several decades has meant just one thing—huge, finger-lickin' caramel and cinnamon rolls, specialties of **Tobie's Eat Shop & Bus Stop,** situated since 1947 on Hwy. 35 halfway between the Twin Cities and Duluth. Tobie's has been for travelers the traditional place to fill up cars and people. The establishment has gone far beyond its humble origins: The bakery now employs 17 full-time bakers. A handsome restaurant, bar, and lounge have been added to an enlarged coffee shop. And there's a 29-unit motel with sauna and hot tub, not to mention a shopping center complete with women's wear, sporting goods, country gifts, and a year-round Christmas store. Call 612/384-7600 for information on prices and events at any of Tobie's facilities and attractions.

9. Spas

The brief spa getaway is a concept that's caught on with increasing numbers of Twin Citians. Whether you're taking time out from a business trip, a longer vacation, or just the everyday stay-at-home routine, you might want to consider one or more of the following facilities. They differ in location and amenities, but not in their primary purpose—to offer the kind of relaxing or invigorating activity that induces a healthful sense of well-being and rejuvenation.

THE MARSH

May 1985 saw the opening of the Marsh, 15000 Minnetonka Blvd., Minnetonka, MN 55345 (tel. 612/935-2202). A self-described "center for balance and fitness," the Marsh offers state-of-the-art equipment and a whole lot more. The rustic three-story building, set on the edge of a picturesque area of untouched suburban wetland, offers a wide variety of facilities and programs. The circuit training/Nautilus room is equipped with a Versa-climber, a Concept II rowing ergometer, and a "Heart Mate," whose computerized display not only monitors the heart rate as you bicycle, but tells how many calories are being burned per hour and per session. (This super-sophisticated machine also has a built-in TV and an AM/FM radio that will exercise your mind—to a degree—while you're exercising the rest of you.)

The Marsh also offers two fully equipped exercise studios, outfitted with spring-cushioned wood floors to absorb the shock of aerobic workouts. At 30 feet by 60 feet, this is the largest spring-cushioned floor in the Midwest. As directed and inspired by Ruth Strickland, the Marsh is also interested in your mental, spiritual, and emotional fitness. Classes, seminars, and lectures by nationally known fitness experts help in this regard. And there is a small dining room serving three healthful meals a day. Membership is open to those 16 and older.

For guests who can only spend a limited number of hours here, there's a variety of facials, massages, and body wraps, in addition to cosmetic makeovers and other health and beauty services. Prices vary according to method and time. A one-hour session of Swedish and Esalen massage is $40 for nonmembers, while there's a $45 charge for nonmembers' for Shiatsu, neuromuscular, and sports massage and a $40 charge for nonmembers who'd like a half-hour of acupuncture. Call 935-2202 for more specific information about services and prices.

You might also want to inquire about full-day, two-day, and three-day Marsh "minivacations" at prices ranging from $150 to $375 for nonmembers. (Although an expansion is being planned that will include overnight accommodations for the Marsh, at this writing they're not yet available on site. Personnel here will make reduced-rate reservations for you, at your expense, in the nearby Minnetonka Marriot Hotel. Do phone the Marsh for more specific information.)

BIRDWING

You'll find a very different kind of spa-getaway at Birdwing Spa, Route 2, Box 104, Litchfield, MN 55355 (tel. 612/693-6064). Opened in spring 1986, this beautiful getaway has lured guests from the Twin Cities (about a 70-mile drive) and from more far-flung places as well. In fact, guests have come from 37 states and 4 foreign countries to visit this luxurious retreat situated on 300 acres of woods and prairie. Names of the groomed trails impart information about the kinds of wildlife you'll encounter here: "Swan's Flight," "Hawk's Prairie," "Pelican Loop," and "Woodduck Cove." Summertime guests enjoy hiking these trails when they're not canoeing, biking, or doing aqua aerobics in the small outdoor swimming pool. During winter at this picturesque property, exercise takes the form of walking, snowshoeing, and cross-country skiing. Wintertime aerobic workouts, though, are held indoors.

But don't get the idea that exercise is all at Birdwing Spa. Austrian-born Elisabeth Carlson, who with her husband Richard owns and runs Birdwing, believes in pampering her guests. Would you rather have breakfast in bed than in the dining room? No problem. Would you like to skip some of the fitness session? That's for you to decide. What you won't want to skip, though, are the "beauty services" which are included, one per day, in the price of your stay. If you come for a week (at a cost of $995 per person double occupancy, $1095 single), you'll receive a full body massage, facial, manicure, pedicure, hair-styling, beauty makeover, and tanning sessions. The weekend package ($285 per person double, $350 single) includes a full body massage, a facial, and two tanning sessions. Additional services can be secured on an individual basis, of course, at ates ranging from $5 for a tanning session to $60 for an "ultimate" two-hour massage.

Meals here are worth writing home about, gourmet items that somehow make 1,300 calories a day seem sufficient. The small shop that's open briefly during your stay sells a cookbook, with which you'll be able to reproduce at home the delicacies you enjoyed here. It makes an appropriate and practical souvenir. The attention really is personalized here, so call to see what Birdwing can offer you.

ESTEE LAUDER SPA

When the Estee Lauder spa opened at Dayton's Department Store at Southdale in August 1990, it became only the ninth such full-service spa in the entire country. It also became a place where Twin Cities women, men, and teen-agers can find "an island of tranquility" right in the heart of one of the busiest centers in the Twin Cities. The services here—everything from facials to body massage to manicures—have proved popular with a diverse clientele. For example, the spa features a specially tailored "Lauder Men's Facial Treatment" designed to clean, energize, and maintain a healthy skin. (Cost: $45 for one treatment, $225 for a series of six.) Then there's the "Teenage Problem Skin Facial Treatment, to regularize oil and eliminate breakouts." (Cost: $25 for one treatment, $125 for six.)

But the majority of clients at this Southdale spa are women, and for them there's a wide variety of services, available individually or as part of a package. Facials come in many forms and at many costs, from the $45 "Skin Perfecting or Thorough Cleansing" treatments to the $70 "Thermal Hydrating Facial," recommended at the change of each season and after exposure to the sun. Body massage, maybe the most popular treatment of all, ranges from the "Re-Vitalizing" ½ hour back massage at $35 to the "Tension Relieving Body Massage" at $45.

Hand and foot treatments include manicures for $12.50, individual nail wraps or nail extensions for $6, pedicures, including foot massage and toenail shaping and polishing, for $25, and rehydrating hand or foot treatments for $10. Waxing prices depend on the area being treated, from $10 for eyebrow shaping to $22 for full arm, $45 for full leg, and $55 for full leg and bikini.

Since the name Estee Lauder means makeup to millions of women, there are, of course, makeup applications ($25) and makeup lessons ($50) available, with the cost of each service applicable toward the price of any Estee Lauder product.

For those with the time and the wherewithal, two particularly popular packages are offered. The "Estee Lauder Spa Express," at $80, lasts about two hours and offers a morning or afternoon of services tailored to your taste. The comprehensive "Day of Beauty," which lasts about five hours and includes lunch, costs $175.

One last point of pride here is that this is the first full-service Estee Lauder spa in the country to offer three features: a shower, dry brushing for hands and feet, and seaweed body wraps. Sooner or later these will probably be available in Estee Lauder spas elsewhere, but they originated here at Southdale.

AVEDA SPA OSCEOLA

And finally you'll want to know about Aveda Spa Osceola, 1015 Cascade St., Osceola, Wisconsin (tel. 715/294-4465), located on the banks of the St. Croix River about 50 miles from downtown Minneapolis or St. Paul. This beautiful European-style spa complex stands amidst 80 acres of unspoiled land in an area long noted for the purity of its air and its natural medicinal waters.

Aveda Spa Osceola, which opened in August 1990, was founded by Austrian-born Horst Rechelbacher, who made his name in the sixties as one of the top hairdressers in the world. (His distinctions include the coveted Intercoiffure Chevalier Award). During a 1963 international show tour, Rechelbacher was injured in an automobile accident in Minneapolis, Minnesota, and by the time his recovery was complete, so was his commitment to living and working in the Twin Cities.

In the late sixties, after opening the first of his six current Horst-and-Friends salons and establishing the Horst Education Center, from which salons throughout the country now recruit stylists, Rechelbacher turned to the intensive study of medicinal herbs, plants, and flowers. During that time he traveled to the Himalayas, which he still visits annually, to study with experts in aromatology. By 1978 he'd founded the Aveda Corporation, which uses the science of flower and plant essences in natural products for the hair, skin, body, and environment. Aveda products are now marketed internationally, and they are, of course, used exclusively on these premises. Given Rechelbacher's philosophy concerning beauty products, it won't surprise you to learn that the meals here are strictly organic; many ingredients are even grown on the premises.

Full-day and overnight packages are particularly popular here with guests who drive in from the Twin Cities or those who fly into the Twin Cities and are then provided shuttle service from Minneapolis/St. Paul International Airport. (Pickup service for any guest is available on request.)

The one-day 8-hour package for women and men includes full body massage, face and body treatment, natural essence scalp treatment, haircut and style, manicure and pedicure. In addition women receive a makeup lesson, while men are provided a skin-care consultation. The total cost, which includes an organic gourmet lunch, is $195.

The overnight package includes all the above plus a night's lodging in one of the truly beautiful guest rooms, gourmet dinner on arrival, breakfast and lunch the following day, one session of professional instruction in yoga, relaxation, stretching and stress-relieving exercise, and use of the spa steam room. Fitness and weight-training equipment are available and so is unlimited outdoor activity and exploration. Prices are $330, single occupancy, $290 per person double occupancy. Aveda Spa Osceola is open year-round. Handicapped accommodations are available. Some rooms have shared baths. For further information and for reservations, call 715/294-4465.

FAMILY FUN

1. RAIN OR SHINE
2. FAIR-WEATHER FUN

The Twin Cities are a mecca for family fun. Some prime entertainment spots have already been covered in earlier chapters, but for those of you with restless youngsters on your hands, this quick, comprehensive alphabetical listing should head off at the pass any threats of boredom. And lest the weather report put you in a quandary, I've divided this chapter into "rain-or-shine" and "better-in-the-sun" activities.

Admittedly this is something of a judgment call. For example, I've listed the Minnesota Zoo as a rain-or-shine attraction because so many of the animals, birds, and other residents here live in huge, beautifully landscaped, but totally sheltered areas that will keep you as comfortable as they are throughout the year. You're in the best position to know which activities will be of most interest to your particular cast of characters, but there's a lot to choose from, as you'll see from the sampling below. Have fun!

1. Rain or Shine

The American Swedish Institute, 2600 Park Ave., Minneapolis (tel. 871-4907). This extravagantly beautiful mansion looks like something out of a fairytale. Families have a fine time here admiring the beautifully wrought woodcarvings of griffins (half eagle, half lion) and other fantastical beings. Upstairs, on the third floor, visitors enjoy seeing turn-of-the-century clothing, tools, and toys, including an exquisitely furnished dollhouse. The Swedish Institute is open Tuesday through Saturday from noon to 4 p.m. and on Sunday from 1 to 5 p.m.; closed Monday. Admission is $2 for adults, $1 for students and senior citizens.

The Children's Museum, 1217 Bandana Blvd., St. Paul (tel. 644-3818). Children get to do all sorts of grownup things here, from operating a crane to driving a bus to playing banker, dentist, or grocery-store clerk. There are two floors of fun here, and parents seem as intrigued as youngsters are.

Hours are Sunday and Tuesday 10 a.m. to 6 p.m., Wednesday through Saturday 10 a.m. to 8 p.m. The museum is closed on Mondays during the school year, but is open seven days a week during June, July, and August. Admission is $2 for adults and children everyday, $3 on weekends September through May. June through August the ticket price is $3 at all times. Children one year or younger can enter free. Senior citizens pay $2 at all times.

The **Children's Theatre,** 2400 Third Ave. S., Minneapolis (tel. 874-0400). This theater is known throughout the world for its imaginative productions of plays for children. Characters like Babar and the Little Match Girl have come to life on this stage in an immense auditorium with wonderful sightlines. Prices are $11.25 to $18.50 for adults, $8.25 to $14.50 for children under the age of 17 and for senior citizens 62 and over.

The **Festival of Nations,** at the Civic Center of St. Paul, 143 W. 4th St., St. Paul (tel. 224-7361), is an annual celebration of the diversity of nationalities to be found in Minnesota. Dozens of countries are represented by costumed Twin Citians, who demonstrate the food, crafts, costumes, music, and dance of their respective countries. Admission is $7 for adults, $4 for children 5 to 16 (no charge for children under 5). For details on this event, usually held the last weekend of April, contact the International Institute of Minnesota at 612/647-0191.

The ***Indian God of Peace,*** located in the St. Paul City Hall and Courthouse at 4th and Wabasha, is a truly majestic figure of white onyx. A good many of the grownups who bring their children here these days first saw this magnificent work of art when they themselves were children. There's no charge for admission of course, but the courthouse is open Monday through Friday from 8 a.m. to 4:30 p.m.

The **James Ford Bell Museum of Natural History,** on the Minneapolis Campus of the University of Minnesota, University Avenue and 17th Avenue S.E. (tel. 624-1852). Enjoy wonderful recreations of animals, birds, and fish in their natural habitat, and on the third floor, visit the popular "Touch and See" room, where children can encounter prehistoric monsters, try on antlers, and consider—usually from a respectful distance—a grinning skeleton. Hours are 9 a.m. to 5 p.m. Tuesday through Saturday, from 1 to 5 p.m. on Sunday. Ticket prices are $2 for adults, $1 for those 3 to 16 years old and for full-time University of Minnesota students with a current I.D. Children under 3 pay no entrance fee. Thursdays are free.

The **Minnesota State Capitol Building,** Aurora and Park Avenues, St. Paul (tel. 297-3521). This magnificent building is a memorable sight for families; also memorable are the free tours that take you past beautiful Minnesota-related paintings and sculpture and up sweeping marble stairways to official government chambers. Tours are conducted every day, leaving from the Information Desk every hour on the hour from 9 a.m. to 4 p.m. Monday through Friday, 10 a.m. to 3 p.m. on Saturday, and 1 to 3 p.m. on Sunday.

The **Minnesota State Fair,** at Como and Snelling Avenues in

St. Paul (tel. 642-2251), has something for everybody. There's a lot to see, a lot to eat, a lot to do during this end-of-summer celebration, and the fact that it's housed in permanent installations means that your good time won't be rained out. The daily newspapers carry full listings of each day's special events. Admission is $4 for adults, $2.50 for seniors and children 5 to 12. There's no charge for children under 6, and no charge for parking. The largest 12-day fair in the country always ends on Labor Day.

The **Minnesota Zoo,** 12101 Johnny Cake Ridge Rd., Apple Valley (tel. 432-9000). You'll meet all manner of wild animals and birds here, in reconstructions of their natural habitats. Wintertime brings superb cross-country skiing opportunities to outdoorsy families who enjoy sharing their trails with creatures of the wild. Others will find plenty to see and ponder in a succession of indoor exhibitions. There's a petting barn here for the youngest members of your group. Admission is $4 for adults, $2 for seniors, $1.50 for ages 6 through 16; children under 5 are free. If you're in town from October through February and can get here on a Tuesday, there's no entrance charge at all.

The **Omnitheater,** in the Science Museum of Minnesota, 30 E. 10th St., St. Paul (221-9400), is popular with audiences of all ages. The huge curved screen and the world's largest film projector literally propel you out into space, down to the ocean's floor, or to places in between. You can go to the Omnitheater early and wait in line, or phone 221-9456 and pay an extra 50¢ per ticket for advance reservations. Ticket prices are $5 for adults, $4 for senior citizens and children 12 and under.

The **Science Museum of Minnesota,** 30 E. 10th St., St. Paul (tel. 221-9454), is a participatory museum that encourages children to try their hand at everything from grinding grain to operating a computer. Exhibits here cover a wide range of times and places, and one visit may well lead to another. If you attend the Omnitheater on the second floor, your admission to the rest of the Science Museum will be only $1; otherwise the cost of entering the museum is $3 for adults, $2 for children ages 4 to 12; children under 4 are admitted free. Hours October through March are Tuesday through Saturday from 9:30 a.m. to 9 p.m., on Sunday from 11 a.m. to 9 p.m.; closed Monday. Hours April through October are Monday through Saturday from 9:30 a.m. to 9 p.m., on Sunday from 11 a.m. to 9 p.m.

Sibley House, Sibley Memorial Hwy. near Hwys. 55 and 13, Mendota (tel. 452-1596). Henry Hastings Sibley was a prosperous fur trader before he became the first governor of Minnesota. His gracious home has been restored to the mid-19th-century authenticity, with furnishings and a remarkable collection of Indian carvings and peace pipes. Admission is $2.50 for adults, $1.00 for children 6 through 15; children under 6, free. The Sibley house is open from 10 a.m. to 5 p.m. Tuesday through Saturday, noon to 5 p.m. on Sunday.

Town Square Park, on the top levels of the Town Square shopping, dining, and office complex at 445 Minnesota St. in St. Paul (tel. 227-3307), is the world's largest indoor park. There's a small playground for children, lots of cozy seating for adults, and a picturesque setting of shrubs, trees, and waterfalls. Come at noon any weekday and you'll hear a musical recital.

The **Twin Cities Model Railroad Club** at Bandana Square, 1021 Bandana Blvd. East, St. Paul (tel. 647-9628), offers children and their elders the chance to see a remarkable exhibit in the process of becoming. Club members are still assembling historic tracks and artifacts that trace the history of railroading in this area during the past 50 years. The exhibit can be seen every day from noon to 9 p.m., but if you want to be able to walk all the way around the layout, plan to visit on Tuesday or Friday evening from 6 to 9 p.m. and on Sunday from noon to 5 p.m.

The **St. Paul Winter Carnival** (tel. 222-4416). The whole city of St. Paul is the setting for this annual late-January to early-February event. What's being celebrated here is not only the variety of wintertime fun, but the fact that by this time of year winter is about to be displaced by spring. Snow sculpture, ice carvings, and piped-in music make a fairyland of inner-city parks. There are parades and contests, and even a treasure hunt. Children can try their hand at ice fishing, and they'll enjoy the food and the fun at the "indoor midway" in the massive St. Paul Civic Center. Daily newspaper listings will keep you informed about what each day's and evening's events and activities will be.

2. Fair-Weather Fun

The Como Park Zoo, Midwest Parkway and Kaufman Drive, St. Paul (tel. 488-5572). Sparky, the performing seal, is everybody's favorite here, but there are lots of other animals to meet in the Primate and Aquatic buildings and in Wolf Woods. The buildings are open daily, from 10 a.m. to 4 p.m. during the winter months, to 6 p.m. during the summer months. There's no admission charge.

Gibb's Farm, 2097 W. Larpenteur Ave., Falcon Heights (tel. 646-8629), is a turn-of-the-century family homesite that enables children to experience for themselves the surroundings of the girls and boys who lived long ago. In addition to the farmhouse, the seven-acre site holds a red barn with tools of that day and a white barn with domestic animals. If reservations are made early enough in the season, first- through sixth-grade schoolchildren who visit Gibbs Farm during July or August can spend a full day attending the farm's old-style school, at a cost of $7.50. Gibbs Farm is open to the public from May 1 through October 31. Admission is $2.50 for adults, $1.00 for children, $2 for seniors.

Historic Fort Snelling, Hwy. 5 at Hwy. 55, 1 mile east of the Minneapolis–St. Paul airport (tel. 726-9430). This faithful restoration of the military post that brought the first settlers to these parts is now one of the most popular of all Twin Cities tourist attractions. Costumed guides encourage visitors to take part in the activities that kept soldiers and their families busy during those early days. Children particularly seem to enjoy the Round Tower, which provided a lookout up and down the Minnesota and Mississippi rivers. The schoolhouse, the blacksmith shop, and the hospital are just some of the fascinating and educational exhibits here. Historic Fort Snelling is open from May through October. Admission is $2 for adults, $1 for senior citizens and children 5 to 16; no charge for children under 5. Hours vary according to the season, so phone in advance for specific information.

The *Jonathon Paddelford* **Sternwheeler,** Harriet Island, St. Paul (tel. 227-1100). Passengers board this authentic 19th-century riverboat on Harriet Island, located on the edge of downtown St. Paul, and sail the Mississippi for a two-hour round trip to within sight of Historic Fort Snelling. A taped narration points out special places and facts of interest—a wonderful way to learn more about Twin Cities history. There are three sailings each day from June through August, and one sailing on Saturday, Sunday, and holidays during May and September. Phone for specific details. Prices are $7.50 for adults, $5.00 for children under 12.

The **Lake Harriet Trolley,** 42nd Street and Queen Avenue South, Minneapolis (tel. 522-7417). Many Twin Cities parents and grandparents can remember riding old-fashioned streetcars, but most children have never had the experience, and so they have a great time on the mile-long ride between Lake Harriet and Lake Calhoun. Just as in the old days, children buy tokens for the ride and a conductor collects them. This line is manned by volunteers, hence the abbreviated hours: Memorial Day through Labor Day, from 6:30 p.m. to dusk Monday through Friday, 3:30 p.m. to dusk on Saturday, and 12:30 p.m. to dusk on Sunday and holidays. After Labor Day, trolley rides continue through October, weather permitting, from 3:30 p.m. to dusk on Saturday and 12:30 p.m. to dusk on Sunday.

Minnehaha Falls/Statue of Hiawatha and Minnehaha, in Minnehaha Park, near the Mississippi River. It was reportedly a description of Minnehaha Falls that inspired Henry Wadsworth Longfellow to write his immortal narrative poem about the Indian brave Hiawatha and the Indian maiden Minnehaha. The two are reunited here in a graceful statue near the falls that bear her name. This whole area is a popular picnicking place for families. It's also the site of many large ethnic picnics, so you may run into costumed Scandinavians of all ages if you get there at the right time.

To get to the statue and falls from Minneapolis, take Hwy. 55 for about five miles; turn left on Minnehaha Parkway and enter the parking lot on the right. From St. Paul it's a lot less complex than it sounds: take Hwy. 94 west and get off at the Cretin-Vandalia exit; at the stop sign, turn left and proceed about three miles, turning right onto the Ford Parkway, which becomes a bridge that crosses the Mississippi River; one block beyond the Ford Bridge, turn left on 46th Street, proceed one block to Godfrey, turn right on Godfrey, drive about a block, and turn left into the parking lot.

Unlike other living-history restorations in the area, **Murphy's Landing,** Hwy. 101 near Shakopee (tel. 445-6900), doesn't confine itself to a relatively narrow point in time. Instead, 50 years of Minnesota Valley history unfolds before visitors as they proceed from the 1840s fur trader's cabin to the 1850 timber farm, and ultimately to a village of the 1890s. The costumes of the guides in each of the settings are consistent with the time period they represent. City children in particular enjoy seeing the farm animals roaming through the lanes; they also enjoy watching the churning, spinning, weaving, and other chores being carried on much as they were in the 19th century. Murphy's Landing, located about 11 miles west of the intersection of I-35W and Hwy. 13, about 1 mile past Valleyfair, is open to the public from May through October. Admission is $4 for adults, $3 for students and seniors; children under 6 are admitted free.

Valleyfair, Hwy. 101 near Shakopee (tel. 445-7600). If you're bringing children to the Twin Cities, you might want to consider spending a day at Valleyfair, an enormously popular theme park that occupies 60 acres and offers attractions for children and grown-ups alike. Many Twin Cities parents appreciate the presence here of the beautiful merry-go-round rescued from the now-demolished Excelsior Amusement Park near Lake Minnetonka. This is one of the most popular amusement parks in the entire Midwest. Come early and stay late. Valley Fair is open from the middle of May through Labor Day and then on weekends until the end of September. During the summer of 1990, ticket prices were $16 for regular admission, $9.25 for people 4 years old to 48 inches tall. Those 62 and older paid $9.25. Children under 3 entered free. Parking costs $2.50. Valleyfair is located about nine miles west of the intersection of I-35W and Hwy. 13, about 1 mile from Murphy's Landing.

Finally, check Chapter XI, "Festivals and Fairs," to see if one may be under way during your visit. They're a sure-fire source of family fun in these parts and will provide you with lots of local color in addition. And consider a family outing at one of the local parks and lakes that have been providing family fun for such a long time. You'll find more information about them in Chapter IX, "Sports and Recreation."

INDEX

GENERAL INFORMATION

ACCOMMODATIONS

Twin Cities

Day-Trip & Excursion Areas

KEY TO ABBREVIATIONS: B = Budget; **M** = Moderately priced; **E** = Expensive

RESTAURANTS

Twin Cities

KEY TO ABBREVIATIONS: B = Budget; **M** = Moderately priced; **E** = Expensive

Day-Trip & Excursion Areas

NOW, SAVE MONEY ON ALL YOUR TRAVELS!
Join Frommer's™ Dollarwise® Travel Club

Saving money while traveling is never a simple matter, which is why the **Dollarwise Travel Club** was formed 31 years ago. Developed in response to requests from Frommer's Travel Guide readers, the Club provides cost-cutting travel strategies, up-to-date travel information, and a sense of community for value-conscious travelers from all over the world.

In keeping with the money-saving concept, the annual membership fee is low — $18 for U.S. residents or $20 for residents of Canada, Mexico, and other countries — and is immediately exceeded by the value of your benefits, which include:

1. Any TWO books listed on the following pages.
2. Plus any ONE Frommer's City Guide.
3. A subscription to our quarterly newspaper, *The Dollarwise Traveler.*
4. A membership card that entitles you to purchase through the Club all Frommer's publications for 33% to 50% off their retail price.

The eight-page **Dollarwise Traveler** tells you about the latest developments in good-value travel worldwide and includes the following columns: **Hospitality Exchange** (for those offering and seeking hospitality in cities all over the world); **Share-a-Trip** (for those looking for travel companions to share costs); and **Readers Ask . . . Readers Reply** (for those with travel questions that other members can answer).

Aside from the Frommer's Guides and the Gault Millau Guides, you can also choose from our Special Editions. These include such titles as *California with Kids* (a compendium of the best of California's accommodations, restaurants, and sightseeing attractions appropriate for those traveling with toddlers through teens); *Candy Apple: New York with Kids* (a spirited guide to the Big Apple by a savvy New York grandmother that's perfect for both visitors and residents); *Caribbean Hideaways* (the 100 most romantic places to stay in the Islands, all rated on ambience, food, sports opportunities, and price); *Honeymoon Destinations* (a guide to planning and choosing just the right destination from hundreds of possibilities in the U.S., Mexico, and the Caribbean); *Marilyn Wood's Wonderful Weekends* (a selection of the best mini-vacations within a 200-mile radius of New York City, including descriptions of country inns and other accommodations, restaurants, picnic spots, sights, and activities); and *Paris Rendez-Vous* (a delightful guide to the best places to meet in Paris whether for power breakfasts or dancing till dawn).

To join this Club, simply send the appropriate membership fee with your name and address to: Frommer's Dollarwise Travel Club, 15 Columbus Circle, New York, NY 10023. Remember to specify which single city guide and which two other guides you wish to receive in your initial package of member's benefits. Or tear out the next page, check off your choices, and send the page to us with your membership fee.

FROMMER BOOKS
PRENTICE HALL PRESS
15 COLUMBUS CIRCLE
NEW YORK, NY 10023
212/373-8125

Date_____

Friends:

Please send me the books checked below.

FROMMER'S™ GUIDES

(Guides to sightseeing and tourist accommodations and facilities from budget to deluxe, with emphasis on the medium-priced.)

☐ Alaska. $14.95	☐ Germany $14.95
☐ Australia $14.95	☐ Italy $14.95
☐ Austria & Hungary $14.95	☐ Japan & Hong Kong. $14.95
☐ Belgium, Holland & Lux-	☐ Mid-Atlantic States $14.95
embourg $14.95	☐ New England $14.95
☐ Bermuda & The Bahamas $14.95	☐ New York State. $14.95
☐ Brazil $14.95	☐ Northwest. $14.95
☐ Canada. $14.95	☐ Portugal, Madeira & the Azores. $14.95
☐ Caribbean $14.95	☐ Skiing Europe $14.95
☐ Cruises (incl. Alaska, Carib, Mex, Ha-	☐ South Pacific $14.95
waii, Panama, Canada & US). .$14.95	☐ Southeast Asia $14.95
☐ California & Las Vegas. $14.95	☐ Southern Atlantic States $14.95
☐ Egypt $14.95	☐ Southwest. $14.95
☐ England & Scotland. $14.95	☐ Switzerland & Liechtenstein. $14.95
☐ Florida $14.95	☐ USA $15.95
☐ France. $14.95	

FROMMER'S $-A-DAY® GUIDES

(In-depth guides to sightseeing and low-cost tourist accommodations and facilities.)

☐ Europe on $40 a Day $15.95	☐ New York on $60 a Day $13.95
☐ Australia on $40 a Day $13.95	☐ New Zealand on $45 a Day. $13.95
☐ Eastern Europe on $25 a Day .$13.95	☐ Scandinavia on $60 a Day. $13.95
☐ England on $50 a Day $13.95	☐ Scotland & Wales on $40 a Day $13.95
☐ Greece on $35 a Day $13.95	☐ South America on $35 a Day. $13.95
☐ Hawaii on $60 a Day $13.95	☐ Spain & Morocco on $40 a Day $13.95
☐ India on $25 a Day $12.95	☐ Turkey on $30 a Day $13.95
☐ Ireland on $35 a Day $13.95	☐ Washington, D.C. & Historic Va. on
☐ Israel on $40 a Day $13.95	$40 a Day $13.95
☐ Mexico on $35 a Day. $13.95	

FROMMER'S TOURING GUIDES

(Color illustrated guides that include walking tours, cultural and historic sites, and other vital travel information.)

☐ Amsterdam $10.95	☐ New York. $10.95
☐ Australia. $9.95	☐ Paris $8.95
☐ Brazil $10.95	☐ Rome $10.95
☐ Egypt $8.95	☐ Scotland $9.95
☐ Florence $8.95	☐ Thailand $9.95
☐ Hong Kong $10.95	☐ Turkey $10.95
☐ London. $8.95	☐ Venice $8.95

TURN PAGE FOR ADDITONAL BOOKS AND ORDER FORM

0690

FROMMER'S CITY GUIDES

(Pocket-size guides to sightseeing and tourist accommodations and facilities in all price ranges.)

- ☐ Amsterdam/Holland $8.95
- ☐ Athens $8.95
- ☐ Atlanta $8.95
- ☐ Atlantic City/Cape May $8.95
- ☐ Barcelona $7.95
- ☐ Belgium $7.95
- ☐ Boston $8.95
- ☐ Cancún/Cozumel/Yucatán . . $8.95
- ☐ Chicago $8.95
- ☐ Denver/Boulder/Colorado Springs $7.95
- ☐ Dublin/Ireland $8.95
- ☐ Hawaii $8.95
- ☐ Hong Kong $7.95
- ☐ Las Vegas $8.95
- ☐ Lisbon/Madrid/Costa del Sol . . $8.95
- ☐ London $8.95
- ☐ Los Angeles $8.95
- ☐ Mexico City/Acapulco $8.95
- ☐ Minneapolis/St. Paul $8.95
- ☐ Montréal/Québec City $8.95
- ☐ New Orleans $8.95
- ☐ New York $8.95
- ☐ Orlando $8.95
- ☐ Paris $8.95
- ☐ Philadelphia $8.95
- ☐ Rio $8.95
- ☐ Rome $8.95
- ☐ Salt Lake City $8.95
- ☐ San Diego $8.95
- ☐ San Francisco $8.95
- ☐ Santa Fe/Taos/Albuquerque $8.95
- ☐ Seattle/Portland $7.95
- ☐ Sydney $8.95
- ☐ Tampa/St. Petersburg $8.95
- ☐ Tokyo $7.95
- ☐ Toronto $8.95
- ☐ Vancouver/Victoria $7.95
- ☐ Washington, D.C. $8.95

SPECIAL EDITIONS

- ☐ Beat the High Cost of Travel . . . $6.95
- ☐ Bed & Breakfast—N. America $11.95
- ☐ California with Kids $14.95
- ☐ Caribbean Hideaways $14.95
- ☐ Manhattan's Outdoor Sculpture $15.95
- ☐ Motorist's Phrase Book (Fr/Ger/Sp) $4.95
- ☐ Paris Rendez-Vous $10.95
- ☐ Swap and Go (Home Exchanging) $10.95
- ☐ The Candy Apple (NY with Kids) $12.95
- ☐ Travel Diary and Record Book $5.95
- ☐ Honeymoon Destinations (US, Mex & Carib) $14.95
- ☐ Where to Stay USA (From $3 to $30 a night) $10.95
- ☐ Marilyn Wood's Wonderful Weekends (CT, DE, MA, NH, NJ, NY, PA, RI, VT) $11.95
- ☐ The New World of Travel (Annual sourcebook by Arthur Frommer for savvy travelers) . . $16.95

GAULT MILLAU

(The only guides that distinguish the truly superlative from the merely overrated.)

- ☐ The Best of Chicago $15.95
- ☐ The Best of France $16.95
- ☐ The Best of Hong Kong $16.95
- ☐ The Best of Italy $16.95
- ☐ The Best of London $16.95
- ☐ The Best of Los Angeles $16.95
- ☐ The Best of New England $15.95
- ☐ The Best of New York $16.95
- ☐ The Best of Paris $16.95
- ☐ The Best of San Francisco $16.95
- ☐ The Best of Washington, D.C. $16.95

ORDER NOW!

In U.S. include $2 shipping UPS for 1st book; $1 ea. add'l book. Outside U.S. $3 and $1, respectively.
Allow four to six weeks for delivery in U.S., longer outside U.S.

Enclosed is my check or money order for $_____

NAME_____

ADDRESS_____

CITY_____ STATE_____ ZIP_____

0690